COUNTRY WALKS AROUND LONDON

Country Walks
Around London

Geoff Garvey
and Leigh Hatts

MAINSTREAM
PUBLISHING

EDINBURGH AND LONDON

Authors' note

All facts in the text have been checked as carefully as possible but the authors and publisher cannot be held responsible for any errors, however caused. Walks 2, 3, 5, 9, 10, 12, 13, 15, 17, 18, 20, 22 and 24 are by Leigh Hatts.

Maps supplied by Pear Technology Services Ltd.

First published in Great Britain in 1998 by *
MAINSTREAM PUBLISHING COMPANY (EDINBURGH) LTD
7 Albany Street
Edinburgh EH1 3UG

ISBN 1 85158 968 6

A catalogue record for this book is available from the British Library

Typeset in Helvetica
Printed and bound in Finland by WSOY

CONTENTS

Acknowledgements   6
Foreword   7
Preface – Ninety Years of *Country Walks*   8
Introduction   9

Walk 1   Runnymede to Windsor (11.5 or 5 miles)   12 *W- Egham*
Walk 2   Paul Nash Countryside (8 or 3 miles)   20 *Met*
Walk 3   Milton's Violet-Embroidered Vale (8 or 4 miles)   26 *1900*
Walk 4   Chesham Switchback (11.5 or 7.5 miles)   30 *Met*
Walk 5   Along the Chess (7 or 5 miles)   37 *Met*
Walk 6   Chorleywood Outback (8 or 6.5 miles)   42 *Met*
Walk 7   The Martyr, the Pope and Ovaltine (10.5 or 7.5 miles)   48 *St Albans*
Walk 8   Three Hertfordshire Houses (8.5 or 3 miles)   56 *Northern*
Walk 9   Dollis Valley and Totteridge Fields (4 or 2 miles)   62 *"*
Walk 10   On the Hertfordshire Border (7 or 5.5 miles)   66 *Liverpool St.*
Walk 11   The Fringe of the Forest (8 or 5 miles)   72 *Vic, Liv*
Walk 12   End of the Line (8.5 or 5 miles)   79 *Central*
Walk 13   Chigwell Circular (3 miles)   85 *"*
Walk 14   The Valley of the Rom (6 or 3 miles)   88 *Liv Romford*
Walk 15   Upminster Fields (8 or 4 miles)   93 *Dist*
Walk 16   Essex Flatlands (10 or 5.5 miles)   98 *Dist*
Walk 17   Over the Hill (6.5 or 3.5 miles)   104 *ChargX*
Walk 18   The Veil of Heaven (6 or 4 miles)   109 *Blackfriars*
Walk 19   Crusader Knights and Roman Ways (9 or 4 miles)   114 *Vic E*
Walk 20   Darwin's Retreat (5.5 or 2 miles)   121 *CharX*
Walk 21   Surrey Valleys and the Ladder of Salvation (11.5 or 5.5 miles) 126 *Cottersham*
Walk 22   Along the Mole (9 or 4 miles)   *Leatherhead* 133 *Watt*
Walk 23   Ancient Woods and Epsom Salts (4 miles)   *Ashtead* 139 *Wic W so*
Walk 24   Hampton Court Deer Parks (5.5 or 3.5 miles)   144
Walk 25   Riverside Villages (6.5 or 4 miles)   150
Walk 26   Along the Thames (4.5 or 2 miles)   *Staines* 159

Travelling in London   163
More Walks   166
Index   167

ACKNOWLEDGEMENTS

Thanks are due to many of the local libraries and local authorities in whose areas the walks are located for valuable help and information. The authors would also like to single out for special appreciation Marion Pleydell, Assistant Curator of the East Surrey Museum in Caterham; Bill Torrens, of the Buckinghamshire County Records and Local Studies Service; Jonathan Catton, Thurrock Museum, Essex; Alan Cooper, Havering Countryside Service; Len Stevens, Havering-atte-Bower; Richard Hellier and Trevor Odell of the Environment Agency; Dr Colin Shrimpton, Syon House; the Rev. Roger Ford, St Margaret's Darenth; Ted Webb, Bulphan; John Bubb, Orsett; Jean Tooke, Caterham; Margaret Whale, Windsor; Mr D. Badger, South Mimms; Tricia Moxey, Epping Forest Information Centre; the Rev. R. Freeman, Church of St Peter and St Paul, Farningham; Elizabeth and Ray Payne, Chesham; Mr F. G. Stickler, the Crown Estate; the Rev. P. Brown, All Saints Laleham and Sheila Hole, formerly of the LT Publicity Office. Valuable assistance was also rendered by the staff of English Heritage, the London Walking Forum and David Ellis and the staff of the London Transport Museum.

FOREWORD

I am delighted to endorse this revival of the long tradition of *Country Walks* books. This guide provides, in glorious detail, the delightful elements of the walks around London. The marvellous chapter headings, a treat in themselves, tempt you to learn more of the joy of walking in the country.

I am keen to encourage the idea of walking as a transport mode for work and also for the undoubted improvement to health walking can bring. I am very pleased that all these walks can be easily reached by public transport and that this book reinforces the benefits of walking for pleasure.

Do enjoy these walks and the wonderful variety of countryside to be found so close to London.

GLENDA JACKSON CBE MP
MINISTER FOR TRANSPORT IN LONDON

PREFACE

NINETY YEARS OF COUNTRY WALKS
The origin of London Transport's *Country Walks* book can be traced back 90 years to when the Metropolitan Railway issued *Country Walks* booklets to encourage off-peak travel to the Chilterns. In 1913 and 1914 the LCC Tramways published *Tramway Trips and Rambles* booklets written by 'The Tramp', and during the First World War posters on the underground carried in red lettering the challenge: 'Why bother about the Germans invading the country? Invade it yourself by Underground and motor-bus.'

In 1931 the Great Western Railway published *Rambles in the Chiltern Countryside* describing 365 miles of rambles. Two years later London's bus and underground services were brought together under London Transport which continued promoting trips to the countryside by producing *Chiltern Strolls and Rambles*, *Surrey and Kent Strolls and Rambles* and *Bucks, Berks, Herts and Essex Strolls and Rambles*.

These early London Transport publications provided 20 walks for an all-area *Country Walks via London Transport* book published, in collaboration with the Ramblers' Association, in 1936. This first book, written by Charles White and illustrated by Eric Ravilious, was followed within months by *Country Walks Second Series*, and in 1937 by *Country Walks Third Series*. By 1939 the first book was in its fourth edition.

Charles White had the run of the new London Transport area which, with Country Buses and Green Line coaches, reached as far as Baldock in Hertfordshire to the north and Horsham in Sussex to the south. The River Thames was embraced from Windsor to Gravesend. Meanwhile, the Southern Railway was promoting walking with its rival paperback *Southern Rambles for Londoners,* which ran into five editions by 1938.

The Second World War halted publication of the London Transport books until 1950, when Charles White resumed updating the walks series. In the mid-1960s he was briefly succeeded by Ron Pigram, whose own Chiltern walks books remain in print more than a decade after his early death. In 1968 Neil Garrie became principal author of the annual publication and, before moving two years later to the LT press office and becoming head of communications for London Underground, introduced an inner London section to compensate for the loss of Country Buses and Green Line to the National Bus Company. He was followed by Leigh Hatts, the main author for almost a decade, who continued the policy of devising new routes. Enthusiastic readers at this time included the historian A.J.P. Taylor, who would occasionally write a glowing review. However, an early casualty of London Transport reorganisation was its publishing arm, along with *Country Walks* which appeared for the last time in 1980.

Almost 20 years later its successor *Country Walks Around London,* is published in response to public demand.

INTRODUCTION

If you're a regular walker you'll already know the great pleasures to be had from tramping the footpaths around London. And if you've never walked further than the nearest park, then don't worry, this book is all you need to take you into some of the most attractive areas of countryside surrounding the capital. All the walks can be reached by public transport and many of them can be started in less than an hour from where you are reading these words.

Why walk? If you're interested in medical reasons your doctor will confirm that most of us don't get enough exercise, and that vigorous activity such as walking could prevent a coronary, help you lose weight and may even extend your life. But all this is secondary to the sheer enjoyment to be found in experiencing the astonishing variety of countryside around London.

The walks in this book have been designed to allow the reader to shorten them should the weather turn or a decision be made to spend longer at some of the places to visit along the way. These range from charming Norman country churches and elegant period houses to the National Rose Garden and even an aircraft museum. And if your interest is in wildlife: the woodlands, heaths, open grass areas and ponds to be found on the walks are prime sites for spotting birds and wild flowers. Each walk also includes background details on pub and café opening times and transport information, with the aim of giving the walker as many choices as possible when planning the walk.

And while there are 26 walks described here, it's worth bearing in mind that the same walk taken in the snows of January, the glorious splendour of a summer's day in July or the dazzling tints of autumn – when picking blackberries is another seasonal bonus – can provide often spectacular contrasts. It's our hope that you'll enjoy the walks that follow just as much as we did when researching and writing them. Good luck, and happy trails!

WALKING HINTS

TRANSPORT

All the walks can be reached by public transport which has been used and checked by the authors. As well as being more environmentally friendly, the absence of any ties to a fixed point of return permits some walks to be linear rather than circular, and also allows for a couple of drinks to be taken safely at the end of a good day out with no worries about getting behind the wheel of a vehicle. For details of public transport and fare zones see page 163.

MAPS AND MILEAGE

Each walk has a basic route map and for those who wish to put the routes in a wider context details are given of the relevant Ordnance Survey Landranger maps and the more detailed OS Explorer and Pathfinder maps, popular with ramblers. Some London street maps also include the countryside.

When calculating time and distance it is worth remembering that a walker makes slower progress over rugged terrain than along a flat, metalled road. The average walking speed for an adult is about three miles per hour on good flat tracks, which slows to about two miles per hour where the going gets rough or climbs. While not necessary for the walks covered in this volume, you will get much more enjoyment out of your journeys into the countryside if you learn how to read a map and use a compass. This will enable you to adapt these walks to take in areas of personal interest – perhaps a local landmark, a church or natural beauty spot – and will even assist accuracy in estimating your time of arrival, taking into account the terrain. Details of these skills and many other useful tips are to be found in *Teach Yourself Walking and Rambling* by Heather MacDermid (Hodder & Stoughton).

EQUIPMENT

To follow the walks described here requires no special equipment, but as you will be spending most of the time on your feet, comfortable, practical footwear is essential. While you can walk perfectly well in town shoes or even modern trainers, the limitations of this kind of footwear show up when the weather becomes wet or muddy underfoot or you need some grip to get up a slippery slope. This is where a good walking boot comes into its own. They may cost a little more, but if fitted correctly by a reputable dealer they'll become your best friends and will last for years.

The sensible walker is also prepared for all contingencies, especially with weather as unpredictable as that produced by the British climate. Take along a small rucksack and put in it the essentials for your trip.

FOOD

An important part of any walk is refreshment and details of pubs and teashops have been included to enable walks to be planned around them. Where pubs serve meals (M) or have a garden (G) these have been indicated in the Food and Drink section at the start of each walk. It's also a good idea to pack some snack food in your rucksack to maintain energy levels. Nuts are an extremely efficient energy provider, as is fruit, but there's no rule saying that you can't have your favourite chocolate bar as well. Incidentally, it's often a good idea to carry a plastic bottle of water as access to drinking water is not always readily available, even in the countryside. In summer a plastic bottle of frozen water can provide welcome refreshment on a warm day.

COUNTRY CODE

The Country Code should be observed at all times. Visitors to the countryside should close any gates behind them, and while farmers have an obligation to keep rights of way clear, walkers are equally obligated not to stray from them. Be aware of the risk of fire, treat livestock and farm equipment with respect and make sure to take your litter home. Finally, dogs are great companions to have on walks, but make sure to keep them under close control, especially near farm animals.

HELP US UPDATE

The authors have taken great pains to ensure that this edition of *Country Walks Around London* is as accurate and up to date as possible. The countryside changes frequently, however, as landmarks disappear, pubs close or change their hours and stiles are suddenly not there any more. If you feel that we've got something wrong or left out something important, we'd like you to tell us. A map reference would be helpful. Please mark your letter 'Country Walks Around London' and send to: Mainstream Publishing Ltd, 7 Albany Street, Edinburgh EH1 3UG.

Please keep in mind that while some walks have a number of possible visits, it is not implied that all of the places mentioned could be visited on a single walk and for many walks this would simply be impractical. It would be wise to tailor those visits requiring more time (the Botanic Gardens at Kew, for example) to one per walk, saving others for a later date. The walk itself should always be the main and most rewarding focus of your interest.

GEOFF GARVEY
LEIGH HATTS

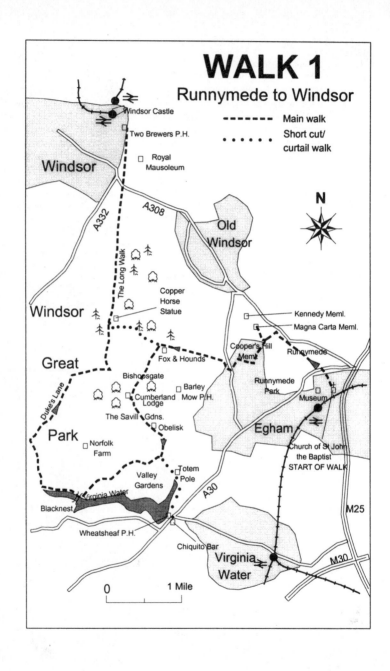

WALK 1
Runnymede to Windsor

- - - - - - - Main walk

• • • • • • • Short cut/
curtail walk

N

Windsor Castle

Two Brewers P.H.

Royal
Mausoleum

Windsor

Old
Windsor

A332

A308

The Long Walk

Copper
Horse
Statue

Windsor

Kennedy Meml.

Magna Carta Meml.

Cooper's Hill
Meml.

Runnymede

Fox & Hounds

Great

Bishopsgate

Barley
Mow P/H.

Cumberland
Lodge

The Savill Gdns.

Runnymede
Park

Museum

Egham

Park

Obelisk

Norfolk
Farm

Church of St John
the Baptist
START OF WALK

Valley
Gardens

Totem
Pole

Duke's Lane

A30

M25

Virginia Water

Blacknest

Wheatsheaf P.H.

Chiquito Bar

Virginia

Water

M30

0   1 Mile

Walk 1: Runnymede to Windsor

Egham – Runnymede – Englefield Green – Virginia Water – Windsor

---

This walk connects two of the most historically significant locations in English history. Starting out close to Runnymede meadow where the Magna Carta was sealed, it traverses the Windsor Great Park to end at the gates of Windsor Castle, residence of English monarchs since its founding by William the Conqueror. Natural beauty along the way includes the water meadows of Runnymede, the birdlife of Virginia Water and an endless variety of trees and plants – as well as deer – in the Great Park, all that today remains of the once vast Windsor forest. And if you want to see trees and flora in even greater profusion, including spectacular exotic specimens from all parts of the world, the Savill and Valley Gardens as well as the latter's heather garden are all inside the park's boundaries and are passed on the walk.

Distance: 11.5 miles, or 5 miles using short-cut. The walk may also be curtailed at 5.5 miles, ending at the Wheatsheaf pub and returning to Egham by bus number 500 (two-hourly service, not operating Sundays or public holidays; details from Tillingbourne Buses on 01252 315900).

Map: OS Landranger 176 (West London Area) or Explorer 160 (Windsor) and 1174 (Staines). Should you wish to work out your own detours or short-cuts inside the park, the Windsor and the Great Park footpath map (50p) produced by the East Berkshire Ramblers' Association is available from Windsor bookshops or by post (cheques payable to East Berks RA, add 40p p&p) from PO Box 1357, Maidenhead, Berkshire SL6 7FP. The Crown Estates' own map of the Great Park (10p) is available from any of the park lodges as you enter the park.

Terrain: Field paths, bridleways and some metalled paths in the park. Muddy in parts after rain. Two easy climbs.

Food & Drink: Barley Mow (Mon–Sat 11am–11pm; Sun 12–10.30pm; winter hours may vary; M/G), Englefield Green; Fox and Hounds (Mon–Sat 11am–3pm & 6–11pm; Sun 12–4pm & 7–10.30pm; M/G), Bishopsgate; Savill Gardens restaurant/cafeteria (same hours as gardens; see box below; M/G); Wheatsheaf (Mon-Sat 11am–2.30pm & 6–11pm; Sun 12–3pm & 7–10.30pm; M/G) and Chiquito Bar Restaurant (Mon–Sat 12–11pm; Sun 12–10.30pm; M/G), both Virginia Water; Two Brewers (Mon–Sat 10.30am–11pm; Sun 12–10.30pm; M) and Waterman's Arms (Mon–Sat 11–2.30 & 6-11pm; Sun 12–3pm & 7–10.30pm; M/G) plus other pubs and cafés, Windsor.

Transport: By National Railways from Waterloo to Egham (outside Travelcard zones)

Start & Finish: Parish church of St John the Baptist, Egham, to Windsor Castle and town where there are trains to Paddington (Central Station) and Waterloo (Riverside Station).

Arriving by train at Egham, turn right outside the main station entrance along Station Road. At the traffic lights use the crossing to keep ahead, shortly turning right at the elegant eighteenth-century bank building into the pedestrianised High Street.

EGHAM

Sited at the foot of a hill crowned by the impressive Royal Holloway College, a late nineteenth-century pile modelled on the Loire château of Chambord, little remains of the old market and coaching town of Egham which underwent the ravages of 1960s modernisation. The pedestrianised High Street retains a few traces of these earlier days, particularly inside the interesting Egham Museum (within the Literary Institute: Tues, Thur & Sat 10am–12.30pm & 2–4.30pm; free), manned by volunteers and a mine of local information. Other notable buildings here are the Red Lion pub dating from the sixteenth century and, further along, Clark Brothers butchers retains its nineteenth-century frontage. Nearby is a monument to the Magna Carta and at the end of the High Street there's an even larger one. Just over the main road from here lies the church of St John the Baptist surrounded by its graveyard with traditional yew trees. The early nineteenth-century church (currently open Mon–Thurs 8.30–9.30am; Wed 10–11.15am; Sunday service 10.30am-1pm; or ☎01784/430964 to request access) is built in the classical style and stands on the site of its Norman predecessor pulled down because it was 'insufficiently large to accommodate the inhabitants'. Inside, among a number of features from the earlier church are two fine early seventeenth-century memorials to Sir John Denham and his two wives.

The walk begins from the St John's lych gate. The ancient lych gate pre-dates the later church and from here you should cross the main road, turning left along Hummer Road. At the end of here cross the bypass to enter Runnymede meadow, maintained by the National Trust. Do not take the tarmac path but keep roughly ahead across the grass picking up the nearest hedge-line. Follow the hedge-line for 50 yards to a kissing gate. Keep ahead beyond this along the grassy path across a field with the dark mass of Cooper's Hill to your left.

RUNNYMEDE

It was here on 15 June 1215 that King John was compelled to agree to the Magna Carta recognising the rights and privileges of the barons, church and freemen and effectively placing the actions of the king under law for the first time. The document concludes 'Given by Our hand in the meadow which is called Runnymede between Windsor and Staines', although the precise spot has never been identified. While the document marked the outcome of a power struggle between the throne and the barons with little regard to the rights of the people at large, the privileges enshrined in the charter became the touchstone of liberties eventually extended to all. In 1957 the American Bar Association set up the first memorial to these events on the site (see below), and nearby in 1965 a monument to the assassinated President Kennedy was set up, on an acre of land now American soil.

On reaching the far side of the field cross two stiles into and out of an enclosure near the Windsor road. From the second stile keep ahead with the road (A308) to your right. When you come in line with a stile in a hedge on the right, turn left along the grassy field path in the direction of Cooper's Hill, topped by the visible memorial (see below), to reach a footbridge. This meadow is maintained in a natural state by the National Trust and in early summer presents a glorious feast of wild flowers, butterflies, dragonflies and singing crickets – sights and sounds that are rapidly vanishing from the factory-farmed landscapes of Britain. The walk continues across the footbridge, but should you wish to visit the Magna Carta monument, turn right to follow the path which keeps close to the trees for about 300 yards to cross a stile to reach the monument; the John F. Kennedy monument is a further 100 yards ahead through a gate on the left.

To continue the walk cross the footbridge over a stream to a kissing gate and keep ahead through an enclosed section to a second kissing gate. Take the stepped path beyond this which leads uphill through trees to eventually emerge at a lane. Turn right here to follow the hedge marking the grounds of the Cooper's Hill memorial. Continue along the road as it becomes paved, with the buildings of London University to the left. It soon bends right, passing the entrance to the Cooper's Hill memorial.

COOPER'S HILL AIR FORCES MEMORIAL

Impressively austere in style and immaculately maintained by the Commonwealth War Graves Commission, this monument erected in 1953 commemorates the 20,455 airmen and women from Commonwealth countries who lost their lives in World War Two, and who have no known grave. Their names are inscribed in successive pages of stone 'books' which line the arcaded galleries surrounding a serene quadrangle. From the observation tower there's a panoramic view over Runnymede, the Thames and, somewhat appropriately, the planes taking off and landing at Heathrow airport beyond. Pope's lines on this hill (written in the eighteenth century) seem eerily prescient:

> On Cooper's Hill eternal wreaths shall grow
> While lasts the mountain,
> Or while Thames
> shall flow

Continue west along the lane beyond the gates of the Air Forces Memorial for a quarter of a mile, passing the Cooper's Hill car park (left) to a triangular green. Bear left with the lane to the main road (A328) leading to the start of Bishop's Gate Road on the right, beyond which expands the open grass of Englefield Green. The walk continues along Bishop's Gate Road.

ENGLEFIELD GREEN

Englefield Green – 'Inga's Field' – preserves the ancient Saxon name of this large open area, originally used as pasture by the local community. In the late eighteenth and early nineteenth centuries it became a fashionable address and a number of substantial houses for the gentry – many connected with the Court at Windsor – were built. The green survived the expropriations of the 1814 Enclosure Act due to the influence of these wealthy incomers and was exempted 'for the adornment of their residences'. The elegant Englefield Green House on the green's east flank and the stately Castle Hill on the west side both date from this time. A wall plaque outside the Barley Mow pub at the southern edge of the green enables identification of these and other buildings around it. The Barley Mow is a fairly venerable edifice in its own right dating from the early eighteenth century. The pub's weather-boarded frontage is perhaps best appreciated with a glass of beer on the green in fine weather; there's a rather less attractive enclosed beer garden at the rear.

From Englefield Green head west – you can glimpse the castellated façade of Castle Hill behind walls to the left – along Bishop's Gate Road for a long half-mile and, when it forks, keep straight on passing the Fox and Hounds pub to reach, a little beyond, the Bishop's Gate entrance to Windsor Great Park.

The Shorter Walk

To follow the shorter walk, just inside the Bishop's Gate turn off the drive to head half-right along a bridleway passing between trees. When you meet a drive turn right through the gate marking the entry to the deer park and keep ahead along the metalled drive. After a quarter of a mile, where an avenue of trees reaches the drive from the left, look for a clump of trees about 150 yards ahead and bear off half-left just beyond it along a broad grass ride. On clear days, off to the right there's a fine view of Windsor Castle in the distance. Continue along the ride for about 300 yards to reach the Copper Horse statue where you rejoin the main walk (see below). If you wish to take in the Savill Garden (see below) before taking the short-cut, this would add an extra two miles to the walk.

The **main walk** continues on a grass path running half-left through the trees to a metalled drive with an enclosure on its far side. Turn left along the drive which soon takes a left bend. You can cut off the corner by following a horse ride through an area of smoothed, turfed ground planted with oak trees donated by the then Commonwealth nations to mark the coronation of George VI in 1937. You will rejoin the drive near to some houses on the left. Keep going in the same direction to reach Cumberland Gate. Pass through the gate and turn left along a metalled drive. Leave the drive where it turns left and go forward over grass alongside the iron fence (left) of the Savill Garden. Keep forward, following the line of the fence, for a good quarter mile to cross a stone footbridge from where a track leads uphill to the Cumberland Obelisk. The entrance to the Savill Garden lies two hundred yards down the drive to the left of the obelisk as you approach.

CUMBERLAND OBELISK AND THE SAVILL GARDEN

Erected to commemorate the Duke of Cumberland (1721–65), nicknamed 'the Butcher' for his brutal treatment of the Jacobites during and after the Battle of Culloden where he commanded the British army, the obelisk stands close to Virginia Water, the lake constructed by the duke – incidentally the park's first ranger – in one of his less destructive moods. The Savill Garden (open daily except 25 & 26 Dec; Mar–Oct 10am–6pm; Nov–Feb 10am–4pm; adults £3.50, senior citizens £3.00, children under 16 free) was designed by Sir Eric Savill in 1932 incorporating plantings from the eighteenth and nineteenth centuries in the Great Park. The result today is a magnificent 35-acre oasis filled with every conceivable flower from roses to rockplants, camellias to hydrangeas, magnolias to rhododendrons all on display in a scenic woodland setting. There are numerous delightful nooks and arbours around the gardens where a cool bottle of wine could be enjoyed on a warm summer's day with a little discretion, although picnicking is not allowed. The self-service restaurant

– also serving tea and snacks – can be visited without entering the gardens proper. There is a picnic area with tables close to the Cumberland Obelisk.

Bear half-left beyond the obelisk to join the drive coming from the left which leads to the Savill Garden entrance. Continue beside the Obelisk Pond (right) and follow the path as it bends along the pond's south side. Where the pond ends, keep ahead along a metalled drive for 200 yards to a cross drive.

A track half-left from here (and signposted) leads to the spectacular brightly painted Totem Pole, a soaring 100-foot-high work carved in Canada from a 600-year-old Western Red Cedar and placed here in 1958 to mark the centenary of British Columbia. The detour there and back would add half a mile to the walk, or alternatively you could continue around the south bank of Virginia Water from the Totem Pole to rejoin the walk beyond the Blacknest Gate at High Bridge. This would enable you to take in the Roman ruins (see box below).

The 5.5-mile walk ends here by following the signs from the Totem Pole to the Wheatsheaf public house, reached by heading south along the lakeside and turning left through trees after half a mile. The bus stop (for buses to Egham) is on the same side as the pub, and 50 yards beyond the car park next door. Time spent waiting for infrequent buses can be passed in the Wheatsheaf pub or the more exotic Chiquito Mexican Bar and restaurant which does a lethal line in cocktails.

Otherwise, the main walk continues by turning right along the drive where soon it gently ascends through silver birches to fork after 50 yards at a house. Keep left following the drive as it winds right to pass the polo ground. Ignore left turns to the Valley Gardens car park and a second left beyond this, but keep ahead between two fenced areas. When you come level with the polo ground's tea pavilion (signed as the Guards Polo Club), a dismal brown structure resembling a bunch of joined-up Portakabins just beyond which lies the white royal box with a distinctive sloping roof backed by flagpoles, turn left at a fork along a gravel track which winds downhill.

This track skirts the edge of Valley Gardens and you'll soon pass a gate leading into the ten-acre heather garden (free admission) which contains a collection of dwarf and slow-growing conifers, as well as maples and other trees renowned for their autumnal splendour. In May and June the Punch Bowl, slightly further into the garden, is ablaze with a spectacular display of rhododendrons and Japanese azaleas.

After 200 yards fork right along a gravel path that falls steeply to a road just before a bridge over Virginia Water.

VIRGINIA WATER
A renowned beauty spot, the artificial lake was laid out by the Duke of Cumberland, Master Ranger of the Great Park, and several follies are dotted around the edge of the lake, among them, close to its southern bank, a pile of Roman ruins from Leptis Magna in Libya donated to the project in 1816 by the Prince Regent (later George IV). The lake is home to a large number of water birds, among the most charming of which are the mandarin duck.

Turn left along the road to cross the bridge – with a waterfall on its south side –

and walk on the grass beside the road, ignoring the private rides to the right, for almost half a mile until you reach another bridge over Virginia Water at Blacknest. Do *not* cross this bridge, but bear right along a wide grass ride beside the water. One of the most tranquil sections of the walk with plenty of opportunities for birdspotting, keep ahead following the lakeside for half a mile until, at the end of the lake, the ride bears down to a small stone bridge leading to a cross track.

Turn right along the track heading roughly north, skirting the eastern edge (left) of the lovely wooded estate of Buckhurst Park. After three-quarters of a mile the track meets a junction at a drive (Duke's Lane). Turn right here and follow the drive (or its grass verges) lined with over-manicured oaks roughly north-east for a mile, with the fields of Norfolk Farm to the right. At a small group of cottages (right) cross over a drive, and after 50 yards bear half-right along another drive which runs clearly uphill in the distance. At the top keep ahead for about 150 yards beyond where another drive comes in from the left. Here, at a junction, turn left on to a track which soon heads downhill close to a fence and trees (right). As you near a pond (left) the colossal Copper Horse equestrian statue of George III appears on the horizon to the right.

Beyond the pond, go forward to an enclosed track reserved for walkers and head for the statue, passing through a kissing gate on the way which alerts you that you are now entering the deer park enclosure. The gargantuan statue of the mentally troubled monarch erected in 1831, eleven years after his death, has him proudly saluting and garbed in a rather outlandish classical toga.

At the statue **the short-cut from Bishop's Gate rejoins the main walk**. The statue also marks the nine-mile point of the main walk, and the reward for your labours comes at the summit of the hill with a stupendous and unforgettable view of Windsor Castle with the long ribbon of the Long Walk stretching towards it. There are plenty of comfortable rocks surrounding the statue's plinth for a longer contemplation.

The two-and-a-half-mile straight drive of Long Walk, the last stage of the hike, is lined with chestnut and plane trees and is often crossed by flocks of grazing deer. Halfway down the Long Walk you'll pass through the Double Gates to leave the deer park. A little beyond here the route crosses the Albert Road with the castle now dominating the view ahead. Peeping above trees to the right is the green copper dome of the Royal Mausoleum founded by Queen Victoria as the tomb for herself and Albert, and which is also the final resting place of the Duke and Duchess of Windsor. At the gates of Windsor Castle (this is the royal family's private entrance) veer left into Park Street where the Two Brewers pub will allow you to rest up your aching feet. A recommended stop for pub food is the Waterman's Arms, reached by following the route to the Riverside train station (see below) and crossing the Windsor Bridge to take the first left into Brocas Street.

WINDSOR AND THE CASTLE

Windsor is an attractive, if somewhat overtly genteel town dominated by the castle which overlooks the north end of the High Street. Entering the High Street from Park Street the parish church of St John the Baptist (open daily 10am–5pm) appears on the right. Dating from 1822 it was built over the remains of a twelfth-century church of the same name and has some interesting interior furniture. Just beyond the church, on the same side, is the elegant and porticoed Guildhall designed by Fitch and completed by Sir Christopher Wren in 1707. If you look closely at the columns you will see that they do not touch the ceiling. The story goes that they were insisted upon by the town's councillors who thought the building would be in danger of collapse without them. Wren, knowing better, disagreed and proved his point by leaving their capitals supporting nothing but air. The Guildhall is flanked by the curiously tilting Market Cross House (known locally as the 'Crooked House') which is itself adjoined by Queen Charlotte Street, recorded in the *Guinness Book of Records* as the shortest street in Britain at just 51 feet 10 inches. Across the road from here lies the Windsor Information Centre, 24 High Street (☎01753 852010; Jan–Mar daily 10am–4pm; Apr–May daily 10am–5pm; June –Sept daily 9.30am–6pm; Oct–Dec daily 10am–5pm) with maps and information on the town and surrounding area.

At the end of the High Street and beyond the bronze statue of a sternly matriarchal Queen Victoria by Boehm, erected to mark her Golden Jubilee in 1887, loom the walls of Windsor Castle (Mar–Oct 10am–5.30pm; Nov–Feb 10am–4pm; adults £9.80, senior citizens £7.20, children £5.60) and the visitors' entrance. Planned by William the Conqueror as a link in a chain of fortresses which dominated the Thames Valley, it dates from around 1070. The castle has been a favourite residence of English monarchs ever since and almost every sovereign has had a hand in extending or restoring it, the present one included after a great fire in 1992 which severely damaged parts of the castle including St George's Hall, recently reopened. The interior is filled with treasures including paintings, tapestries, frescoes and various *objets d'art* displayed in richly decorated apartments.

To reach the train stations continue north along Thames Street (the High Street's continuation); the Central Station (for trains to Paddington) is a short way along here on the left. To reach the Riverside Station (for trains to Waterloo) you should follow Thames Street, which bends right and then left to a junction near Windsor Bridge, where you should turn right into Datchet Road. The station is a short distance ahead on the left.

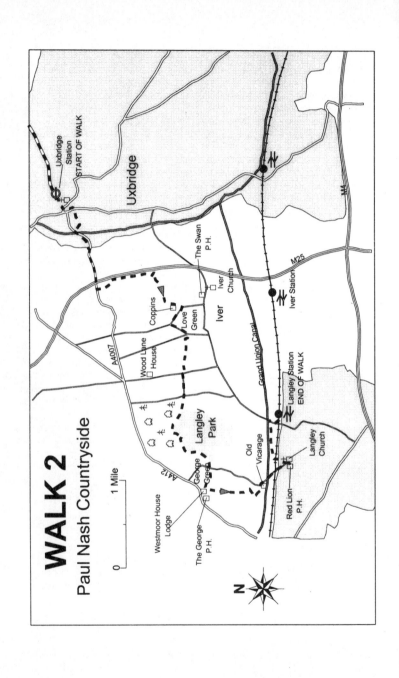

WALK 2
Paul Nash Countryside

Uxbridge Station
START OF WALK

Uxbridge

The Swan
P.H.

Iver
Church

Iver

Wood Lane
House

A4007

Coppins

Love
Green

Grand Union Canal

Langley Park

Old
Vicarage

Langley Station
END OF WALK

Iver Station

M25

M4

Red Lion
P.H.

Langley
Church

Westmoor House
Lodge

A412

George
Green

The George
P.H.

0   1 Mile

N

Walk 2: Paul Nash Countryside

Uxbridge – Iver – Langley Park – George Green – Langley

Artist Paul Nash (1889–1946) designed the moquette upholstery for the seats on London's red double-decker RT buses. In 1936 a pair of his posters, using photography and collage, promoted season tickets for work and pleasure. At the Royal College of Art he was tutor to Eric Ravilious who produced the woodcut illustrations for Green Line coach timetables and London Transport's *Country Walks*. Nash is best known as a painter although his work extended to designing book jackets, rugs, stage sets, ceramics, glassware and even Tilly Losch's bathroom. He was also a guidebook writer and a photographer. This walk explores what Nash called 'the real country only fifteen miles from London' which inspired him in his early years as an emerging artist. The climax is at Langley, where he found the church enthralling and in whose churchyard he is now buried.

Distance: 8 or 3 miles.

Map: OS Landranger 176 (West London) or OS Pathfinder 1158 (Hillingdon & Wembley), 1174 (Staines, Heathrow Airport and Richmond) and OS Explorer Map 3 (Chiltern Hills South).

Terrain: Field paths, bridleways and roads.

Food & Drink: Uxbridge has several pubs and cafés. The Swan at Iver (11am–3pm & 6–11pm; Fri–Sat 11am–11pm; Sun 12–10.30pm; M inc. cream teas Sat–Sun 3–5pm/G); the George (12–11pm; Sun 12–3pm & 7–10.30pm; M/G) at George Green; the Red Lion (11am–11pm; Sun 12–10.30pm; M/G) at Langley.

Transport: Metropolitan line to Uxbridge (Travelcard Zone 6). Return by Beeline bus 458 (Sunday's only) or Buckinghamshire CC bus 459 (Mondays to Fridays shopping hours) (outside Travelcard zones) from Iver to Uxbridge or National Railways from Langley (outside zones) to Paddington. Buckinghamshire bus enquiry line ☎0345 382000 Beeline ☎01753 524144.

Start & Finish: Uxbridge in Middlesex to Langley in Buckinghamshire. The shorter walk ends at Iver.

UXBRIDGE
Paul Nash used the now demolished GWR Vine Street Station in 1909-8 when travelling to and from his art classes at Bolt Court off Fleet Street. Opposite the spacious 1938 underground station is the eighteenth-century Market House. This hides St Margaret's, which dates from the fourteenth century and has a fine hammerbeam roof and is now well known as The Ark – a combined church, arts centre and café. In 1645 the Crown Inn was the venue for an abortive peace

negotiation between representatives of Charles I and Oliver Cromwell. The town was a stopping point for London stage coaches, and even after the arrival of the railway there were still around 60 inns. The Battle of Britain was planned at Uxbridge RAF base in a room 64 feet below ground. The police station in Windsor Street is now the Old Bill pub.

On leaving Uxbridge underground station go ahead along Windsor Street at the side of the Market House to pass the Nave and the Queen's Head. At the main road use the crossing (right) to keep forward with the old burial ground to the left. Cross the second main road, Trumper Way, on the crossing at the tip of the burial ground. On the far side of the road go left for a short distance to turn right down Wellington Road.

At the far end cross Fray's River and keep ahead on the metalled path across the playing field. On reaching a road continue ahead to meet the main Rockingham Road at a junction. The Dolphin is opposite. Turn left to cross the Grand Union Canal and follow the road down to the General Eliot. Here, cross the road to the Riverside Way junction to find a footpath on the left running behind the bus stop and alongside the River Colne. Pass behind the Pipemakers Arms and a row of back gardens. When the path joins the pavement cross the bridge to leave Greater London and enter both Buckinghamshire and the Colne Valley Park.

Do *not* be tempted down the footpath to the left but continue along the Slough Road (there is a pavement on the left) to cross the M25. At once take the metalled path on the left which runs downhill to the old road. Go left over a stream, through a gateway and turn right to follow a path alongside the motorway (left). The path crosses the Colne Brook, and later there is a view to the right of a recently created lake. As the path curves away from the motorway the water is more visible. Do not go ahead into a field but follow a fence (left) with the Colne Brook over to the right through the trees.

On reaching a stile by a gateway go right to cross the Colne Brook at an entrance to Delaford Manor and Cottages. Here a bridleway bears round to the right on a crunchy driveway in front of two cottages. At the end go left to find a gate leading to a long fenced path running alongside the manor's garden. After a gateway, the path runs gently uphill and bears slightly right. On meeting an abandoned cottage at Coppins Farm the track becomes the metalled Coppins Lane. There is a glimpse of Coppins (right) rising above the wall, which has 'Coppins' carved in a stone above a doorway.

COPPINS

In the Middle Ages a farmhouse here was the home of the Copyns family. The present nineteenth-century building was first occupied by John Mitchell who arranged Queen Victoria's theatre outings. Later the house was the home of a lady-in-waiting before Princess Victoria, Edward VII's daughter, moved here in 1925. On her death it passed to the Duke of Kent who had just married Princess Marina of Greece. Flowers and vegetables were sent from here weekly to the couple's Belgrave Square house. The Queen, Princess Margaret and Prince Philip all visited here as children. The Duke of Kent was killed on active service in 1942 and the Duchess continued to live here until her son, the present Duke of Kent, married in 1961 and took up residence. The house ceased to be a royal residence in 1972.

The lane meets Bangors Road South. To the left there is the village of Iver. **To end the walk here go left along the road to a bus stop.**

IVER

The village appears in the Domesday Book as Evreham. St Peter's Church dates from the Saxon period when builders included some Roman bricks. On the north side the thirteenth-century nave pillars are supporting Norman arches. There is a brass to Ralph Aubrey who was Chief Clerk to the Kitchen in the household of Catherine of Aragon when she was married to Prince Arthur, Henry VIII's elder brother. Opposite the lych gate is the sixteenth-century Swan inn. The eighteenth-century Bridgefoot House by Iver Bridge was the home of architect G.F. Bodley (see page 84).

The main walk continues to the right away from the village to pass the Coppins main entrance. After 300 yards turn left at a junction by the bus stop (there is a wall letterbox) to walk down Love Green Lane. On reaching a garage (left) go half-right (through iron railings under an oak tree) across a small triangle of grass and over a driveway to a road. Go right for a few yards to walk up the third of three driveways on the left. There is a plantation of young trees to the right, and as the path turns there is a view (left) of stables. On reaching a gateway go to the right on an enclosed footpath running alongside fields (right). Later there is a long line of dark trees before the straight path reaches a gate leading on to Wood Lane.

Wood Lane House is a quarter of a mile to the right and on the right opposite a garden centre on the now busy Wood Lane.

WOOD LANE HOUSE

The house was built in 1901 for the Nash family when Paul was 12 years old. The Bloomsbury Group's Dora Carrington called it a 'curious house' after visiting Paul's younger artist brother during the First World War. When Paul regularly caught the 10pm train from Paddington after art classes and cycled home in the dark, he was often moved by the shapes and shadows he observed. He was concentrating on landscape drawing with 'The Colne' and 'Tree Group, Iver Heath'. The heathland, to the north, had been a popular haunt of highwaymen including Dick Turpin, who pounced on the Uxbridge–Windsor coaches. Other work from this period includes 'Landscape at Wood Lane', 'Window of the Morning Room' and 'Bird Garden' (now in Cardiff's National Museum of Wales) showing part of the garden in 1911. The following year he staged his first exhibition thanks to an introduction to Sir William Richmond by a local resident. The works of Paul and John Nash can be seen at the Imperial War Museum.

The walk continues down Bellswood Lane opposite. After just over three-quarters of a mile the road meets Billet Lane at Ashen Cross. Go ahead to pass Treal Farm (now a new house). At the far end go through a gap into the woodland of Langley Park.

LANGLEY PARK

This was a royal estate given by Charles I to Sir John Kedermister (see page 25). The present house was built in 1756 for the third Duke of Marlborough who thought his grandfather's Blenheim Palace to be too far from London. Sir Robert Harvey was squire here from 1856 until 1931. The house, now owned by Buckinghamshire County Council, has been the headquarters of BPB Industries since 1984. The 130-acre park, where deer can be spotted, is part of the Colne Valley Park which stretches from Rickmansworth in the north to Staines in the south. In the north-east corner of Langley Park is the formal Temple Gardens which affords a view of Windsor Castle. The columns at the park's George Green gateway echo the pillar featured in several Paul Nash watercolours, and in his oil painting 'Pillar and Moon'.

Follow the path ahead and soon there is a glimpse of Langley Park mansion half-left. Stay on the winding gravel path until reaching the stable block. Go right on the metalled estate road to cross the end of the main tree-lined drive by the mansion's gateway (left).

Take a rough path ahead which runs alongside the garden. This soon bears left to a kissing gate at George Green Field. Follow the path through the parkland with a lake over to the left in front of the house. The path bears round to the right to a lodge (left) between new and old gateways at Langley Park's George Green entrance.

At the T-junction beyond the white lodge keep ahead up George Green Road to pass Westfield Lane (left), and reach the main road at George Green. To the left is the lodge at the entrance to Westmoor House. (The Green Man is opposite, but it should be reached by way of a pedestrian bridge to the left outside the George on George Green.)

WESTMOOR HOUSE

The house dates from 1664 and was formerly known as Langley Marish Rectory. Paul's grandfather lived here as lay rector of the parish, having inherited the position purchased by an ancestor giving the Nash family the right to receive tithes. The parish priest was a 'perpetual curate' known as the vicar. Paul often stayed here having tea under the mulberry tree in summer and celebrating Christmas in winter. The family remembered Disraeli calling.

Walk back along George Green Road for a few yards to go right down a footpath opposite the timber-framed Elizabeth Cottage. This footpath is known as Westfield Lane but it has the feel of a footpath. After a stile the way runs through woodland before continuing south in a straight line between high hedges. Soon after a double bend the path meets a stile. Go ahead on a metalled path to a road.

Turn right for a short distance to find a stile on the left next to a gateway. Cross the stile and go straight ahead across the field towards a point between the two pylons. At the far end of the field go over a stile by a gate. At once bear left to follow the fence to another stile by a road. Go right to pass the Old Vicarage.

THE OLD VICARAGE

This was the residence of the 'perpetual curate' in the 1890s when young Paul Nash drove past here with his grandfather on their way to church. The first Langley parish priest to live here was W.D. Scoones who had 12 children and served from 1856 to 1891. It ceased to be the vicarage in 1964.

Beyond the Old Vicarage there is Langley Manor School. Stay on the road to cross the Slough arm of the Grand Union Canal and the Paddington–Slough railway line. The road runs downhill into Langley passing the Chestnuts (left). Ahead at a bend are almshouses flanking Langley Church.

LANGLEY CHURCH

St Mary's parish is also known as Langley Marish after the de Marisco family who held the manor under Edward I. In 1960 Nikolaus Pevsner described the church as 'a great surprise' and 'one of the most rewarding in Buckinghamshire'. It is largely twelfth-century with traces of earlier Norman work, a fifteenth-century porch and a seventeenth-century tower. As a child young Paul enjoyed riding to Sunday morning service here in a dog cart with his grandfather from Westmoor House with people waving and curtseying. Much later he recalled those visits in the 1890s: '... the inside of the church was so enthralling that it was difficult to keep up an appearance of interest in the service. From the family pew in the choir, I had a view of the congregation beyond the screen and of the exquisite little chain library on the far wall. More constantly my eyes strayed to the clear glass east window where the branches of trees showed through or to the lovely painted vault above, pale, clear, blue painted with golden stars and bunches of corn.' The Kedermister Library, often consulted by the poet John Milton, was founded in 1623 by Sir John Kedermister of Langley Park. The Kedermister monument is to the left of the high altar. The corn which fascinated Nash was probably the sheaf on the hatchment.

Paul, who died in 1946, and his wife Margaret are buried at the side of the walled Harvey grave. (Go down the right side of the church and turn sharp right to leave the metalled path. The Harvey plot is to the left.) The church is open on the first Sunday afternoon in June to September. Wild's Almshouses were rebuilt in 1955, but the original foundation stone has been renewed and set in the garden wall showing the names of three members of the Nash family as trustees. Paul Nash's great grandfather lived at Langley Hall, which stood in Kedermister Park to the south.

Retrace the route to the modern almshouses and bear right up an enclosed footpath at the side. The path runs ahead between grass to a road. Cross the end of Maryside and before reaching the line of bollards blocking traffic bear left on to a footpath. The way runs uphill to cross the railway. Before crossing canal bridge 8 bear right to go down on to the towpath. Follow the towpath, with the water to the left, to pass through a gate at Langley Business Park, where there is a mile marker. At the bridge go up the steps to the road. Turn right to reach the crossroads where a path (half-left) runs up to Langley Station.

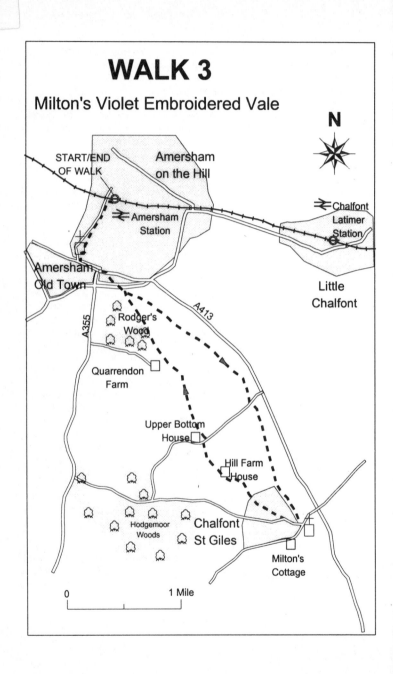

WALK 3

Milton's Violet Embroidered Vale

N

START/END
OF WALK

Amersham
on the Hill

Chalfont
Latimer
Station

Amersham
Station

Amersham
Old Town

Little
Chalfont

Rodger's
Wood

A413

A355

Quarrendon
Farm

Upper Bottom
House

Hill Farm
House

Chalfont
St Giles

Hodgemoor
Woods

Milton's
Cottage

0   1 Mile

Walk 3: Milton's Violet-Embroidered Vale

Amersham – Chalfont St Giles – Amersham

Amersham in the Chilterns has a mill at each end of the town which stand as testimony to the River Misbourne's once strong flow of water. This is not so today, especially during hot summers or when the course is affected by water extraction, but the Misbourne valley villages remain attractive with good linking footpaths. This route goes down into the Misbourne valley to visit both Old Amersham and the 'violet-embroidered vale' of John Milton, who chose the healthy Chiltern hills when escaping from the London plague. The return is over high ground with views across the valley.

Distance: 8 miles or 4 miles.

Map: OS Landranger 176 (West London) or OS Explorer 3 (Chiltern Hills South).

Terrain: Mainly field paths with two steep climbs.

Food & Drink: Old Amersham has several pubs and cafés including Carrington (8am–7pm; Sat–Sun to 6pm) opposite the church. The Fox and Hounds (11.30am–3pm & 6–11pm; Sun 12–3pm & 7–10.30pm M/G) & Teatime teashop (10am–5.30pm; Sun 1–5.30pm) are at Chalfont St Giles.

Transport: Metropolitan line to Amersham (outside Travelcard zones – special Travelcard available). Return from Chalfont St Giles (outside zones) by Chiltern Rover bus 305 to Uxbridge for Metropolitan line or Beaconsfield for National Railways. The Shires/Network Watford Bus enquiry line ☎01923 673121.

Start & Finish: Amersham in Buckinghamshire. The shorter walk ends at Chalfont St Giles.

AMERSHAM-ON-THE-HILL
The village has grown up around the station which opened here, rather than in the town below, in 1892 as a result of protests by the Drake family who wanted to preserve the view from their mansion.

Turn left out of Amersham Station and go left again under the railway bridge. At once cross the road to go right up a path by the side of the railway embankment to reach the top of Parsonage Wood. On reaching another road go left for a few yards before following a path back into the trees. The way, much used by commuters, later widens before reaching the far end of the wood with a view across Old Amersham. Continue downhill on the narrow metalled path. At a junction bear left and right to cross the River Misbourne, and enter Amersham churchyard.

OLD AMERSHAM

Amersham Church is partly twelfth century with plenty of memorials to the Drake family of Shardeloes. In 1682 a Drake built the nearby Market Hall which dominates the High Street. Every year on 19 and 20 September the road is closed for the annual fun fair marking the church's patronal festival. In the film *Four Weddings and a Funeral* it was the King's Arms which provided the exterior shots while the nearby Crown was used as the interior for the bedroom scene after the first wedding. The Griffin was a billet for Cromwell's troops in the civil war. On the same side is No. 60 The Broadway, once used as a prison, which has a notice issued in 1811 by the magistrates of the Hundred warning against 'Common Beggars, Ballard Singers and other Vagrants'. The award-winning Amersham Museum, opposite the King's Arms, is open summer weekends 2.30–4.30pm, admission 75p.

Bear left before the church to reach Amersham High Street. Turn left and use the crossing before continuing along the High Street to pass the Griffin (right) and No. 60 (right) with its notice. At the roundabout (by Fox's) cross the bottom of Gore Hill to the former Bury Farm, on the corner, and Bury Cottage.

BURY FARM

Bury Farm, at the bottom of Gore Hill, was the family home of Guilielma Springett who was visited here by Pennsylvania's founder William Penn (see pages 41 and 87) just before their farmhouse wedding at nearby Chorleywood in 1672.

Just before Bury Cottage go over the stile by the gate to follow the wooden fence (left) round to the left. Beyond a cattle grid the path crosses a field to go under a road. Use the stiles and fenced path on the left to avoid any mud. Enter a long field and walk ahead to pass a stile on the right. Keep forward to a stile at the bottom of the slope at the far end.

A path runs ahead along the side of a field. Soon after crossing a track, the hedge ends and the path becomes the field boundary as it runs across open country. Over to the left is a mill on the River Misbourne. Later the path is by a high hedge hiding waterworks. Go over the stile, and another by a gate. When the hedge falls away there is a view of the Ivy House pub with its Gothic windows. Continue forward across the large field towards a stile in the hedge ahead. At the stile go half-right across a smaller field to a gateway.

Cross a lane to a stile and continue ahead to a second stile. Go forward, with rising ground to the right, keeping to the right of the pylon. Go over a stile and follow the path ahead running through woodland. At a road, where there is a ford road sign, go ahead past the Old Mill's entrance and take the rough track ahead while the road swings left to ford the Misbourne.

After a line of houses the path enters more woodland where the way is joined by another wide path to run directly to Chalfont St Giles.

To end the walk here look for the bus stop in the main street.

CHALFONT ST GILES

The village, which has a green, carefully tended pond and a line of little shops, was the film location for 'Warmington-on-Sea' in the *Dad's Army* film with the Crown becoming Captain Mainwaring's bank. John Milton, who came here in 1665 to escape the Great Plague in London, completed *Paradise Lost* and started *Paradise*

Regained in Milton's Cottage at the west end of the main street (open daily except Mon, Mar–Oct 10am–1pm & 2–6pm; admission £2). The sixteenth-century house was bought by public subscription in 1877 to prevent it being dismantled and shipped to America. St Giles Church has monuments to the local Fleetwood family, one of whom – George Fleetwood – signed Charles I's death warrant.

The walk continues at Up Corner at the side of the Crown. As the road bends to become Silver Hill continue ahead up the footpath. At the seat bear right to pass William Shakman House. The Fox and Hounds is over to the right as the path meets School Lane. Go right and left to follow the main road past Jasmine Cottage. At a junction go ahead along Dodds Lane.

At the far end go ahead up Hill Farm Lane and past the entrance to Hunter's Lodge. The rough lane gently climbs up through the trees passing several hidden residences. Eventually the lane passes the entrance to Hill Farmhouse. At Hill View turn right. Just beyond the farmhouse (right), where the lane turns sharp right, continue ahead to find a hidden signpost (left). Here bear right down to a stile by a gate.

Keep forward by a fence (right) as the way runs downhill and widens. Soon there is a view of Upper Bottom House Farm down into the valley. Continue downhill as another path joins from the left. At the junction by the farm go right along Bottom House Farm Lane. When the buildings (left) end, turn left into a farmyard. Pass a round water tank (right) to go ahead up steps to a stile. Continue uphill to a stile by gates.

Bear half-left in the direction of a pylon to a stile in a hedge. Here there is a view ahead of the water tower at the top of Amersham's Gore Hill. Turn half-right to walk towards the trees passing the pylon (left). Cross a stile and walk past Day's Wood (right) to the corner of the field. Cross the stile by the gate and continue alongside a hedge (left). Over to the right is the Misbourne valley and a first glimpse of Amersham.

Before the hedge curves round to Quarrendon Farm (left) bear half-right at a waymark post across the field to a field corner. Continue in the same direction to a stile on the edge of Rodger's Wood. The path clips the corner of the wood to reach a stile from where there is a view of Amersham in the valley. Follow the path half-left as it runs downhill across two fields. At the bottom of the hill go over the stile by the gate and turn left to follow the path into Amersham. Retrace the outward route to the station at Amersham-on-the-Hill.

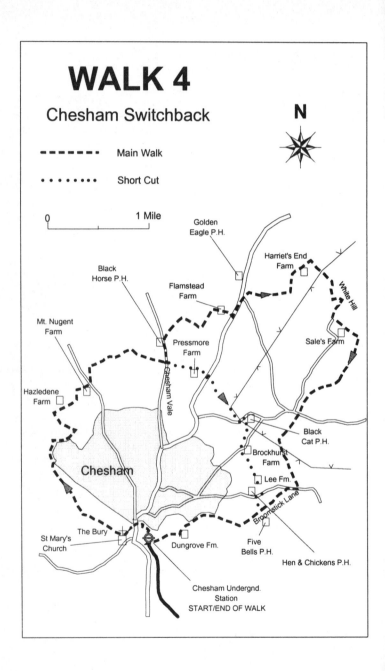

WALK 4

Chesham Switchback

N

- - - - - - - Main Walk

· · · · · · · Short Cut

0 _____ 1 Mile

Golden Eagle P.H.

Harriet's End Farm

White Hill

Black Horse P.H.

Flamstead Farm

Mt. Nugent Farm

Pressmore Farm

Sale's Farm

Chesham Vale

Hazledene Farm

Black Cat P.H.

Chesham

Brockhurst Farm

Lee Fm.

Broomstick Lane

St Mary's Church

The Bury

Dungrove Fm.

Five Bells P.H.

Hen & Chickens P.H.

Chesham Undergnd. Station
START/END OF WALK

Walk 4: Chesham Switchback

Chesham – Ashley Green – Botley – Chesham

This walk provides an exhilarating day out in the Chiltern Hills, one of the most picturesque walking areas in the south-east and within surprisingly easy reach of central London by tube. Rising west of the busy country town of Chesham in Buckinghamshire, these hills are a walker's paradise and there are countless rambles to be had along the dense network of footpaths meticulously maintained by the Chiltern Society. This walk takes in a good stretch of the ridges, 'bottoms' and wide grassy slopes as well as quite a few of the beechwoods which flourish in the soil of this enchanting chalk country. Whilst in this area keep an eye out aloft for red kites which have recently been introduced to the Chilterns and are now breeding successfully.

Distance: 11.5 miles, or 7.5 miles using short-cut.

Map: OS Landranger 165 (Aylesbury and Leighton Buzzard area) or OS Explorer 2 (Chiltern Hills North).

Terrain: Mostly field paths, bridleways and country roads. Some of the bridleways and farm surrounds can be poached up by animals after heavy rain – sturdy footwear is advised. Five easy climbs on the longer route, two on the shorter.

Food & Drink: Black Horse (Mon–Sat 12–3pm & 6–11pm; Sun 12–3pm & 7–10.30pm; M/G), Chesham Vale; Black Cat (Mon–Sat 5.30–11pm; Sat 11am–11pm; Sun 12–10.30pm; M/G), Lye Green (short-cut only); Hen and Chickens (Mon–Fri 11am–2.30pm & 6–11pm; Sat 11.30am–3pm & 6–11pm; Sun 12–2.30pm & 7–10.30pm; M/G), Botley (short-cut only); Golden Eagle (Mon–Thurs 11.30am–3pm; Fri–Sat 11.30am–11pm; Sun 12–10.30pm; M/G), Ashley Green; Five Bells (Mon-Sat 11am–2.30pm & 6–11pm; Sun 12–3pm & 7.30–10.30pm; M/G), Tyler's Hill; George and Dragon (Mon–Sat 11am–11pm; Sun 12–10.30pm; G) and other pubs, Chesham.

Transport: London Underground Metropolitan line to Chesham (outside Travelcard zones).

Start & Finish: Chesham underground station.

Turn left outside Chesham station to head downhill along Station Road to the town centre. When you meet the High Street turn right to a roundabout with a war memorial and then left along The Broadway, passing a church on your left and an ancient timbered building to the right. At a second roundabout take the zebra crossing (left) across the road to enter Lowdnes Park. Head roughly south-west (or half-right) over the grass, with a pond to the left, to reach St Mary's Parish Church whose tower is visible above trees.

CHESHAM AND SAINT MARY'S CHURCH

The Buckinghamshire town of Chesham dates back to Saxon times when it was called Caesteleshamm, and is mentioned as Cestreham in the Domesday Book. Gradually changed into Chesham, the river which rises in hills to the east of the town also lost its Saxon designation of Isene to become the Chess. Saint Mary's (open daily all day) dates from the thirteenth century and is almost certainly built on the foundations of an earlier church; a fragment of a Norman window in the north transept is evidence of this. All later periods have contributed to the amalgam of mainly Gothic styles. An elegant interior (somewhat marred by a jarring modern mural by John Ward R.A.) has an interesting fourteenth-century *piscina* (basin for washing the chalice after mass) in the sanctuary and a seventeenth-century oak communion table in the south transept. In the porch, take a look at the fourteenth-century stoup, or font, and, just outside, at the ancient puddingstones – chunks of conglomerate rock used as cornerstones at the entrance to the south porch and at the base of various buttresses. These 'goldstones' were accorded holy status by the druids and may also testify to the importance of this site in prehistoric times. A pamphlet available in the church gives a more detailed description of the interior. Unlike many churches today, St Mary's has a devoted congregation and is packed to the doors for its Sunday service.

Follow the metalled path uphill to the right of the church to pass the weather-boarded 'Guides Hut', just beyond which a double gate (left) leads to a grassy path through a field with the tree-line on your immediate left. From a gap in the upper left corner of the field the path runs down to two stiles, which you cross to reach a field from where you'll see the first broad panoramic view over the Chiltern folds, towards Hundridge and Missenden.

Avoid the path running downwards, but take the path to the right signed 'Chartridge Lane'. This path keeps to the upper slope of the field, close to trees on the right. Pass through a kissing gate into another large field and keep ahead to reach a second kissing gate. Go through this to follow an enclosed path running behind the back gardens of houses before winding right to reach the main road (Chartridge Lane). Here you turn left. Follow the road as it meanders right and then left. As it turns leftwards, and just after you pass Berkely Avenue (a side road on the right), you will see a red post box. As you pass the box, cross the wide grass verge behind it to reach a small enclosed footpath that runs along the backs of gardens before turning left towards a field. Go under a waymarked bar stile and head down the slope towards Portobello Farm, the group of buildings in the far field corner. Cross a stile into a lane and turn left.

About a third of a mile along this attractive lane (keep an eye out for speeding traffic) you'll come to a footpath by a gate on the right signed 'Hazeldean Farm' (the chimney of Hazeldean Farm can just be seen on the lower slopes of the hill). Follow this concrete track until it turns left to the farm, where you should keep ahead through a narrow gate to follow a field path climbing up the side of a field to Captain's Wood. When you enter the beechwood try to keep the line of the yellow waymarked public footpath through the wood. Pick your way upwards through bracken, evading any fallen trees, and after about 100 yards you will meet a track that runs along the top edge of the wood. When you reach it, turn left along the track for a short distance.

You will soon see Mount Nugent Farm in the field to your right and a stile. Do *not* cross this stile but keep ahead along the same track until, almost in line with the farmhouse's distinctive gable, a smaller track forks to the right. Take this track which keeps close to a wire fence for about seventy yards until you come to a second stile beneath a gnarled old beech. Cross this stile and keep ahead with the farm buildings to your right. Go over the grass to another stile and cross this to turn left along the farm drive. When you reach a road, cross over to pick up the next path directly opposite.

After a few yards this path turns sharp left to run beside the back gardens of houses, with a field on your right. After passing into a second field follow the path as it makes an obvious turn to the right to run alongside a fence, with hedge-line to the right. At the far end of this field the path makes a left turn for about 50 yards to pass around a projecting spur of a wood; it then curves right and, beyond a gate, plunges between the trees. It cuts through the wood soon to wind right to reach a broken stile at a field; there's an attractive view from here overlooking a sheltered little vale. Go downhill now, with the hedge to your left and the wire fence and field to your right. Pass through a kissing gate to reach a gap in a lower hedgerow and a dirt track. Turn right along the track with a hedge to the right and fence to the left. After a good quarter of a mile you'll come to a road at Chesham Vale. To take the short-cut (see below) you will keep ahead here while the main walk (go to p.34) turns left along the road to reach, after 250 yards, the Black Horse pub.

The Shorter Walk

To continue along the shorter route, cross the road at Chesham Vale (facing a sign saying 'The Vale') and head uphill through the farmyard of Pressmore Farm. You will soon reach a gate leading to an enclosed track. Go through this and follow a track which continues to climb. When the path divides, fork left with a house and hedgerow to your left. The path continues uphill with the hedge now to your right and fence and field to the left. Keep ahead beyond a stile at the brow of the hill and continue your line to cross two more stiles until you reach a lane. Veer left along the lane to reach a junction facing a holly hedge. Turn right here (passing Pressmore Cottage) to reach a major road (A416).

Cross the road and turn left to pick up the next path facing a car showroom. Signed 'Lyecrome Road', the path continues beyond a stile keeping close to a hedgerow to the right. After 100 yards the path bends right before turning left to head south-east towards electricity pylons. Ignore a stile and follow the hedgerow, keeping this to your right as you approach an electricity substation. Keep ahead to pass through this area along the concreted path, with the station to your left, to reach a lane. Turn left along this lane for 75 yards to a stile and footpath on the right, close to the Black Cat pub with a (very basic) beer garden and restricted opening hours.

Cross the stile and follow the path with the hedge-line to your left to head across the field half-right to a stile in the far corner. Cross the stile and follow a mature laurel hedge (left) protecting a garden behind. The footpath soon emerges at a road (B4505). Turn right along here passing the sixteenth-century Brockhurst Farm, with its equally ancient (and listed) granary whose south side has been converted into a garage complete with incongruous metal doors. Just beyond the farmhouse turn left along a path signed 'Botley'. This crosses a field to join a hedge. Keep ahead with the hedge to your left and at the field corner maintain your line along a path which becomes enclosed with trees to the left. Emerging into another field keep the same direction with a hedgerow now to your right. Over to the left you may be able to spot (in summer) some of the exotic animals in the children's area of Lee Farm.

LEE FARM

Lee Farm is one of a number of 'pick your own' farms which have sprung up in this area. Strawberries, blackberries, raspberries, gooseberries, redcurrants (all late June onwards), asparagus (mid-May to late June) and other vegetables are available for picking. Affable proprietor Richard Birch has also set up a children's farm to keep the offspring happy while mum and dad are culling the fruit and veg in the adjacent fields. Llamas, pheasants, turkeys, guinea fowl, chickens, ducks and geese are on hand to entertain.

Keeping ahead through the farmyard of Lee Farm leads you to a road where you should turn right. Go along here for 50 yards before turning left down Tyler's Hill Road opposite the Hen and Chickens pub. Follow the road – in fact a pleasant country lane – as it descends to Bottom Lane, where the short-cut rejoins the main walk (page 35).

The **main walk continues** by crossing the road from the Black Horse pub and taking a hedged cart-track heading north-east. After passing a few settlements, the stony track runs uphill between hedges with fields stretching upwards on either side. After a quarter of a mile the track turns boldly right into private property, but your path continues to climb – now between trees – keeping the same line. When it reaches a height of 525 feet the track bends right to reach a metalled lane and gate. Pass through the gate to continue along the metalled lane to reach Flamstead Farm.

The path continues through the farmyard to follow the drive on the far side to meet a main road (A416). However, the farmer is not sympathetic to walkers and has attempted to divert them around the farm by means of signs. If you prefer not to exercise your right to follow a legal footpath (and a possible confrontation) turn left with the sign and then right to pass between farm buildings. Ahead, and to the left of a wooden power pylon, cross a stile into a field. Head half-right across the field towards a lofty horse chestnut and a second stile. Cross this to enter the farm drive where you would have ended up had you continued through the main farmyard.

At the end of the farm drive turn left along the main road (A416) into Ashley Green, a small settlement scattered along the main road. You'll soon reach the sombre Victorian church of St John the Evangelist fronting the green, which gives the village its name. From the war memorial in front of the church head half-right over grass to a wooden structure resembling a summer house. This is, in fact, the reconstructed well house which used to cover the village's well head (no longer visible) before the days of mains water. Should you require refreshment, the Golden Eagle pub lies 100 yards north from here on the left of the main road. The walk continues to the right of the well house along a track to the side of the old village school, now the Ashley Green Community Association.

Cross a stile beside a gate and bear right, descending across a small field to a kissing gate. Beyond this follow an enclosed path around the property of Thames Water. Do not cross a stile on the far side of this enclosure but turn right along an enclosed path, often overgrown in summer. This descends gently downhill to a stile. Cross this and keep ahead, skirting a field edge with trees to the left. Keep ahead at a cross path towards the valley of Hockeridge Bottom. This is a wonderfully open stretch of countryside, especially picturesque in summer when the hills are covered in golden wheat, invaded by quite a number of crimson wild poppies.

When the field track reaches lower ground at a field corner, follow it as it swerves leftwards uphill to run beside a small wood. Soon the way passes between the buildings of Harriotsend Farm and runs down the farm drive to a sunken lane. Turn right along this delightful lane, flanked with dense foliage in summer, as it drops to offer another look at Hockeridge Bottom as it runs, right, to White Hill. The lane climbs out of the valley and, when it veers left near the top of a sharp rise, bear right along a track (to the left of Spring Meadow Farm) that enters a belt of trees. The track soon makes a left turn to climb to Sale's Farm.

When you reach the farm keep ahead along a short fence to a stile. Cross the large field beyond along a path which should be free of crops aiming towards a telegraph pole on the horizon. At an unmetalled farm drive on the far side, turn right to meet a lane. Cross the lane to continue along a gritted bridleway heading in a roughly south-west direction towards a wood. Go through the wood, which can be a bit of a bog after rain, and on the far side keep ahead to follow the edge of a large field with a hedge and wood to your left. When you come to a stile on the right, cross this to keep forward over another large field. The farmer is not conscientious about maintaining the right of way here and you may need to follow the example of local ramblers and tread through any crops. Your path lies to the right of a telegraph pole, aiming for a metal gate and stile beyond an enclosed track on the far side. At the time of writing the stile is broken and you may need to clamber over the gate. Once beyond the gate/stile keep forward along a fence (right). When the fence turns right towards buildings keep ahead to follow the grassy path as it bends left towards a gate and stile at a road.

Cross the stile and the road (B4505) beyond to enter an enclosed footpath opposite. This soon passes a horse-riding stables (left). At the end of the enclosed section, keep ahead across a field aiming toward a power pylon. Cross a stile in a hedgerow on the far side of the field and another beyond to keep forward over another large field. Just before you come in line with another power pylon to the left, turn left across the field towards a stile in a hedgerow. Cross the stile and maintain your line across another field heading towards a wood. Follow the path as it skirts the edge of the wood (right) to reach a stile. Cross this stile keeping the same direction to follow an enclosed path by a house garden. This soon meets the Chesham Road in the village of Botley. Turn right along the road for a good hundred yards to reach Broomstick Lane, opposite the post office and village shop. Turn left along this lane which, after a few houses, turns into a pleasant flint track running beneath a leafy bower in summer.

At the foot of this track you will reach a junction where the **short-cut joins**

the main walk. For refreshment, turn left up Tyler's Hill Lane for 200 yards to reach the Five Bells pub with a decent selection of beers and a garden.

The walk continues down Bottom Lane, opposite. Initially paved, this lane – heading roughly south-west downhill – soon degenerates into a rough flint way for about 300 yards or so until trees appear ahead and the track widens at a signposted footpath crossing. Leave the trackway here and cross over a stile by a gate into the field on the right, and go half-left over steeply rising grassland to cross a pair of stiles, the second in a dilapidated state. Keeping the same direction, continue over a second meadow, gradually leaving the hedge-line on the right, and follow a path that picks up another hedgerow on the right behind which lie school playing fields followed by a couple of houses. Keep forward (with the farm buildings of Dungrove Farm ahead to the left) to meet a track by a mature oak. Cross a stile on the other side of the track and keep ahead over a grassy field to cross another stile to the right of Dungrove Farm.

Once over the stile – this area tends to become a quagmire after rain – turn right along a rutted track between hedgerows. Fifty yards along here you will come to another stile on the left. Cross this to head in a roughly southerly direction with the hedge-line to your right and the farm buildings across a field to the left. You will soon pass a stile on the right. Ignore this and continue for another 100 yards to a second stile. Cross this to follow a narrow and well trodden path half-left over a field. After about 100 yards the path dips towards a stile with a fine view over Chesham beyond, and St Mary's Church from where the walk started out.

Cross the stile, and another soon after it, to follow a steeply falling enclosed path between bushes. On lower ground turn left along a line of rusted iron railings and then right to a footbridge over the Metropolitan line. On the far side of this, turn right along a path to reach the entrance to Chesham tube station. If you are looking for refreshment, there's a short-cut from the footbridge to the George and Dragon (see below).

For refreshment in Chesham the only pub with a (basic) beer garden is the George and Dragon, a venerable old drinking den dating from 1715, reached by turning left at the foot of Station Road for 100 yards along the pedestrianised High Street. To take the short-cut from the footbridge above, keep ahead down steps opposite the bridge to reach the end of East Street. Turn right along the main road for a short distance and then right again into Market Square with its monumental clock. Beyond the clock the pub lies along the High Street to the left. The only possibility for lighter refreshment is a McDonald's at the start of the High Street.

Walk 5: Along the Chess

Little Chalfont – Latimer – Sarrat Bottom – Rickmansworth

The River Chess rises at Chesham and flows south for ten miles down through Buckinghamshire and Hertfordshire to Rickmansworth where it joins the River Colne and the Grand Union Canal. Dragonflies might be seen on warm summer evenings and swans are always somewhere on the river. This walk from Latimer is largely through waterside meadows and flower-filled fields, with just a farm shop and a pub on top of a hill for refreshment. The shorter walk also climbs out of the valley to run across Chorleywood Common.

Distance: 7 or 5 miles.

Map: OS Landranger 165 (Aylesbury), 166 (Luton and Hertford) & 176 (West London);. OS Pathfinder 1139 (Watford and Rickmansworth).

Terrain: Field paths and lanes. Can be muddy.

Food & Drink: Cock Inn (11am–3pm & 6pm–11pm; Sat 11am–11pm; Sun 12–10.30pm; M/G) at Church End; the Sportsman Hotel (12–3pm & 6–11pm; Sat 11am–11pm & Sun 12–10.30pm; M) opposite Chorleywood Station. Rickmansworth has several pubs, and at weekends food is available at Batchworth Lock Canal Centre at the end of Church Street.

Transport: Metropolitan line to Chalfont & Latimer (outside Travelcard zones). Return by Metropolitan line from Chorleywood or Rickmansworth (outside Travelcard zones).

Start & Finish: Little Chalfont in Buckinghamshire to Rickmansworth in Hertfordshire. The shorter walk ends at Chorleywood.

Leave Chalfont & Latimer Station by the up (to London) platform. Turn right down the station approach and go sharp left into Bedford Avenue. (Opposite there is a short-cut to Bedford Avenue but, as the notice indicates, passengers use this path across a car park at their own risk.)

Follow this residential road along the side of the railway line and go right at the junction into Chenies Avenue. Continue over a crossroads and at Beechwood Avenue (left) keep forward down a short private road. A path runs into the trees. Go through the fence gap ahead and take the main right fork. The wide woodland path curves past a pit and downhill. Shortly after joining another path there is a junction. Look to the left to find a stile under the trees.

Go over the stile into a field and walk ahead. Up on the hill is the red-brick Latimer House, reached later. Cross a road at gates and continue across a small field to a third gate. Take the metalled driveway ahead which crosses the River Chess. Bear round to the right to follow the driveway as it climbs uphill

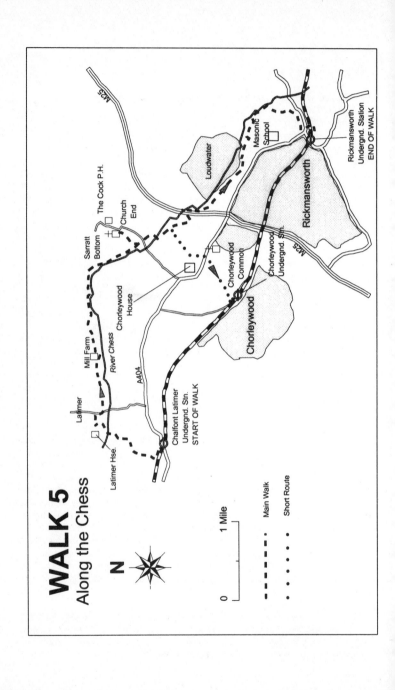

WALK 5
Along the Chess

N

0   1 Mile

- - - - Main Walk
· · · · Short Route

Latimer

Latimer Hse.

Mill Farm

River Chess

Chorleywood House

A404

Chalfont Latimer
Undergnd. Stn.
START OF WALK

Sarratt
Bottom

The Cock P.H.

Church
End

Chorleywood
Common

Chorleywood
Undergnd. Stn.

Chorleywood

M25

Loudwater

Masonic
School

Rickmansworth

M25

Rickmansworth
Undergnd. Station
END OF WALK

giving a view down to the right of the river. At gates go ahead to a road by the entrance to Latimer House (left).

LATIMER HOUSE

Once the home of Lord Chesham, Latimer House is now the Coopers & Lybrand conference centre. The red-brick house by Edward Blore, on a site where Charles I was held prisoner, dates from 1863. The church alongside the driveway was enlarged in 1867 by architect George Gilbert Scott who had stayed with his uncle at the rectory opposite years before. Latimer Cottage was the home of the Latimer House butler.

Turn left past the Latimer House entrance and, just before Latimer Church (left) and Latimer Cottage (right), go right through a small gate waymarked Chess Valley Way. A path swings left to a kissing gate. Continue forward down to a second kissing gate and follow a narrow hedged path to reach Latimer village green.

LATIMER VILLAGE GREEN

The heart and harness of a horse which served in the Boer War are buried beneath the stone near the war memorial. The road from the south crossed the Chess by ford until 1898.

At the grass triangle with its parish pump go right, and where the houses end go left over a stile. Cross a second stile and bear half-left to leave Buckinghamshire and continue along the valley just inside Hertfordshire. The high path gives a view down on to the river which is now the county boundary. In the wood below are traces of Flaunden's thirteenth-century church which became redundant in 1838 when a church was added to the new village one and a half miles to the north. Beyond a stile and gate there is a lonely tomb beneath two oak trees. William Liberty who died in 1777 wished to be buried near his house, which stood on the hill behind.

Beyond another gate the path runs above a stream from the Chess before passing through Mill Farm farmyard at Chenies Bottom. On the left is the farm shop, open daily 7.30am to 5pm (closed 1 to 2pm) selling eggs and local honey. Ice cream is also available.

At Chenies Bottom turn left up the road to find a stile by a gate on the right. Once in the field go forward along the top of a bank and then cut a corner to the stile ahead. Go ahead to another stile. Cross a field (there may be some horse jumps here) to a stile in the far left-hand corner. A path runs through trees before becoming fenced as it double bends to run nearer the River Chess. The way is occasionally boarded, and afterwards a second stile meets a lane at a bend. To the right there is a ford.

Do not cross the river but keep forward along the concrete road. The surface changes before the way reaches a corner white cottage at Sarrat Bottom. Turn right along the narrow road and at a junction continue ahead. Eventually the lane becomes a footpath and meets a stile.

The path runs ahead below a bank (left) with the river to the right. Soon there is a view (left) of the strip lynchets, a medieval field system, on the hillside. Keep along the bottom of the field to a stile in front of two cottages. The path running uphill on the far side of the buildings leads to the church and pub at Church End.

CHURCH END

Church End consists of Holy Cross Church, almshouses built in 1821 and the Cock Inn. The church was built about 1190 and extended in the following century when the wall paintings in the south transept were added. The tower is Tudor. In 1804 the vicar decided that the little church should be restored as 'the walls were green and dangerous, the floors were all in holes and uneven, and an extended or opened-out cheese box was used to keep out the draughts through the front door'. Sixty years later there was a major restoration carried out by George Gilbert Scott (who worked on Latimer Church). Richard Baxter, who wrote the hymn 'Ye holy angels bright', is known to have preached from the pulpit in the seventeenth century.

Continue ahead along a track to a road. Cross over to a kissing gate and follow the side of the field. At the far end go through a gap and bear round to the right towards the river. The path is boarded as it approaches a bridge. Once across the Chess go forward for a few yards to a path junction. Go left through a kissing gate (ignoring an early path on the left) and follow a woodland path ahead to a T-junction.

The Shorter Walk

For the shorter walk go right over the stile to follow a woodland path uphill, ignoring all turnings. Later the way is flat and straight. On meeting metalled road at a bend go left downhill. Soon there is a wide expanse of grass to the right and a view of Chorleywood House. Keep on the estate road to reach a lodge at a main road. Opposite is Chorleywood Common with a view of the church to the left.

Cross the road to a car park and follow the long worn path running half-right down the middle of the grass clearing in the wood. At the far end keep ahead to pass the right side of a small group of trees which surround a pond. To the right is Child's Farm by Darvill's Works. Do not continue on the gravel path by the pond but take the right fork to head for the far end of the white terrace. Over to the right there is the Rose and Crown.

The path meets the road opposite a Hire Economy Centres corner shop. Go down the road opposite called Colley Land to pass the Chorley Wood Community Arts Centre (right) and the Old Bakery further down the hill. On meeting a road below the railway embankment go left for Chorleywood Station. (Shire Lane and the shops are to the right under the bridge.)

CHORLEYWOOD

The area was known as Chorley Wood by 1730 and the name was still two words on the Underground station signs as late as the 1970s. Christ Church on the common was designed by George Street and completed in 1870 with the landmark tower added in 1882. The architect of Chorleywood House, now apartments, was Lady Ela Russell – her father, the Duke of Bedford, was the landowner. The attractive houses on the north side of Colley Land were built in the 1890s – garden produce is sometimes on sale at Ivy Cottage. The homely St John Fisher Church in Shire Lane opened in 1955 when Hill Cottage, originally designed by Charles Voysey, was converted. The architect planned his own house, The Orchard, built in 1900 on the same side further up Shire Lane. Two doors away, and almost opposite Chalfont Lane, is another Voysey house, now called Holly Bank.

The main walk continues to the left to meet a metalled Chorleywood Estate road. Go right through a gateway to follow the metalled road over the centre of a field. The road becomes enclosed to pass through a gateway and reach a main road. Turn left to follow the pavement over the M25. Once on the far side go right into the Colesbridge Mill Watergardens entrance. Bear right and round a bend to the Watergardens gates where the footpath runs ahead on the right. Follow the long fenced path to eventually reach a stile with a view across paddocks. Bear half-left on a wide grass path running between fences to join a track from a stables. Where the track swings to the right keep forward on another grass path. Beyond barriers and an iron stile the path is enclosed. After a road the way continues between gardens. Later there is woodland on the left. Another path joins from the right and again the path is soon alongside a row of gardens. At the far end the path turns sharp left below a bank on to a wide way to reach a road.

Cross over to find, a few yards uphill on the left, a gap where a path runs down the bank to a path junction. Continue ahead on a fenced path which is at first alongside a field before bending through trees to reach the Chess by a low bridge. Continue downstream on the wide grass way with the river to the left. The Royal Masonic School for Girls can be seen up on the hill (right). On reaching a playing field entrance bear right to continue on an enclosed path which, after running under trees, reaches the back of Our Lady Help of Christians Church on the edge of Rickmansworth.

At once turn right across grass to join a road running past a school (left). At the end of the road go ahead on a path running up a grassy bank. At the top continue ahead until reaching a lamp-post with a Chess Valley Walk waymark. Here turn left across the grass to find, behind the last tree, a footbridge spanning a road. Cross the bridge and keep ahead to cross a second bridge over the railway. Turn right to reach a road. Cross over to go right under the railway and left up to Rickmansworth Station.

RICKMANSWORTH
The town, which once had many mills, lies at the confluence of the Rivers Colne, Chess and Gade and the Grand Union Canal. Our Lady de Insula Chapel in the original and now demolished St Mary's Church may be a reference to the church's island site created by the rivers and streams. The present church building is mostly an 1893 restoration by Blomfield with a tower surviving from 1630. The large east window is by Burne-Jones. Nearby in Church Street, there is the sixteenth-century Feathers pub. Basing House, between the library and Watersmeet Theatre in the High Street, is where William Penn (see pages 28 and 87) lived for the first five years of his married life from 1672. The house, which has a stone from America, is now the museum (open Mon–Fri 2–4pm & Sat 10am–4pm; admission free). At the east end of the High Street is St Joan of Arc School which embraces The Elms where Marian Cross spent the summer of 1857, the year she first used the pseudonym 'George Eliot'. The railway, which caused the town to change, reached here in 1889.

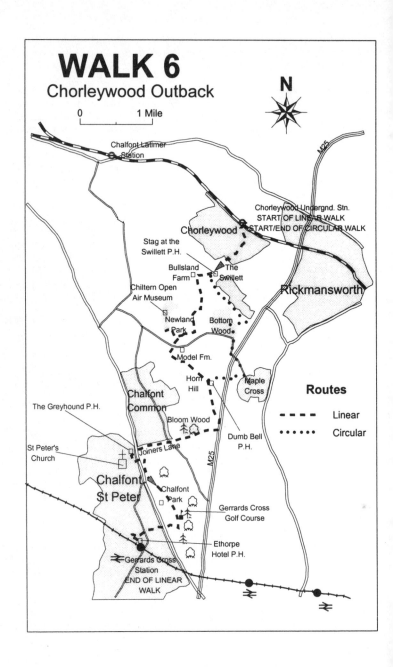

WALK 6
Chorleywood Outback

0   1 Mile

N

Chalfont Latimer Station

M25

Chorleywood Undergnd. Stn.
START OF LINEAR WALK
START/END OF CIRCULAR WALK

Chorleywood

Stag at the Swillett P.H.

Bullsland Farm

The Swillett

Rickmansworth

Chiltern Open Air Museum

Newland Park

Bottom Wood

Model Fm.

Horn Hill

Maple Cross

Chalfont Common

The Greyhound P.H.

Bloom Wood

Dumb Bell P.H.

St Peter's Church

Joiners Lane

M25

Chalfont St Peter

Chalfont Park

Gerrards Cross Golf Course

Ethorpe Hotel P.H.

Gerrards Cross Station
END OF LINEAR WALK

Routes

- - - Linear

· · · · · Circular

Walk 6: Chorleywood Outback

Chorleywood – Horn Hill – Chalfont St Peter – Gerrards Cross

This walk may be completed as a circular hike based on Chorleywood or as a slightly longer linear route ending at Gerrards Cross train station. Directions for each route are given in the text. Both walks offer pleasant, easy rambles through the gently rolling landscape of the lesser Chilterns, where beechwoods thrive on the chalky soil. On both walks there's an optional detour to the fascinating Chiltern Open Air Museum where farm buildings from the past have been rescued, restored and set up in 45 acres of parkland.

> *Distance*: 8 miles (Gerrards Cross linear route) or 6.5 miles (Chorleywood circular route).

> *Map*: OS Landranger 176 (West London area) or OS Pathfinder 1139 (Watford) and 1158 (Hillingdon).

> *Terrain*: Field paths and country lanes. Waterproof footwear is recommended as some parts tend to be very muddy after rain.

> *Food & Drink*: Stag at the Swillett (Mon–Sat 11am-3pm & 5.30–11pm; Sun 12–3pm & 7–10.30pm; M/G), Chorleywood; Dumb Bell (Mon–Thur 11–3 & 5.30–11pm; Fri–Sat 11am–11pm; Sun 12–30pm & 7–10.30pm; M/G), Horn Hill; Greyhound (Mon–Sat 11am–11pm; Sun 12–10.30pm; M/G) and Myrtle Tree tearoom (Mon–Sat 9am–4.15pm), Chalfont St Peter; Ethorpe Hotel (Mon–Sat 10am–2.30pm & 5.30–11pm; Sun 12–3pm & 7–10.30pm; M/G), Gerrards Cross.

> *Transport*: London Underground (Metropolitan line) to Chorleywood (outside Travelcard zones). On the linear route, the return journey is from Gerrards Cross train station (outside Travelcard zones)

> *Start & Finish*: Both walks start out from Chorleywood underground station. The linear route ends at Gerrards Cross train station.

Leave Chorleywood Station by the car park on the 'down' (or 'from London') platform, using the car park steps to descend to a road (Lower Road) where you turn left to a junction. Cross this into Capell Way which brings you to Hubbard's Road, a steep hill lined with houses. Turn right uphill as far as a turning on the left called Copman's Wick; turn along here to a narrow enclosed path on the right marked by a 'no cycles' sign. Keep ahead along this enclosed path, ignoring a stile which soon appears on the left, and across a cul-de-sac to eventually emerge at Rendlesham Way. Continue the short distance to the junction above, bearing right along Stag Lane to the Stag at the Swillett pub, just visible in the distance.

Taking a track to the right of the pub the walk reaches the countryside; keep forward at the first near allotments to a field beyond a stile. Do not take the tempting path round to the left (this is the return route for the circular walk) but instead veer to the right over rough grass towards the left edge of a wood and into a valley where you will meet a stile. Cross this and the sloping field beyond to a second stile leading into a lane fronting the farmyard of Bullsland Farm. You may be inspected here by the farm's dogs, who are friendly and wear computer-linked bleepers on their collars. Turn left along the lane to pass through a white metal gate and continue along a rough metalled path with farm buildings to the right. This becomes a pleasant country track running between hedgerows and, beyond a bend near an orchard, soon plunges downhill towards a field. At the foot of the hill turn right between two old gateposts and follow the path through bushes to reach Shire Lane by a gate.

Swing leftwards here along this good and pleasant leafy track which marks the county boundary between Hertfordshire and Buckinghamshire. After half a mile look for a waymarked stile into the grounds of Newlands Park, on the right. Cross this and keep forward over the grass, crossing a drive to a sports ground. Follow the fence of an all-weather sports field (right) and beyond this keep ahead across a cricket field veering slightly right to a stile in a hedgerow.

The walk continues across the stile, but should you wish to visit the Chiltern Open Air Museum, follow the instructions in the box below.

THE CHILTERN OPEN AIR MUSEUM

Opened in 1976 as an agricultural history museum with the aim of rescuing threatened farm buildings and machinery, the Chiltern Open Air Museum is a registered charity largely run and staffed by local volunteers. Besides ancient barns, stables, granaries, farmhouses and cottages – all fully equipped with period furniture and implements – some of the more unusual buildings the museum has saved include a fully functioning forge, a toll house and gate, an Edwardian cast-iron public lavatory and a charming Victorian corrugated-iron chapel complete with porch and bell tower. They have all been imaginatively laid out in a natural park of meadow and woodland, complete with village green which often features pageants, displays of country crafts and dancing. The farmyard of Chiltern Farm – maintained as a traditional working farmstead with sheep, cattle and poultry – appeared in the television drama *Bramwell*. There is also a cafeteria. (Museum open Easter to Oct; weekends & bank holidays 11am–6pm, Tue–Fri 2-6pm, closed Mon; adults £4.00, children £2.50, concessions £3.50.)

To reach the museum, at the end of the fence by the all-weather sports field (see above) turn right across the grass to meet a concrete path close to a brick wall. Turn left along the path to pass through a metal gate into the grounds of Buckinghamshire College. On meeting a drive, with a student hall of residence beyond, turn right. Follow the drive as it bends to the right to meet the main college drive. Turn left along here for about 100 yards to a security gate at the college entrance. A few yards beyond this gate on the right is the entrance to the museum. When you have visited the museum retrace your steps to continue the walk.

Cross the stile (see above) into a field and set a course half-left over the grass, passing at first beneath the branches of some mature oaks. Try not to drift too far left, keeping a pond (often dried up in high summer) circled by trees to your left. If you find yourself off course and reach a lane by the Model Farm you'll need to walk right along the lane to reach the next path. Beyond the width of the field is a stile set in the bushes standing close to an isolated tree. Cross the stile to pass through a screen of trees to a lane.

Directly opposite, another stile and signposted path leads on, passing to the left of a bungalow and glasshouses to a field where the path keeps beside a hedge (left) to another stile in the corner. Cross this, immediately *turning left* over a second stile. Now follow the left edge of a large field (probably filled with inquisitive ponies from the local riding centre) towards Brawlings Farm in the distance. You should abandon the hedgerow when it turns away, striking towards a stile to the left of the farm buildings. Cross this into a field and follow a hedge on the right to another stile on a narrow lane.

A few yards right, and opposite, a signposted path leads half-right over rising ground towards the hamlet of Horn Hill (which cannot be glimpsed at first). After climbing gently to 350 feet you will begin to see two prominent white buildings and notice that your path leads to the far one, at another stile leading into a lane. Cross this stile and turn right to reach the Dumb Bell Inn with a beer garden, a good place for refreshment.

Here, at Horn Hill, the two walks divide. Details of both the circular and linear routes follow.

Circular Route

From the stile mentioned at the end of the last paragraph (about 150 yards north of the Dumb Bell Inn) proceed almost directly opposite to take an enclosed signed footpath to the left of Crooked Billet cottage. This path dog-legs around the perimeter of a farm before reaching a field at a kissing gate. From here it follows a right-hand hedge-line over gently falling pastures interrupted by a stile to reach a second stile in the field corner. Cross this and the corner of the field beyond to a footbridge over the M25 motorway. Once over the footbridge keep ahead across a field towards trees. On reaching the trees turn left to follow the field edge downhill with a hedge and fence to the right. When you reach a lane turn left to pass under a viaduct carrying the M25.

Beyond the viaduct follow the lane as it curves uphill through trees. About 100 yards beyond the viaduct leave the road on the right by a stand of beech trees (with the M25 beyond) to follow a path running parallel to the road, heading north. Where the road swings away to the left keep ahead along the path into Bottom Wood, a delightful beechwood where a glorious sea of bluebells covers the woodland floor in late April and early May before the leaf canopy above closes. The path keeps close to the right margin of the wood. Do *not* allow yourself to be tempted off course by a broad track on the left after 100 yards or so, but press on along the main border track. Soon the path descends suddenly to the lower part of the wood and, not far ahead, when you meet a waymarked crosspath, turn right along a path which leads to the edge of the wood and a stile facing a rising field. Keeping ahead, at the top of the rise turn left along a grassy path which runs at first near to house gardens (right) to a stile in the field corner. Cross the stile and keep ahead with the hedge to the right. Your destination, close to Bullsland Farm passed near to the start of the walk, is visible ahead. The path continues through the upper pastures of fields for another half a mile, passing a couple of stiles en route, until it runs in a broad right curve to another stile, rejoining your outward path near the allotments at the Swillett. Retrace your route from here to the Stag at the Swillett pub (and your last opportunity for refreshment) and Stag Lane to reach Chorleywood underground station.

The Linear Route

To follow the Gerrards Cross route, walk forward past the Dumb Bell Inn (left) and keep ahead by a track (signed 'Public Bridleway No. 2') as the lane swings left. This tends to be very muddy underfoot in inclement weather and after 500 yards, with a view of the M25 motorway to the left, it meets another lane at a corner. Keep ahead in the same direction following the lane to a bridge over the M25. Don't cross the bridge but take the lane to the right immediately before it signed 'public footpath' (sign damaged at time of writing). The path follows the line of the M25 leaving the metalled road after 50 metres at a bend to continue beyond an iron gate (this area may have rubbish deposited by fly-tippers).

Keep ahead for a short distance along a gravelled lane. On entering a field turn right and away from the motorway following a line of trees on the right. The line of the path now runs over the crest of a rise, then descends half-left across a field to a lane. Cross the lane to head uphill following the line of trees to the right. Continue with the trees on your right skirting the edge of Bloom Wood, ignoring tempting woodland paths (unless you wish to explore further), for another half a mile to reach a stile at a main road.

BLOOM WOOD

Bloom Wood is typical of the beech woodlands of the area. The common beech (*Fagus sylvatica*) is a European native and grows to a height of thirty to fifty metres. Wildlife find its triangular nut (beech mast), which is rich in oil, a valued food source and these were once gathered and used in pig-feeding. Beech leaves were also used in the past to stuff mattresses, and the eighteenth-century diarist John Evelyn said they were superior to straw because they would 'continue to be sweet for seven or eight years'. Today, in the age of interior springing and latex rubber, the fallen autumn leaves are left to lie in a dense golden carpet, a dazzling sight on the woodland floor.

Cross the stile and go downhill along Joiners Lane, almost opposite. This road takes you for a half a mile, and with increasing speed, down to the Misbourne valley and Chalfont St Peter. Reach the village centre by taking the garishly painted subway beneath the A413 to break surface opposite the picturesque Greyhound Inn.

CHALFONT ST PETER

Not so interesting or attractive as its sister village St Giles (see Walk 3), the former medieval settlement of Chalfont St Peter suffers from an accumulation of urban sprawl, a featureless modern shopping centre and the busy A413 bypass which slices it in two. In the midst of all this, the sizeable Georgian 'brick box' church of St Peter, which replaced its collapsed medieval predecessor, was drastically 'gothicised' by the Victorians but does contain a number of interesting fifteenth-century brass memorials. However, it's not often open outside service times except for weekday afternoons (2–4pm) in June and July. A number of sixteenth- and seventeenth-century buildings have survived the demolition hammer, including the Greyhound Inn. For lighter refreshment there's also the Myrtle Tree tearooms serving home-made cakes and pastries and reached by turning right after the church along Market Place (No. 8).

The walk continues along the High Street passing a clutch of other pubs – the George, the White Hart and the Poachers – before turning left along Chiltern Hill (the first turning). This crosses the main dual carriageway of the bypass by its special bridge. On the far side of this turn off immediately along the asphalt footpath on the right that runs gently down near the road. Where it joins a small private carriageway keep ahead, passing the entrance to the Chalfont Heights residential estate, beyond which (and before a roundabout) the footpath is located beyond a stile in trees to the left.

Cross the stile and proceed through trees to walk ahead over grass. Keep ahead along the path, faint in the smooth turf that runs forward over the lower levels of Gerrards Cross golf course. Keep an eye out for wayward flying golf-balls and for a series of white posts which confirm and mark the right-of-way as it passes through a plantation of conifers, keeping to the left of a cricket field to follow a line of trees to another white marker post indicating the footpath. Beyond this the path passes to the left of buildings and meets a cross path. Keep ahead over grass towards trees, with the golf clubhouse to the right. Beyond a gap in the trees take care to avoid a track on the left and continue forward by a narrow, well-marked path that loiters under a grove of spruce before running along the banks of the River Misbourne with the buildings of Chalfont Park on the opposite bank. Once an eighteenth-century mansion, this has been substantially enlarged and is now a research laboratory for an industrial firm. Just beyond the house a pleasant narrow path forks right to follow the riverbank, rejoining the main path further along.

At a stile the path crosses the stream by a little bridge beneath the shade of trees. Once across the bridge, follow the driveway a short distance to a ford at a stream and stile on the right. Cross this into a field heading half-right over grass to two stiles on the far side, separated by a drive. Once across both stiles pass beneath the spreading branches of a brace of venerable sycamore trees, to another stile. Once over this, carefully cross the A413 Chalfont St Peter bypass to a path on the opposite side which ascends a gentle gradient to another stile. Cross this and follow the path which climbs through woodland to a road. Cross the road to the right picking up an enclosed footpath on the other side which proceeds between houses and gardens. Beyond another road the path, now metalled, continues ahead and finally emerges at a junction almost facing Orchehill Avenue.

If you wish to go directly to the train station, keep ahead along Orchehill Avenue taking the first road on the left (Orchehill Rise) which leads, beyond a bend, to a footpath on the right. This descends the hill to Gerrards Cross station. Alternatively, if you're seeking refreshment don't enter Orchehill Avenue, but turn left along the main road to reach the Ethorpe Hotel, 300 yards ahead on the right, with a restaurant and pleasant beer garden. To reach the station from here turn right along the road immediately beyond the hotel and follow the road as it bends left to a T-junction. Turn right here along Ethorpe Close and, when this bends to the right, turn left along an enclosed public footpath. This will lead you to the entrance to the train station.

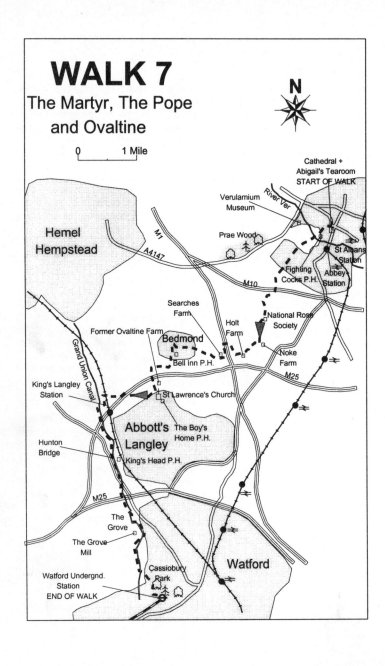

WALK 7
The Martyr, The Pope and Ovaltine

0   1 Mile

N

Cathedral +
Abigail's Tearoom
START OF WALK

River Ver

Verulamium
Museum

Prae Wood

Hemel
Hempstead

M1

A4147

St Albans
Station

Fighting
Cocks P.H.

Abbey
Station

M10

Searches
Farm

National Rose
Society

Holt
Farm

Former Ovaltine Farm

Bedmond

Noke
Farm

Bell Inn P.H.

M25

Grand Union Canal

King's Langley
Station

St Lawrence's Church

**Abbott's
Langley**

The Boy's
Home P.H.

Hunton
Bridge

King's Head P.H.

M25

The
Grove

The Grove
Mill

Watford

Watford Undergnd.
Station
END OF WALK

Cassiobury
Park

Walk 7: The Martyr, the Pope and Ovaltine

St Albans – Bedmond – Abbots Langley – King's Langley – Watford

---

This walk has its start in the urbane, ancient city of St Albans and encompasses a stretch of countryside known to the ancient Britons and Romans as well as to Nicholas Breakspear, the only English pope, who was born near the village of Bedmond. There's the option of visits to the Verulamium museum and the gardens of the National Rose Society, and the longer hike concludes with a pleasant stroll along the towpath of the historic Grand Union Canal.

> *Distance*: 10.5 or 7.5 miles. The shorter walk ends at the railway station at King's Langley where there are also Green Line buses to Watford.

> *Map*: OS Landranger 166 (Luton, Hertford and surrounding area) or OS Pathfinder 1119 (St Albans) and 1139 (Watford).

> *Terrain*: Mostly field paths, country roads and canal towpaths. Muddy in parts after rain. No climbs.

> *Food & Drink*: Ye Old Fighting Cocks (Mon–Sat 11am–11pm; Sun 12–10.30pm; M/G) and Abigail's Tearoom (9.30am–5pm; Sun 11am–5pm; G), both St. Albans; Bell Inn (Mon–Sat 11am–4pm & 5.30-11pm; Sun 12–4pm & 5.30–10.30pm; M/G), Bedmond; Boys' Home (Mon–Sat 11am–11pm; Sun 12–3pm & 7–10.30pm), Abbots Langley; King's Head (Mon–Sat 11am–4pm & 7–10.30pm; Sun 12–3pm & 7–10.30pm; M/G), Hunton Bridge.

> *Transport*: National Railways to St Albans City Station. If arriving by rail at the Abbey Station turn right up Holywell Hill and Chequer Street for a quarter of a mile to reach Market Square and the Tourist Information Centre, and begin the walk from there. By underground to High Barnet and then LT Bus 84 (a one-hour journey) to St Albans City Station. St Albans, King's Langley and Watford stations all lie slightly outside Travelcard Zone 6 necessitating a supplementary fare on a one-day Travelcard.

> *Start & Finish*: St Albans Cathedral to Watford underground station. The shorter route ends at King's Langley Station for trains to Euston or Green Line buses 501 or 747 to Watford and the underground.

If arriving by rail from London climb the steps to the right as you exit the station and cross the bridge. Continue ahead (with a view of the square tower of the cathedral above the city's skyline) along Victoria St to reach (after half a mile) the Market Square. Cross the road and pass the Tourist Office (April–Oct: Mon–Sat 9.30–5.30pm, Sun 10.30–4.30pm; Nov–Mar Mon–Sat 10am–4pm), turning left to reach French Row.

ST ALBANS

French Row is a reminder of the French occupation in the early thirteenth century. In the Fleur de Lys Inn, heavily restored but retaining much of its original timber framework, King John of France was imprisoned after his defeat by Edward the Black Prince at the battle of Poitiers in 1356. Many of the other buildings in this atmospheric street date from the fourteenth century. At the end of French Row the fifteenth-century Clock Tower houses 'Gabriel,' the curfew bell, striking on the hour and older than the tower itself. From the tower (open April–Sept Sat, Sun and bank holidays 10.30am–5pm; small charge) there are fine views over the town and the surrounding countryside. Before the Reformation, candles were sold to pilgrims visiting the cathedral at Waxhouse Gate opposite.

At the end of French Row cross the High Street at the traffic lights to turn left to go through the small Waxhouse Gate. Go ahead passing the pleasant terrace of Abigail's Tearoom (left) to follow the footpath around the north side of the cathedral – or 'Abbey' as it's known by locals – to arrive at the main west entrance.

ST ALBANS CATHEDRAL

In about AD 303 according to legend a Roman soldier, Albanus, was led out of Verulamium (see below) and beheaded for giving shelter to a priest and refusing to deny his conversion to Christianity, then a sect being vigorously persecuted by the Roman Emperor, Diocletian. A church was built on the execution site, followed in the eighth century by an abbey (now the cathedral) as the tomb of St Alban, the first Christian martyr in England, became an object of pilgrimage. Roman tiles and stone from the now abandoned Roman city were used by the Normans to build an enlarged church and tower.

The beautiful carved oak watching chamber at the eastern end of the church's nave – the longest in England at 84 metres and decorated with medieval wall paintings – where monks guarded the shrine of the martyr day and night, dates from the early fifteenth century. The shrine was wilfully destroyed during the Dissolution, but the thousands of fragments of Purbeck marble were painstakingly recovered and reconstructed in the last century. Note the relief on the west side depicting the saint's martyrdom. A tour of the church is best made with the guide 'A Visit to St Albans Cathedral' (available at the entrance, price 30p).

Nicholas Breakspear, who was to become Pope Adrian IV in 1154, attended the Abbey School but was refused admission to the Benedictine order for being 'insufficient in learning'. He then entered a French monastery, became a cardinal and found his route to Rome. The fourteenth-century Abbey gateway facing the cathedral's main entrance is all that remains of the great Benedictine Abbey, also destroyed during the Dissolution. Earlier, this same portal had been besieged by John Ball and his followers during the Peasants' Revolt in 1381.

From the west entrance take the path right to a gate leading into George Street. Turn left to pass through the Abbey gateway and walk down Abbey Mill Lane – St Alban would have walked up this road to his execution on the hill outside the Roman city. Keep right where the road divides. The Fighting Cocks pub is on the left.

YE OLD FIGHTING COCKS

This ancient octagonal timber-framed building is one of the oldest inns in England, and with its position overlooking the river has kept much of its character despite having suffered extensive 'improvement'. It's said to have been a medieval pigeon house and fishing lodge. The building was part of the monastery until the Reformation, when it became an inn. For a time it was a centre of cockfighting, hence the name.

Cross the River Ver and follow the path ahead with a lake to the right. Ignore all turnings (except if you are visiting the museum – see box below) and soon the way passes beside the impressive remains of the ancient walls (right) pierced by the London Gate of the Roman city of Verulamium, now lying beneath the parkland beyond after being excavated in the 1930s and 1950s.

VERULAMIUM

Roman Verulamium was one of the largest and most important of the towns established by the Romans in Britain. Roman armies conquered this area in AD 43 and a new town was laid out just over five years later close to the capital of the subdued Catuvellauni tribe, now in Prae Wood (see below). The city was sacked in AD 61 in the rising led by Boudicca, and then rebuilt on a grand scale. Verulamium remained a vibrant municipality until its decline in the fifth century as the empire succumbed to barbarian invasions. Among the visible remains are a rare and well-preserved theatre (April–Oct 10am–5pm daily; Nov–Mar 10am–4pm; adults £1.50, £1.00 concessions, children 50p), a mosaic pavement and hypocaust in a bath-house in the park, as well as an outstanding Verulamium Museum (Mon–Sat 10am–5pm; Sun 2–5pm; £2.80 adults, £1.60 children and concessions) with more fine mosaics and discoveries from the excavations.

To reach the museum (near the tenth-century St Michael's Church on the far side of the park) take the path alongside the lake to the right immediately after crossing the river at the Fighting Cocks. Continue along the lakeside to a bridge (left). Cross the bridge, passing to the right of a children's pool and keep ahead to the Inn on the Park café where you should turn right to follow the path to the museum car park.

Continue forward following the line of the Roman wall to reach a road beyond a footbridge. Cross this and take the footpath ahead which runs between a playing field and new houses (right). The path, becoming enclosed, crosses three roads. Where the houses end bear left on to a rough path and soon turn right, through a gap in the fence, to follow a path up a sloping field. On the hill to the right lies Prae Wood.

PRAE WOOD

Prae Wood is the site of the great *oppidum* or tribal capital of the Catuvellauni, a tribe that controlled a chunk of territory embracing most of Hertfordshire and areas beyond, prior to the Roman conquest of AD 43. This settlement, of which earthworks survive, spread down the hill to the banks of the River Ver, and the discovery of a number of rich 'warrior graves' burials close by has confirmed the power and prosperity of the tribe's ruling elite. After taking and sacking the Catuvellaunian stronghold, the Roman army moved the centre of the new Roman town closer to the river.

On reaching a wood go left and, when the trees end, right to cross a footbridge over the M10 motorway. Keep ahead over the bridge and follow the edge of Park Wood (right) to reach a lane. Go right along the lane for 200 yards and turn left into Furzebushes Lane. This road bears left to a sharp right turn. Do *not* go right, but keep forward to enter a field and turn half-right to climb up to a lane by the entrance to the National Rose Society.

ROYAL NATIONAL ROSE SOCIETY

The Royal National Rose Society was founded in 1876 to extend knowledge and appreciation of the rose. The society (which prides itself on an unstuffy approach to the subject) maintains over 30,000 plants consisting of more than 1,650 different varieties and species in 12 acres of superb gardens. (Open mid-June to late October; Mon–Sat 9am–5pm; Sun & bank hols. 10am–6pm; adults £4.00, kids under sixteen free.)

Go to the right along the lane and, at the end of the Rose Society's ground, turn left to find a footpath (signed 'Noke Lane'). When the garden (left) ends keep ahead to a wooden stile on the far side of a field. Keep forward across a further field. At a fence ahead, stay to the right of the drinking trough to follow a track running down to Noke Farm. Turn right following the waymark, and veering wide of the farm and any hay bales, to find a wooden stile leading to a lane. Cross this and turn right along the lane for 100 yards to go left up the private road to Holt Farm.

Follow the rough road past the farmhouse and a barn (left) to continue ahead with trees to the left – along what is now a bridleway – crossing a field to meet a crosspath fronting the motorway. Turn right at this junction to follow the path roughly north alongside the motorway to Blunt's Lane. Go left across the bridge and, after a short distance, turn left down Searches Lane, a metalled road flanking the motorway. After quarter of a mile you arrive at the picturesque Searches Farm.

SEARCHES FARM

Founded in the fourteenth century by one of Norman origin named Seriches, the farm's title was later anglicised to Searches and came under the manorial control of the nearby manor of Windridge. The venerable red-brick farmhouse (private) has one of only three cruck roofs (arched timbers used in roof supports) known in Hertfordshire and contains sections of original fifteenth-century wattle and daub plastering. The present owner, retired farmer John Wadlow, uses the elegant old granary as a garage and claims that the carved stone garden curio nearby is a relic from the original House of Commons at Westminster, destroyed by fire in 1834. If you pass by on the first Sunday of the month the surroundings will resound to the gun cracks of clay pigeon shooters who use the farm for their gatherings.

Keep ahead after the farm entrance to follow an enclosed footpath and bridleway. When this joins a road at Millhouse Farm (left) keep the same direction for half a mile along the metalled road to reach Bedmond.

BEDMOND

Now a rather characterless dormitory village hedged in by motorways, Bedmond's main claim to fame is as the birthplace of England's solitary pope. Nicholas Breakspear, or Pope Adrian IV as he became, was born here about 1100 at the eponymous Breakspear Farm which was demolished in the early 1960s. As a cardinal he is believed to have visited his old home in about 1150, four years before his elevation to the papacy.

Go left along the High Street to pass the Bell Inn (left), with a beer garden, and East Lane. Beyond a small roadside memorial to Nicholas Breakspear (right) continue ahead downhill to pass Studd Cottage (right) and a bus stop. Go right up Sheppey's Lane. Ignore turnings to the left and right, keeping ahead for quarter of a mile until the track dips. About 25 yards beyond two oaks (right) turn left along an unmarked crosspath which bisects a field to reach a footbridge over the M25. Cross the stile on the other side and keep ahead, passing on the left what used to be the Ovaltine Farm.

THE OVALTINE MODEL DAIRY FARM

Built during the 1930s, this model farm supplied the Ovaltine factory at King's Langley (see below) with the milk and eggs needed to make the malt extract 'wonder drink' Ovaltine. Known as Parsonage Farm, it still retains its Sussex farmhouse-style buildings, now converted into a private residential complex, once used in the beverage's advertisements.

When the path crosses the main farm drive keep ahead and, at a crosspath, turn right to walk along the side of Abbots Langley village. After 50 yards there is a path on the left which leads to St Lawrence's Church. To visit the church and village follow the enclosed path, crossing one road, to a metal gate giving access to the leafy churchyard where the way runs between a line of lofty elms to the church.

ABBOTS LANGLEY

Mentioned in the Domesday Book, the village of Abbots Langley derives its name from the Saxon long 'ley', a clearing in a wood. It later came under the authority of the Abbot of St Albans. Facing the village's High Street, which has a number of old buildings, St Lawrence's Church was begun when Pope Adrian was a child, and he possibly saw the completed building when he returned, as a cardinal, to Bedmond. His village friends sent gifts to Rome when he was elected to the papacy, and in 1159, on hearing of his death, they attended a requiem mass in the church. He is buried in St Peter's in Rome but a plaque on the south wall of the church records his association with the parish.

Built of stone and flint with a squat tower, the church's interior – with Norman arcades, a fine south chancel with medieval frescoes and an early fifteenth-century octagonal font – has many interesting architectural features. When locked the key can be obtained from the vicarage, just behind. The land occupied by the pig farm (see below), formerly Parsonage Farm, is the site of the first matches played by the Abbots Langley Cricket Club founded in 1845, and now well into its second century. For refreshment, opposite St Lawrence's lych gate is the curiously named Boys' Home pub.

The walk continues ahead beyond the turn off to the church. Where the path enters a field beyond a wooden barrier, keep forward to turn right along a crosspath at the end of the field to reach a gate, in the far corner. Turn left on to a farm drive which runs gently downhill to another footbridge over the M25. Beyond the bridge there is a view of King's Langley and the Ovaltine factory.

OVALTINE FACTORY

Ovaltine was launched in 1865 by a Swiss company founded by chemist George Wander, who was investigating the nutritional value of barley malt. The King's Langley factory was begun in 1913 when the company then used its own barges to bring coal from Coventry on the nearby Grand Union Canal – a 10- to 14-day return journey. Today more than half the Ovaltine produced here is exported and the factory – the world's largest producer of malt extract – supplies this commodity to the food industry for the manufacture of biscuits, breakfast cereals and home brew kits.

Continue ahead to pass the entrance to the former, and boarded up, Ovaltine Egg Farm with its elegant roofs, half-moon courtyard and well, where the way bears right and then left under the railway bridge. The path meets a main road at the southern edge of King's Langley.

To end the shorter walk here (7.5 miles), turn left to the train station a quarter of a mile ahead on the left; buses to Watford use the stop to the right of where you emerge.

To continue the longer walk also turn left and head south for 300 yards. Just beyond a new office building (right), and before the station, turn down a path on the right. Beyond a stream the path meets the Grand Union Canal. Go left across the bridge and down the steps (left) to reach the water and walk south along the canal (with the canal on the left). This stretch of the hike forms part of the Grand Union Canal Walk launched in 1993, which opened up the towpath to walkers along the whole of the canal's route.

THE GRAND UNION CANAL

The Grand Junction Canal, as it was originally called when started in 1793, took 12 years to complete. The M1 of the eighteenth century and 143 miles in length, it served to link London with Birmingham, a city then being transformed by the industrial revolution. Along the canal was transported a multitude of goods which included the southbound Cheshire salt, Staffordshire pottery and Yorkshire paving stone and coal, as well as the northbound imports from the empire. But the canal's domination of the carrying trade lasted only 30 years and from 1838, when a parallel railway competed for trade, the canal entered upon a slow decline. It was to fight the competition of the railway that brought about, in 1929, the amalgamation of this canal and others into the Grand Union Canal. Although the canal system played a key role in carrying war materials during World War Two, the Grand Union and other canals were finally defeated as a viable economic proposition by the coming of the motorway age. It is in the age of leisure that the Grand Union, no longer a commercial waterway and now managed by British Waterways, is finding a new role as a tranquil and often scenic escape from the frenetic urban conurbations it helped to create.

A quarter of a mile after a picturesque lock with its lock-keeper's cottage there is a view of St Paul's Victorian Church at Hunton Bridge. To get refreshment here, ascend the steps to the bridge and turn left to the King's Head (with an extensive beer garden on the canal) 50 yards down the road on the right. The waterside path, a favourite haunt for anglers and herons, continues under the bridge and beyond two locks the way bends beneath a road. Just before a motorway the path leaves the water for a short distance. After another lock the path crosses the water via a brick footbridge and, beyond a bend, runs under the balustraded bridge 164 which carries the drive to The Grove, an elegant eighteenth-century mansion designed by Sir Robert Taylor. The ornamented bridge was the price the canal company had to pay to cross the aristocratic acres of this home of the dukes of Clarendon. Shortly beyond the bridge the house comes into view on the west bank.

At an S-bend the canal passes Grovemill House and then flows under a road. Soon the path switches back to the west bank before two locks.

After nearly half a mile cross bridge 167 – its steps leading up to the lock behind the bridge worn by generations of users – just beyond another lock, and enter Cassiobury Park.

CASSIOBURY PARK

Cassiobury House, the once magnificent home of the earls of Essex, was pulled down in 1927, but the grounds remain as a park. Originally part of the lands of St Albans Abbey and mentioned in the Domesday Book, after the dissolution of the monasteries Henry VIII granted the manor to Sir Richard Morison, a virulent propagandist in the king's war against the papacy, in 1545. Later the estate passed into the hands of the Capel family, and when Lord Capel was raised to the earldom of Essex by Charles II after the Restoration as a reward for his loyalty during the civil war, he set about creating a befitting family seat. It was in this period that the house was extended and embellished with one of the finest landscaped gardens in England by Moses Cook and, later, Humphrey Repton. Many of the modern park's trees – cedars, oaks and beeches – are the estate's only survivors. When the earls of Essex began to break up the estate in the early 1900s in response to financial pressures, Watford Council purchased 75 acres for a 'people's park and pleasure ground'. Later acquisitions increased the park's dimensions to its present 190 acres.

The house itself was put up for sale in 1922 and the surviving catalogue is evidence of a still splendid interior. But it remained unoccupied after the sale, prior to its subsequent demolition. Nothing survives today, but a sumptuous grand staircase in carved wood by Grinling Gibbons was rescued and is now in the collection of the Metropolitan Museum of Art in New York.

After crossing a stream, just inside the park, bear right. Beyond the model railway – with its scaled down steam-engine ever popular with children who ride in carriages behind – the path joins a stream. Shortly after a footbridge (right) bear half-left across the grass towards a car park near a small wood. Roughly a quarter of a mile north of the wood, in an area now built up, was the site of Cassiobury House, and in the basements of some dwellings in Temple Close the house's Tudor cellars survive. Keep ahead through the car park and exit into Gade Avenue, shortly turning left up Cassiobury Park Avenue. Just beyond Swiss Avenue (right) there is Watford underground station (Metropolitan line).

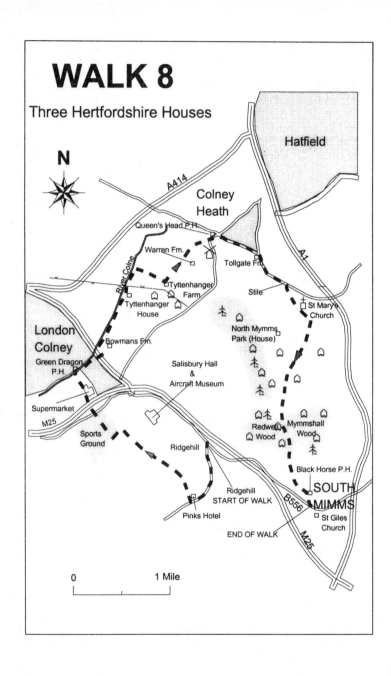

WALK 8

Three Hertfordshire Houses

N

Hatfield

A414

Colney
Heath

Queen's Head P.H.

Warren Fm.

Tollgate Fm.

Tyttenhanger
Farm

River Colne

Stile

St Mary's
Church

Tyttenhanger
House

North Mymms
Park (House)

Bowmans Fm.

London
Colney

Green Dragon
P.H.

Salisbury Hall
&
Aircraft Museum

Supermarket

M25

Sports
Ground

Ridgehill

Redwell
Wood

Mymmshall
Wood

Black Horse P.H.

SOUTH
MIMMS

Ridgehill
START OF WALK

Pinks Hotel

B556

St Giles
Church

END OF WALK

M25

A1

0   1 Mile

Walk 8: Three Hertfordshire Houses

London Colney – Colney Heath – South Mimms

This is a roughly circular walk which passes across the grounds of three historic mansions and visits a delightful old church. In between these sights there's the option of visits to a remarkable aircraft museum and a working farm. The varied scenery en route includes a stroll along the banks of the River Colne as well as undulating woodland on the return leg to the village of South Mimms.

> *Distance*: 8.5 or 3 miles. The shorter walk returns from London Colney by the number 84 bus to High Barnet underground station. On the longer route allow yourself sufficient time for any visits.

> *Map*: OS Landranger 166 (Luton, Hertford and surrounding area) or OS Pathfinder 1119 (St Albans) and 1120 (Hatfield).

> *Terrain*: Mostly field paths and country roads. Muddy in parts after rain. Two easy climbs.

> *Food & Drink*: Green Dragon (Mon–Sat 11am–11pm; Sun 12–10.30pm; M/G) London Colney; Bowmans Farm cafeteria (daily 9am–5.30pm; M/G); The Queen's Head (Mon–Sat 11am–11pm; Sun 12–3pm & 7–10.30pm; M/G) and Cock (Mon–Sat 11am–11pm; Sun 12–3pm & 7.30–10.30pm; M/G), both in Colney Heath; Black Horse (Mon–Thur 11am–3pm & 5.30–11pm; Fri–Sat 11am–11pm; Sun 12–3pm & 7–10.30pm; M/G), South Mimms.

> *Transport*: London Underground to High Barnet (Northern Line) then bus 84 from outside to Ridgehill, which lies just beyond the Zone 6 boundary. If you're buying an ordinary ticket it's cheaper to get the return.

> *Start & Finish*: The walk sets out from the Ridgehill bus stop on the 84 route from High Barnet. It ends at South Mimms from where the 84 bus will return you to High Barnet underground station.

From High Barnet underground station turn right up the ramp outside the station which emerges at a junction. Cross at the crossing to the opposite side of the main street and walk uphill to the Felix and Firkin pub with an exotic red lion projecting precariously above the 84 bus stop. Ask the bus driver to drop you at the Ridgehill stop which lies beyond South Mimms and comes immediately after the bus passes beneath the M25. Add 'near the Pinks Hotel at Rectory Lane' if necessary, as some drivers aren't always familiar with the route.

From the bus halt turn left along Rectory Lane, just north. Follow the lane as it winds first up then downhill to pass a wood on the right, a quarter-mile beyond which lies Pinks Hotel and restaurant. Just beyond the hotel turn right at a signed footpath. The path follows the side of the hotel to reach a stile, and beyond this continues between hedgerows; a view of Shenley Lodge appears half-right beyond trees. Keeping ahead in a northerly direction, negotiate your way beyond two gates which may bar your path and continue uphill. After nearly a quarter of a mile the way runs up to a fenced area with a pair of oaks to the left. Keeping ahead, follow the concreted path over the brow of the hill from where there's a magnificent view over the Colne valley and, on clearer days, St Albans, the square Norman tower of its Abbey projecting above the town. Follow the concrete path, which soon becomes a track, downhill passing a fenced area to the right after which a view of the chimneys of Salisbury Hall provides a backdrop to the De Havilland Aircraft Museum. At the foot of the hill the walk continues over a stile, but you should follow the track as it bends to the right if you wish to visit the aircraft museum.

SALISBURY HALL AND THE MOSQUITO AIRCRAFT MUSEUM

The moated seventeenth-century manor house (currently privately owned and closed to the public) of Salisbury Hall is the third on the site since the original was erected in Saxon times. In 1471 the Earl of Warwick and Salisbury set out from here to meet his death at the battle of Barnet, and there are traces of Tudor work dating from the residence of Sir John Cutler, Henry VIII's treasurer. Charles II and his seductive mistress Nell Gwynn later used the house for regular assignations. This was also the home, for some years, of Churchill's mother whose son was a frequent visitor here. During World War Two the mansion became the top-secret design centre of the De Havilland Aircraft Company where the wooden high-speed unarmed bomber the Mosquito was planned and where the first prototype was built. The original hangars adjoining the historic house are now home to the Mosquito Aircraft Museum (Mar–Oct: Tue, Thurs & Sat 2–5.30pm; Sun & holidays 10.30am–5.30pm; adults £4, children & senior citizens £2; family ticket for four £10) run by 500 enthusiasts volunteers who spend much of their spare time restoring the numerous vintage aircraft on display. The museum's star exhibit is the remarkably well preserved first Mosquito bomber ever built, which has an insurance tag of £5 million.

The walk continues by crossing the stile (see above) at the foot of the hill to follow a hedge and ditch (right) traversing University College and Hospital sports ground. These grounds are also used on weekdays by Arsenal Football Club, and don't be surprised to see a few multi-million-pound soccer stars firing into the goals in the flanking fields. On reaching a concrete path turn left (west) to follow a path between hedges. When you reach a crosspath (signed '21 Shenley') turn right along this with a ditch and hedge to the right, to emerge at a main road (the B556). Cross the road to follow a signed footpath through trees to a footbridge over the M25 with another view of St Albans ahead.

Once over the footbridge cross a stile into a field (right) and bear half-right to follow a hedge (with a supermarket behind) to a second stile in the far corner. Once across the wooden stile keep forward along a line of trees to cross another stile and a stream. Do *not* cross the River Colne footbridge unless you wish to call in at the Green Dragon pub but turn right to pass a row of houses and the old ford and road bridge in London Colney.

To end the walk here (3.5 miles) the 84 bus has a stop on the main road and will return you to High Barnet underground station.

THE GREEN DRAGON AND LONDON COLNEY

On the opposite bank of the River Colne lies the picturesque Green Dragon pub, founded in 1648 during the English civil wars. The green dragon was the crest of one of the local militias. The pub, or inn as it then was, came into being to provide coach travellers journeying between London and St Albans with food and overnight accommodation when the river was too high to cross. The village of London Colney has a few interesting old houses, but is today an overspill suburb of St Albans.

Pass the ford, veering right to the main road and the Bull Inn. Cross the road here and follow Lowbell Lane to where a viaduct carries the London Colney bypass over the road. Once under the bridge turn immediately left along an unsigned track which follows the embankment down to the River Colne. At the river turn right to follow the bank northwards. To the right across a field a pair of grain silos tower above Bowmans Farm. Should you wish to visit the farm take footpath 4 & 5 (signed from the river) on the right; further signs will guide you to the farm's car park and entrance. The walk continues along the riverbank.

BOWMANS FARM

Built on the site of a seventeenth-century farmhouse which burned down in 1933 and covering 1,100 acres, Bowmans Farm (open daily 9am–5.30pm; adults £3.50, children and concessions £2.50) has turned itself into one of the main educational farms in the area and is open to the public. A tour of the farm takes in the milking parlours (milking daily 1–3pm), poultry houses, pig farm and visits popular 'personalities' including Ben the giant shire horse and William the bull. There's also a pets corner and children's adventure playground, as well as a farm shop and cafeteria serving teas and snacks. You may visit the latter without charge, and from the farm's car park there's a fine view of Tyttenhanger House.

Continue north along the riverbank where the tower and weather-vane of Tyttenhanger House soon appear behind trees to the right.

TYTTENHANGER HOUSE

There has been a house on this site since the early fifteenth century and the previous one was visited by Henry VIII and Catherine of Aragon. The present brick mansion was built in 1654 for author Sir Henry Blount, and was possibly designed by Inigo Jones. Many noted guests stayed here including John Evelyn, the seventeenth-century diarist. The interior (not open to the public) has a magnificent staircase, chapel and some fine Elizabethan panelling.

Continue along the the riverbank until, about 100 yards beyond a power pylon, you come to a signed footpath on the right by a fledgling oak. Turn right along this, passing through a green metal gate, and follow the bridlepath east along an embankment between gravel pits. When the path emerges on to a farm track bear right, soon taking a left close to another power pylon to pass through the farmyard of Tyttenhanger Farm with cattle sheds to the right. Go ahead to follow the track which bends around to the left and then straightens to cross an open field in a north-easterly direction with a view (half-right) of Warren Farm in the distance. On the far side cross a ditch and wooden stile in a line of oaks. Across the stile the path continues along a fence to the right, beyond which there's a glimpse of a sailless windmill poking its dome above the trees. Cross another stile ahead and then bear half-right through the bushes on Colney Heath to reach a road by a bridge. Turn left to go over the bridge and follow the road to the centre of Colney Heath village. On the junction there's the first of two pubs here, the Queen's Head, while a little way down the road to the left there's the Cock, a free house offering Benskins beers. Both serve meals and snacks (not Sunday) and the latter's outdoor seating area is perhaps the more attractive of the two.

The walk continues by turning right at the junction along Tollgate Road. Follow the road which leaves the village in a south-east direction to pass Tollgate Farm before it bears half-left to go downhill. A good three-quarters of a mile from the junction a stile appears on the right with a view beyond of North Mymms Park mansion in woodland.

NORTH MYMMS PARK

One of the finest country houses in Hertfordshire, North Mymms Park was constructed in the sixteenth century by Sir Ralph Coningsby. In the following century, when his grandson was sent to the Tower of London for supporting Charles I, the house was ransacked. Laid out on the H-plan of the late Elizabethan style the house is two storeys high, with large windows and a central porch fronting a small cupola. An impressive doorway is flanked by Tuscan columns. The house has had a variety of owners throughout its history and is not open to the public.

Cross the stile (signed 'St Mary's Church') and walk through the trees towards the left side of the house (in the distance). After about 100 metres bear half-left keeping a long wire fence to the left and two clumps of trees to the right. Go over a wooden stile in bushes ahead to cross a footbridge spanning the infant River Colne. Keep ahead over the grass, passing through two gates to cross North Mymms Park drive, to reach St Mary's churchyard in the trees. Cross a wooden stile and go through a kissing gate, which are both opposite the church's west door.

ST MARY'S CHURCH

A fine fourteenth-century church whose predecessor was mentioned in the Domesday Book, St Mary's (open daily 9am–5.30pm) is well worth a visit. The church has had quite a few distinguished patrons including Thomas More, a frequent visitor to the then Carthusian church, whose family seat was nearby. Some of his *Utopia* was written while staying there. Inside, there's a fine Elizabethan panelled pulpit and many monuments of interest including, on the north wall of the chancel, a brass from around 1360 dedicated to parish priest William de Kestevene, with detail of God the Father holding the representation of the priest's soul in a canopy above. The nameless priest was identified by the shield of arms at his feet when a search in 1949 discovered documents and seals bearing the same arms in the archives at Westminster Abbey. The chancel also has a large wall monument to John Somers who framed the Declaration of Rights of 1689 laying down the conditions under which the crown was offered to William and Mary. An informative leaflet describes the interior in more detail. Just to the north of the church is the seventeenth-century vicarage. To the south the splendid nineteenth-century wrought-iron screen designed by Sir Ernest George marks the private entrance to the gardens of North Mymms Park.

The walk continues past the church (left) and leaves the churchyard by Church Cottage (right) to follow the drive to a junction. Turn right to walk southwards along a metalled lane which follows a holly hedge (right).

Where the metalled way swings to the right keep ahead up a rough enclosed path. The path rises to a felled area, Cangsley Grove. Keep ahead, following the track as it descends and climbs again to enter Redwell Wood, a verdant bower in summer. The final descent emerges at a road junction. Take the road left going downhill into the village of South Mimms. As you enter the village the welcome sign of the Black Horse pub (with garden) signals the end of the walk.

To return to High Barnet continue to the top of the road (Blackhorse Lane) turning left along the main road for 50 yards to the 84 bus stop fronting a petrol station. Any waiting time could be used to view the church of St Giles with its serene graveyard and antique tombs, visible behind the White Hart pub opposite. Built in the twelfth century, it has had later additions and alterations and was severely knocked about by Cromwell's troops in the mid-seventeenth century. Some interesting interior furniture includes a fine early sixteenth-century screen in the Lady Chapel and a twelfth-century stone font. The church is kept locked outside service times but names and phone numbers of the churchwardens are posted in the porch, and if it's convenient one of them may be able to come along and open it for you.

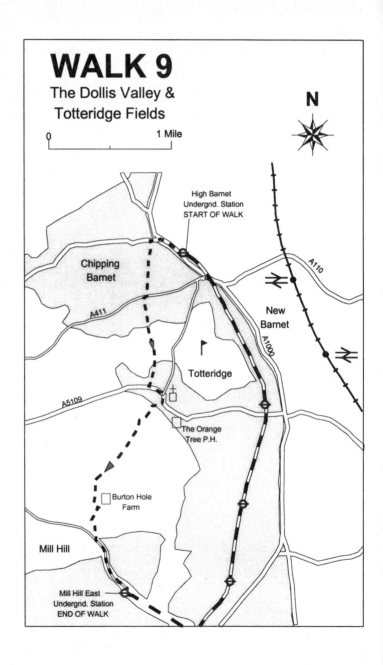

WALK 9

The Dollis Valley &
Totteridge Fields

N

0   1 Mile

High Barnet
Undergnd. Station
START OF WALK

Chipping
Barnet

A411

A110

New
Barnet

A1000

Totteridge

A5109

The Orange
Tree P.H.

Burton Hole
Farm

Mill Hill

Mill Hill East
Undergnd. Station
END OF WALK

Walk 9: Dollis Valley and Totteridge Fields

High Barnet – Chipping Barnet – Totteridge – Mill Hill

Totteridge has been described as having 'the finest example of traditional English countryside in the London area', and this rural landscape is defended from encroachment by a vigilant Barnet Council which also maintains its footpath network well. This route makes use of those paths to view the countryside where the nearest milking herd to central London graze. There is even a farm shop.

Distance: 4 or 2 miles.

Map: OS Landranger 176 (West London); OS Pathfinder 1140 (Barnet and Enfield).

Terrain: Field paths and road. All climbs are gentle and the only steep hill is a descent.

Food & Drink: Barnet has plenty of cafés and the Victoria Bakery in the High Street sells picnic food. Ye Olde Mitre Inn (11am–11pm; Sat 11am–3pm & 7–11pm; Sun 12–10.30pm) in Barnet. The Orange Tree (11am–3pm & 5.30–11pm; Sat 11am–11pm; Sun 12–10.30pm M/G), Totteridge. Railway Engineer (11am–11pm; Sun 12–10.30pm; M/G) at bottom of Bittacy Hill by Mill Hill East Station.

Transport: Northern line to High Barnet (Travelcard Zone 5). Return by LT bus 251 from Totteridge (Zone 4) to Totteridge & Whetstone Northern line station or catch the Northern line from Mill Hill East (Zone 4).

Start & Finish: High Barnet to Mill Hill. The shorter walk ends at Totteridge.

A steep path leads away from High Barnet Underground station to a road junction where there are London Loop waymarks. Cross the top of Meadway to continue up Barnet Hill, passing the Felix and Firkin with its landmark lion (left) and the more modest Mitre (right) to reach the church at Chipping Barnet.

CHIPPING BARNET
'Chipping' is Old English for the 'market', which is held here on Wednesdays and Saturdays. The famous Barnet Horse Fair survives as an annual September event. The keyhole of St John's Church at the top of the hill is level with the dome of St Paul's Cathedral ten miles away. However, Barnet's church falls not in the London diocese but St Albans, reminding us that Barnet was a Hertfordshire town before becoming a London borough. The many pubs were once coaching inns. This was the last stop before London and General Monck stayed at Ye Olde Mitre in 1660 on his way from Scotland to London to prepare for the Restoration. Samuel Pepys dined opposite at the Red Lion (now Felix and Firkin) which was later a Tory inn; the Whigs patronised the Green Man at the far end of the High Street. Barnet Museum is in

Wood Street (open Tue–Thu 2.30–4.30pm; Sat 10am–12pm & 2.30-4.30pm; admission free).

At the church bear left into Wood Street, and just before reaching Barnet Museum go left at the side of the Register Office into Old Court House Recreation Ground. Go ahead through the park but keep to the left of a fenced bowling green to find, on the far side, a long straight path. Follow this path which runs gently downhill, later passing tennis courts, and reach a road. Opposite are shops. Turn right and left into Leeside. At the far end continue on a metalled path down into the Dollis Valley crossing the line of the Dollis Valley Greenwalk and, again, the route of the London Loop, just before the Dollis Brook.

DOLLIS BROOK

The brook, an important ecological corridor for the capital, rises near Arkley and later joins the Mutton Brook to form the River Brent which flows into the Thames opposite Kew Gardens. 'Dollis' may be derived from the Saxon word 'dwllice' meaning 'erratic'. The Dollis Valley Greenwalk follows the stream as far as Hendon before turning east with the Mutton Brook to end on Hampstead Heath.

A footbridge takes the walk across the Dollis Brook to begin a gentle ascent out of the valley towards Totteridge on the hill ahead. The way runs between meadows. There is a school over the hedge (left) before the path crosses the top of a residential road. Beyond the approach to Oaklands (right) there is a kissing gate, and soon the way is grassed. At a road turn left passing a bus stop just before a fork at the cross in Totteridge. Bear round to the right on the road signposted Whetstone to pass the cattle pound (left behind hedge) and the church.

TOTTERIDGE

Totteridge was a Hertfordshire village until 1965 when it became part of north-west London. The great yew tree was here when the previous church was on the site. The present Georgian church was built in 1790 although the weather-boarded bell turret dates from at least 1706. In the year of the battle of Waterloo,1815, the congregation included the future Cardinal Manning whose father and brother are buried in the churchyard, under the holly tree by the new north-east corner of the church. Just outside the lych gate and behind a hedge is the village cattle pound. The Orange Tree pub is along the road to the east by the duck pond on the edge of Totteridge Green.

To end the walk here look for the bus stop on the main road. Pass Garden Hill House (right) and at the entrance to The Darlands go right through the gates. A wide enclosed path soon bends and runs gently downhill on the edge of a wood with views north over hilly countryside. At the bottom of the hill the wooded path runs straight for three-quarters of a mile with a field to the right. At a kissing gate bear half-left across the field towards the huge National Institute for Medical Research building on the hill at Mill Hill, to another kissing gate. Ignore the right-hand path signposted 'Long Ponds' and follow the way ahead running alongside Folly Brook.

At the gateway to the modern Folly Farm (right) turn left to walk on a metalled lane alongside a cricket ground with the view dominated again by the research building. The lane bears left to a junction. Only turn left along Burton Hole Lane to visit Burton Hole Farm where milk, cream, eggs and jam can be purchased between 9.30am and 3.30pm daily except Mondays. The walk continues to the right up the road between the entrance to Hillview Road and the postbox. There is a pavement to the left. At the top of the hill go left into Eleanor Crescent, a narrow track. After a few yards go right through a kissing gate into a wood.

Follow the path ahead (ignoring any left branch) to reach barriers at the junction with Partingdale Lane and The Ridgeway. Cross the main road ahead and go left. There is a bus stop and a view before the road runs down Bittacy Hill. The proximity of the station is indicated by the Railway Engineer (right) at Bittacy Road. Continue ahead for a short distance to find Mill Hill East Station on the right.

MILL HILL EAST STATION

This station, which until recently still had a wooden platform, retains its original 1867 building from the time when this was a through LNER line to Edgware. The name was just Mill Hill Station until the 'East' was added in 1928. The present one-stop branch line became part of the Northern line in 1941 during the Second World War to serve the nearby Inglis Barracks. The planned Underground extension to Edgware over the former LNER line was abandoned although part of the track bed remains. The viaduct over the Dollis Brook is the underground's highest point above street level.

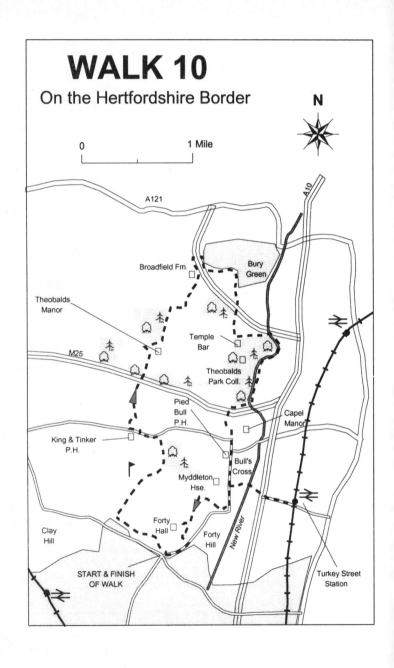

WALK 10
On the Hertfordshire Border

N

0   1 Mile

A121

A10

Broadfield Fm.

Bury Green

Theobalds Manor

Temple Bar

M25

Theobalds Park Coll.

Pied Bull P.H.

Capel Manor

King & Tinker P.H.

Bull's Cross

Myddleton Hse.

Clay Hill

Forty Hall

Forty Hill

New River

START & FINISH OF WALK

Turkey Street Station

Walk 10: On the Hertfordshire Border

Forty Hill – Whitewebbs Lane – Bury Green – Temple Bar – Bulls Cross – Forty Hall – Forty Hill

---

The ceremonial entrance to the City of London, depicted in so many old prints of London, is to be found in a Hertfordshire wood. This corner of the county, just a few yards across today's Greater London boundary, was also the final stop for King James of Scotland before he made his entry into the capital to claim Elizabeth I's throne. His legacy, in the form of an artificial river, lives on in the rural corner of Enfield where this circular walk across parkland and fields begins.

Distance: 7 or 5.5 miles.

Map: OS Landranger 166 (Luton and Hertford) or OS Pathfinder 1120 (Hatfield and Cheshunt) and 1140 (Barnet and Enfield).

Terrain: Field, woodland and park paths and road.

Food & Drink: King and Tinker (11am–3pm & 5.30–11pm; Sat 11am–11pm; Sun 12–3pm & 7–10.30pm; M/G) in Whitewebbs Lane; Pied Bull (11am–11pm; Sun 12–10.30pm; M/G) at Bulls Cross; Forty Hall cafeteria (11am–5pm except Mon in winter) at Forty Hall. Goat Tavern (11am–11pm; Sun 12–10.30pm; M/G) at bottom of Forty Hill.

Transport: National Railways to Enfield Town then LT buses 191, 231 or W10 to Clay Hill (Travelcard Zone 5). Return by LT buses 217, 310, 311 or 317 from Turkey Street (Zone 6) to Enfield, or National Railways from Turkey Street to Liverpool Street.

Start & Finish: Forty Hill to Clay Hill in Enfield. The shorter walk ends at Turkey Street.

At the roundabout at the bottom of Clay Hill turn into Forty Hill, the road with pedestrian and cycle access only. Beyond a large ornamental gate (left) turn left under an archway to follow a woodland footpath. After a short distance there is a pond and the bed of the former New River to the left.

THE NEW RIVER
The river is an artificial watercourse cut between 1609 and 1613 from a point on the River Lea just below Ware in Hertfordshire to Islington forty miles away. It was the idea of goldsmith Sir Hugh Myddleton to bring fresh water to the capital from the countryside, although landowners opposed the idea. James I fell into the water near here in 1622 during an inspection of work, but he knighted Myddleton later that year. The New River, although still part of Thames Water's network, ceased to be used for supply purposes following the recent completion of the London Ring Main. This

section near Forty Hall became redundant in the 1850s when the river, originally constructed to follow contours, was straightened out above Enfield.

Stay on the path which, by an entrance to Forty Hall grounds, is signed 'Mile & a Quarter Footpath'. Continue forward with farmland seen through the trees to the right. Eventually there is a junction of paths. Here the New River disappears to the left. Down to the right, at a lower level, is a footbridge spanning the Turkey Brook. Bear right, not to cross the bridge, but to go over the stile and follow the path (alongside the field) signed 'Mile & a Quarter Footpath' and Whitewebbs Lane. The Turkey Brook is to the left.

TURKEY BROOK

The brook rises near Potters Bar and flows across Enfield Chase. The name comes from nearby Turkey Street, alongside which the stream later flows before joining the River Lea. Turkey Street appears first on early nineteenth-century maps, having been Tokestrete in the fifteenth century.

The water winds along with the path, occasionally disappearing. At one point a bridleway is alongside instead of the Turkey Brook. At a stile go left over a concrete bridge spanning the Turkey Brook, now swollen by the Cuffley Brook. Continue ahead with a field to the right. When the path turns right by a junction go right through the squeeze stile. Another redundant stretch of the New River is to the left. Later the path turns left over the old river. Follow the woodland path, which is later by a field, before reaching a road beyond a stile at Whitewebbs Lane. Turn left along the road for a few yards to join a path running between the road (right) and a bridlepath. Soon the narrow path leaves the bridleway to join the road just before the King and Tinker.

KING and TINKER

The name is thought to recall an incident, featured in a ballad, when James VI of Scotland passed through this area on his way south to accept the crown having become James I on the death of the last Tudor monarch, Queen Elizabeth. In the crowd waiting for the king was a tinker who wondered aloud how they would recognise the new king. A stranger next to him suggested that James would be the only man wearing a hat. Looking around the tinker suddenly realised that everyone was bareheaded except for the stranger. Another suggestion is that James called in here while out hunting and sat with the tinker in the entrance which resembles a church porch. The inn, which has a low beamed ceiling and inglenook fireplace, is at least 400 years old, although the site may have been a pub for longer. Duck and grouse are often on the menu and traditional cider is available. The large garden, with a children's play area, has a bird house made from a beer cask. Open lunchtimes and evenings (see above).

At the pub cross the road to go over a stile by the entrance to stables. At first the way is fenced. Follow the fence on the left to a stile by a cottage. On drawing level with a miniature windmill, the path makes a sharp right turn. Beyond a footbridge go left to follow a field boundary (left). Go over the stile by the gate and walk ahead, down into the valley, towards a lonely waymark post. Turn right for a few yards to find a footbridge and a stile before continuing north. The oak tree marks the approximate point where the rising path passes out of Greater London into Hertfordshire.

A footbridge carries the path over the M25. From the gate and the top of the steps there is a view back to the City of London in the south. Continue north up the side of the field. When the trees to the left end, keep ahead to a point slightly to the left of Theobalds Manor.

On meeting a lane known as Old Park Ride turn left. After a few yards turn right through a gap and walk towards Home Wood. Follow the trees (left) as the path runs gently downhill; after a slight bend the ground rises again. Stay by the trees (left) and at the field corner turn right with the boundary. Before the next corner turn left to go behind a fence and over a ditch to a stile. There is a view north-east across a bypass with the tower of Broxbourne Church just visible above houses.

Continue ahead down the field following the line of oaks (left) to a stile by a gate at the bottom. Follow the track, which soon runs up to Broadfield Farm. At the buildings bear right to find a stile and the path running between the buildings and the Flamstead End Relief Road. On the far side join a concrete farm road which continues north towards the glasshouses.

At a junction go right to cross the bypass to Bury Green, and at once go right on to a wide track running south parallel to the main road. After a short distance there is a cemetery to the left. At the far end turn left on to a long straight path running down the side of the cemetery.

On reaching a residential road, Woodside, go right and left to pass Warrenfield Close (a building right) and meet Burygreen Road. Opposite is a house called Noss Mayo. Turn right along Burygreen Road. When the houses end the hard surface gives way to rough. Beyond Bury Green Farmhouse the road becomes a bridleway and runs downhill. Ignore a left turn and stay ahead to reach the dual carriageway. Cross (with great care) to find the path continuing in the wood opposite. Ignore any turnings and keep forward to a major junction by Temple Bar.

TEMPLE BAR

Temple Bar, which may have been designed by Christopher Wren, was the entrance to the City of London at the West end of Fleet Street from 1670 until 1877. In its early years heads of executed prisoners were displayed on the top. The archway was dismantled when it was found to be too narrow for the increasing traffic, and after a decade of storage the stones were brought here to be made into the entrance to brewer Sir Henry Bruce Meux's Theobalds Park estate. Lady Meux, a former barmaid at his Horseshoe Tavern on the site of the Dominion in Tottenham Court Road, was the driving force for bringing the gateway here.

Walk past the front of Temple Bar (right) and along Theobalds Lane, which is now the main metalled driveway to Theobalds Park (see below). After a quarter of a mile the road passes the entrance to the Tesco staff playing field (right) just before crossing the New River. At once go right through a kissing gate to follow the path along the riverbank. Across the water (right) there are views of Theobalds Park mansion.

THEOBALDS PARK

This mansion, dating from 1763, is the successor to the original Theobalds which stood at the east end of Theobalds Lane near Theobalds Grove Station. It was James I's last stopping place on his journey from Scotland to London on his accession, and where he died – Charles I was proclaimed king at the gate before setting out for London. Cromwell pulled the house down.

Ahead, early on, is a view of the Canary Wharf tower on the Isle of Dogs thirteen miles to the south. Later, to the left can be seen the square tower of Waltham Abbey two miles away. Beyond is Epping Forest.

The path bends where the water widens for a rare island in a man-made river. On reaching a bridge cross the water to follow a narrow fenced path running just inside woodland. Cross the old Theobalds Park drive (cut off by the M25) and go ahead up the steps to the new drive. Turn left to leave Hertfordshire and re-enter Greater London before crossing the M25.

On the far side look on the left for the way down to a gap or stile. Cross the field to a gate and go right past the lodge, where there is a stile at the gateway. Walk up the former Theobalds drive, now known as Gilmour Close, to meet a road at a bend at Bulls Cross. Go ahead past Myddleton Cottages (right), Bullsmoor Lane (left) and the Pied Bull (right).

BULLS CROSS

Bulls Cross was known as Bedell's Cross in the fifteenth century when the junction with Whitewebbs Lane and Bulls Cross was a crossroads. The north–south road, incorporating the old driveway, is the former Ermine Street built by the Romans to link London and Lincoln. Bullsmoor Lane was moved south at the request of the occupants of the seventeenth-century Capel Manor, whose 30-acre garden now includes the *Gardening Which?* trials garden (entrance in Bullsmoor Lane; open summer weekends). Gardening writer Frances Perry (1907–93) grew up at the Pied Bull, a former Enfield Chase kennels which only became a pub in 1790 – hence the very low ceiling. Frances Perry, who was inspired by E. A. Bowles (see below), later lived for more than 50 years two doors away at Bulls Cross Cottage, which she saw being built.

The walk continues south past the Pied Bull (right) and Bulls Cross Cottage. Later the pavement changes sides before reaching the entrance to Myddleton House opposite Turkey Street.

MYDDLETON HOUSE

Named after New River founder Sir Hugh Myddleton, the house dates from 1815. It replaced a house occupied since 1724 by the family with the controlling interest in the New River Company; descendant Henry Carington Bowles, who died here in 1918, was the New River's last governor. His son, the famous gardener E. A. Bowles, was born in 1865 and lived here continuously until his death in 1954 when the house was still without electricity or a telephone. As a concession to the cook there was gas in the basement, but Bowles opposed the phone because he feared it would distract him from gardening. The garden, which embraces part of the old filled-in loop of the New River, is now home to the National Iris Collection and retains many E. A. Bowles features including his 'Lunatic Asylum' area where a contorted hazel is known as

'Harry Lauder's Walking Stick', Enfield's market cross and an Edward VII pew from Sandringham Church. Open Mon–Fri 10am–4pm and Sun 2-5pm; admission £1.80 (concessions £1.20).

To end the walk here turn left along Turkey Street to the main road where there are buses to Enfield reached by way of a subway. Continue along Turkey Street to reach Turkey Street Station.

The main walk continues ahead past Turkey Street (left). The walled road crosses the old course of the New River before running downhill to cross the Turkey Brook. Just before the bridge, go right over a stile to find a wooden footbridge spanning the Turkey Brook. Cross the water into Forty Hill Fields, which form part of Forty Hall Park.

FORTY HALL PARK

Forty Hall Park embraces the site of Elsynge Palace where Edward VI heard of his succession to Henry VIII, who had died in Whitehall. The present house, called Forty Hall (but still 'Four Tree Hall' as recently as 1822), is on a new site and dates from the 1630s (see below). The lime walk, damaged in the 1987 Great Storm, is as old as the house. Two hay crops are cut here each year.

Turn right to follow the brook. Stay by the stream for quarter of a mile before turning left on to a narrow path which runs up a bank to the wide lime walk. Walk ahead up the wide grass avenue to the mansion ahead. On reaching the pond bear round to the right to reach the house on the far side of the water.

FORTY HALL

Designed by Inigo Jones, Forty Hall was built between 1629 and 1636 for Sir Nicholas Rainton, a Lord Mayor of London. In the nineteenth century the house was owned by the Meyer family. Nearby Jesus Church, now a parish church, was built in 1835 for Christian Meyer after his children rebelled against walking to Enfield Church on a hot Sunday morning. In 1895 Forty Hall was purchased by E. A. Bowles's father for his eldest son Sir Henry Ferryman Bowles, and it remained in the family until 1951 when Derek Parker Bowles sold the house to Enfield Council (open Thur–Sun 11am–5pm; admission free; the cafeteria at the back is open daily except winter Mondays).

Leave the Forty Hall garden by taking the path almost opposite the cafeteria at the back of the house. The path bears left on the south side of the garden to run down to a kissing gate on Forty Hill Road. Opposite is Forty Hill House. Turn right down the road, passing Goat Lane (left), before reaching the Goat Tavern. Continue past the shops and the archway (right, and where the walk started) to the roundabout at the bottom of Clay Hill. The bus stop for Enfield buses is across the road in Myddleton Avenue to the left.

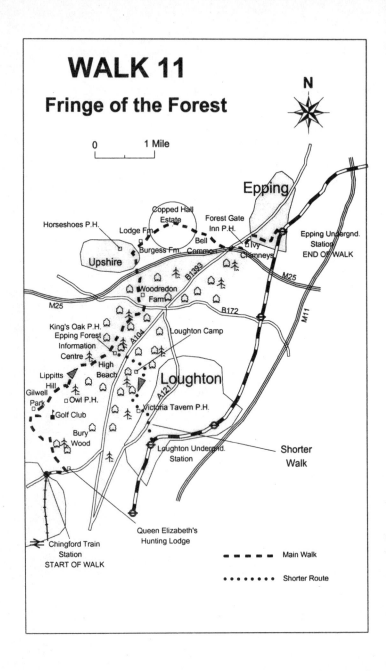

WALK 11

Fringe of the Forest

N

0   1 Mile

Epping

Copped Hall
Estate

Horseshoes P.H.

Lodge Fm

Forest Gate
Inn P.H.

Bell
Common

Burgess Fm.

Ivy
Chimneys

Epping Undergnd.
Station
END OF WALK

Upshire

M25

B1393

Woodredon
Farm

B172

M25

M11

King's Oak P.H.

Epping Forest
Information
Centre

A104

Loughton Camp

High
Beach

Loughton

Lippitts
Hill

Gilwell
Park

Owl P.H.

A121

Golf Club

Victoria Tavern P.H.

Bury
Wood

Loughton Undergnd.
Station

Shorter
Walk

Chingford Train
Station
START OF WALK

Queen Elizabeth's
Hunting Lodge

- - - - -   Main Walk

· · · · · · ·   Shorter Route

Looking down the Long Walk from the Copper Horse statue, Windsor Great Park
(walk 1, Geoff Garvey)

John Milton lived in this cottage in Chalfont St Giles when he came here in 1665
to escape the Great Plague *(walk 3, Leigh Hatts)*

ABOVE: In the Chilterns on the
Chesham Switchback
(walk 4, *Geoff Garvey*)

LEFT: Latimer House is built on
the site of a house where
Charles I was held prisoner
(walk 5, *Leigh Hatts*)

The Chiltern Open Air Museum *(walk 6, Geoff Garvey)*

The former Ovaltine Farm which in the 1930s supplied milk and eggs to the Ovaltine Factory *(walk 7, Leigh Hatts)*

The Green Dragon pub, London Colney. The pub was founded in 1648 during the Civil War *(walk 8, Geoff Garvey)*

Queen Elizabeth's Hunting Lodge, Chingford, built by Henry VIII in 1543 and restored by Elizabeth I in 1589 *(walk 11, Geoff Garvey)*

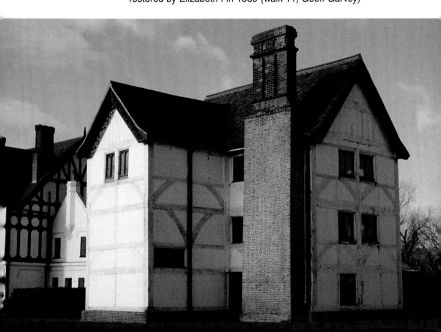

Built in the reign of Henry VIII from old ships' timbers, the King's Head, North Weald Bassett was formerly the home of the village butcher before becoming an alehouse in 1750 *(walk 12, Geoff Garvey)*

The church of St John the Evangelist, Havering-atte-Bower, with copies of the seventeenth century double stocks and whipping post in the foreground
(walk 14, Geoff Garvey)

RIGHT: Lesnes Abbey, founded in 1178 by Richard de Lucy as an act of penance for the murder of Thomas à Becket *(walk 17, Leigh Hatts)*

BELOW: St John's Jerusalem was founded in the late twelfth century by the Knights Hospitallers of the Order of St John of Jerusalem *(walk 19, Geoff Garvey)*

LEFT: Lord Bennett's tomb as seen from Mickleham Church
(walk 22, Leigh Hatts)

BELOW: The Epsom Well, once one of the most sought after cures in Europe
(walk 22, Geoff Garvey)

The Hampton ferry has run since at least 1519
(walk 24, Leigh Hatts)

Looking across the Thames to Syon House. Catherine Howard, fifth wife of Henry VIII was imprisoned here before her execution. After Henry's death in 1547 his body rested at the house where it was mauled by dogs. *(walk 25, Leigh Hatts)*

Walk 11: The Fringe of the Forest

Chingford – Lippitts Hill – High Beach – Upshire – Epping

This walk runs northwards to Epping along the high scarp on the western approaches of the magnificent forest. The woodland's cloak breaks often enough to allow some fine views far over London. The forest itself is a 'green lung' for east London and a naturalist's paradise with a rich variety of wild flowers and birds. Rabbits and squirrels are abundant and easy to spot, but to glimpse a stoat, weasel or badger will take more patience and searching.

Distance: 8 or 5 miles. The walk may be curtailed at five miles by taking a short-cut at High Beach to Loughton tube station.

Map: OS Landranger 167 (Chelmsford, Harlow and surrounding area) and 177 (East London area), or OS Pathfinder 1140 (Barnet), 1141 (Loughton) and 1121 (Epping).

Terrain: Field paths, bridleways and country lanes. Waterproof footwear is recommended as some parts tend to be very muddy after rain.

Food & Drink: The Royal Forest Hotel, Chingford (Mon–Sat 11am–11pm; Sun 12–10.30pm; M/G); Butler's Retreat, Chingford (Mon–Fri 9am–7.30pm & Sat–Sun 9am–5pm 0181 5242976); the Owl, Lippitts Hill (Mon–Sat 11am–3pm & 6–11pm; Sun 12–10.30pm; M/G); Royal Oak (Mon-Sat 11am–11pm; Sun 12–10.30pm; M/G), High Beach; tea houses, High Beach (open daily). Victoria Tavern (Mon–Sat 11am–2.30pm & 6–11pm; Sun 12–3pm & 7–10.30pm) and other pubs, Loughton (short-cut only); Horseshoes, Upshire (Mon–Thurs 11.30am–4pm & 6–11pm, Fri & Sat 11.30am–11pm, Sun 12–4pm & 7–10.30pm); Forest Gate Inn (Mon–Sat 11am–2.30pm & 5.30–11pm; Sun 12–3pm & 7–10.30pm; G), Epping.

Transport: National Railways from Liverpool Street or Walthamstow (Victoria Line) or LT Buses to Chingford. Return journey by London Underground (Central line) from Loughton (shorter walk) or Epping (longer route). All stations are within Zone 6.

Start & Finish: A linear walk starting out from Chingford train station and ending at Loughton (5 miles) or Epping (8 miles) underground stations, both on the Central line.

Exiting from Chingford train station turn right along Station Road. Fifty metres ahead take Bury Road on the left should you not wish to visit Queen Elizabeth's Hunting Lodge. The walks join on the edge of Bury Wood (see below). Otherwise keep ahead, along what is now Rangers Road, as it ascends the hill to the Royal Forest Hotel visible through the trees. To the right of the hotel stands Queen Elizabeth's Hunting Lodge.

QUEEN ELIZABETH'S HUNTING LODGE

Queen Elizabeth's Hunting Lodge (open Wed–Sun 2-5pm or dusk in winter; adults 50p, children free) is a tall, half-timbered building commissioned by Henry VIII and completed in 1543. Skilfully constructed from massive oak timbers, its height provided a viewing platform (now enclosed) from where the royal visitors to the forest could watch the hunt and even shoot game with crossbows. It is unlikely that Henry ever used the lodge, but his daughter Elizabeth I apparently did and carried out a restoration in 1589 after it had fallen into disrepair. This included the addition of the impressive Tudor fireplace on the ground floor. The building later passed into private hands and served as a farmhouse and a Victorian tearoom. Since 1878 it has been owned by the Corporation of London and now houses the Epping Forest Museum which has displays on the house's history and former uses. Adjacent to the hunting lodge on its eastern side is Butler's Retreat, a fine old nineteenth-century weather-boarded barn, converted into a tearoom in 1887. In its heyday there was seating for 600 trippers escaping the city for the country air. Today it seats a modest forty diners, but is very pleasant and serves meals as well as snacks, and is noted for its hearty breakfasts.

From the car park behind the Royal Forest Hotel next door to the hunting lodge, go through an exit on its east side between tree stumps (to the side of a building used by the Orion Harriers club). Follow the fence to the end of the hotel ground and then head half-left downhill across Chingford Plain heading for Bury Road where it meets the start of Bury Wood, a dense wood of tangled hornbeam and oak that stretches for a good half a mile to the right of the road. Follow the road for about 700 yards, and just before reaching the end of the wood turn left along a gravel track that runs along the back gardens of the first line of houses on the left. In 200 metres, when the track bears slightly right beyond the last house, turn right to the side of a house to follow a narrow path through trees to reach a rough lane with a footpath sign. Turn left in the direction indicated by the sign and keep ahead, following the fence of a horse paddock, to cross a stile at the end of the lane. The ground here can be a bit of a quagmire after rain but once you're through it the path runs over grass to another stile near the far right field corner. Cross this stile and continue uphill along the right side of the next field to enter a small wood ahead by an iron gate. The path leads out to the entrance to Gilwell Park.

GILWELL PARK

A memorial to Baden-Powell (or Lord Baden-Powell of Gilwell, as he was dubbed in 1929), the founder of the Scout movement, Gilwell Park was purchased in 1919 to provide an activity and camping centre for London's urban scout troops. The hundreds of neckerchiefed scouts to be seen in and around the facility on most days take part in canoeing, shooting, archery and orienteering, in addition to the more traditional pursuits.

Do not enter Gilwell Park but bear right past its gate and follow the drive lined with tree stumps for 300 metres to the road. Here turn left for 150 metres to a waymarked drive on the right (signed 'Lippitts Hill') which enters West Essex Golf Club. Keep ahead along the metalled drive, and once in sight of the clubhouse keep an eye out for airborne golfballs from a tee to the right. Beyond a small pond on the left, turn left along a gravel track, keeping ahead as it gently climbs with a line of trees to the right. From this rising path you have a surprise view of north London opening up behind you – the chimneys in the foreground mark the Brimsdown power station. On the crown of the hill the track bears right, keeping close to a hedge. Soon the hedge-line and track bear right again, before passing a strategically placed seat on the golf course (left), where the track makes a right turn heading in a north-east direction to offer more splendid views (left) before running down to a dilapidated swing-gate at Lippitts Hill.

Turn right up the lane to a bridleway signed 'Mott Street' 50 yards ahead on the left. To continue the walk you should turn left along here. However, if you're in need of refreshment keep ahead for 150 metres into the village of Lippitts Hill where there's the rather featureless, modern Owl pub. It does have a pleasant beer garden though, if somewhat blighted by an unpleasant tannoy system which summons customers to collect their meals.

The walk continues along the Mott Street bridleway. Keep to the right side of the farm drive, soon turning right to follow an enclosed path which runs round to a swing-gate. Go through this and on by a field path that runs, in line with electricity poles, across to a little iron gate on the far side. Here, if conditions are muddy, it's best to keep on to the field corner and follow the right side of three meadows to reach a lane, turning uphill towards High Beach. If the ground is firm, go through the iron gate and on by a straight bridleway that leads to a white iron gate at a little metalled drive with the delightful name of Pepper Alley. This leads in turn to Mott Street, a lane taking you uphill towards the forest at High Beach. Follow the lane and go straight ahead upon reaching a crossroads. After another 200 metres you will emerge into the open again at High Beach.

HIGH BEACH AND EPPING FOREST

High Beach has been a popular weekend picnicking spot for generations of Londoners since 1882 when Queen Victoria came here in great pomp to 'open the Forest to the people' after its purchase by the Corporation of London. Queen Victoria's Oak in the middle of Queen's Green fronting the King's Oak pub is a striking red oak planted at the time to commemorate the royal visit. In fact, the tree planted by her withered almost as soon as she had turned her back, and this one is a replacement hastily substituted by embarrassed officials. High Beach is also, at 350 feet, one of the highest points of the forest with extensive views over the Lea valley towards Waltham Abbey. The name High Beach may refer to the layer of pebbles and sand upon which it stands, but some prefer to spell it 'Beech'. The Epping Forest Information Centre (open summer daily 10am–5pm; winter 11am–dusk; admission free) is located behind the King's Oak pub (with outdoor tables) and has maps and guidebooks as well as displays relating to the forest.

The Shorter Walk

To end the walk at Loughton, from the Epping Forest Information Centre take the wheelchair path to the right of the five-barred gate exit from the car park. Follow this for some 75 yards to take another right after a bench, also on the right. This bends around to the left to reach a track. Turn right along the broad track for 100 yards, then turn left along a crosspath and keep ahead along the track, soon to meet a road (the A104). Cross the road and take the path immediately opposite heading roughly south-east. Follow this path as it winds through a particularly scenic and peaceful stretch of the forest. After about a third of a mile you will arrive at a crosspath, the broad Three Forests Way bridleway. Turn right along this, soon passing a grassy picnic area (left). In the trees to the right are the remains of Loughton Camp.

LOUGHTON CAMP

Once you reach the pits and uneven ground that mark this Iron Age fortified settlement which was spread over some six acres, there is not a great deal to see. Following on the heels of the Romans who tended to settle on the forest fringes, in the seventh and eighth centuries the Anglo-Saxons used the forest as a source of timber and grazed their cattle here too. Their influence is reflected in the name they gave to this area (the 'ton' of Loughton stands for 'town'). It was in this period, too, that the forest lost its 'wildwood' character as many of the ancient trees, such as small-leaved lime, were felled to make way for beech, oak and hornbeam, trees with greater economic potential. The rights to graze animals in the forest and to pollard trees, particularly beech, for firewood were jealously guarded by the local population here for centuries, and in 1878, when these rights were withdrawn by the City of London Corporation who had been given control of the forest by an Act of Parliament, there was a furious revolt by those who felt deprived of their birthright. Gradually the law was made to stick and the curious hangover from these times is the large number of pollarded beeches uncut for over a century which send branches shooting high into the forest canopy from stubby trunks little more than six feet high.

Keep ahead along the bridleway which gently descends through the woods. When the path rises again after about half a mile go forward until the way levels, keeping an eye out on the left for a 'no mountain bikes' sign with an S-bend in the stream down the bank behind. Just beyond the sign turn left off the path to descend the bank half-left to pick up another path running south-west with a stream to your left. Follow this path as it soon crosses a footbridge over the stream and then recrosses it at another footbridge. Now with the stream to your left, the path soon leaves the stream and skirts a pond to reach a road. At the road bear left for 50 yards to take a path on the right. This will lead you to Forest Road.

Continue along Forest Road passing a number of welcoming pubs, the most pleasant of which is the second in line, the Victoria Tavern, with a leafy beer garden and aviary. At the end of Forest Road bear left outside the police station to cross the main road (A121) into Station Road, soon passing Lopping Hall built as a compensation for the ending of lopping rights in 1878, with an elaborate relief over the doorway. When Station Road meets a junction, cross the road to enter the station approach to Loughton underground station (Central line).

To continue the main walk, keep forward, following the road north-east (beyond Queen Victoria's Oak) for 500 yards beyond the little Tea Hut, another High Beach institution which has occupied the same site for over 50 years and is rarely shut. You will come to a point where the road splits after bearing leftwards. Go along the right fork for only 30 metres or so, then strike obliquely left into the forest, aiming to pass between two massive beeches, the first sadly decaying. You may notice a faint track heading half-right; this is the old

Verderer's Ride (see box below) that ran through the woods to the main road (A121) near the Wake Arms. The track now joins a bridleway, and when it meets a fork keep right and then ahead for half a mile ignoring turn-offs. You will soon find that the ground falls away sharply on the left – make sure to keep to the upper slopes.

EPPING FOREST

Epping Forest's 6,000 acres are all that remains of the ancient forest of Waltham which 300 years ago covered 60,000 acres and was a forest in the original meaning of the word – that is, land over which the crown had hunting rights. Once it had appropriated the forests in the late Middle Ages, the monarchy jealously guarded its property, and the fines levied on those who broke the numerous Forest Laws, such as poachers and trespassers illegally grazing their livestock, proved a useful source of revenue. These offences were tried in the verderer's courts, the verderer being a specialised type of magistrate appointed to protect the king's rights. Today their role has been reversed: the four verderers are now elected every seven years by those having the necessary property qualification (on the forest edge) and act in the interests of preserving and maintaining the forest for the recreation and enjoyment of the public.

When the bridleway emerges at a road at the top of a hill, cross this to a metalled drive (Woodredon Farm Lane) almost opposite. This leads to Woodredon Farm; take a glance at the pretty Georgian farmhouse on the right before passing through the lodge gates bearing the 'no through road' sign that keeps the next mile of the walk free of vehicles. A little ahead, and after passing a mansion on the left, the drive winds leftwards to discover an isolated bungalow before another turn leads downhill to a bridge over the M25 motorway. Continue along the track for a further quarter of a mile which brings you to Laundry Cottage (left) from where a path downhill to the road, and left, leads into Upshire.

UPSHIRE

Upshire is just a wayside settlement near the forest, and the distinctive wooden tower of the late Victorian St Thomas's Church is a useful landmark. Just beyond the church's lych gate on the same side is the diminutive Horseshoes pub with outdoor tables a bit too close to passing traffic in front, and a poky beer garden behind. To end the walk here, there are buses from the stop opposite the church to Epping underground station (Service 2000; Mon–Sat 11.41am, 2.41pm & 4.41pm). There's also bus 517 to Enfield and Waltham Forest reached by continuing past the Horseshoes for three-quarters of a mile to the Princes Field Road terminus (Mon–Fri 5 & 35mins past the hour; Sat 10 & 40mins past the hour; Sun 1min past the hour).

From Laundry Cottage – if you're not going into the village – take a track bearing half-right passing before a picturesque huddle of weather-boarded cottages to reach the road. Keeping the same direction, cross to the grassy path opposite which leads gradually away from the road, passes behind a group of trees and runs out opposite Burgess Farm, another attractive timbered house. Leaving the farm buildings on the left, continue by the lane directly opposite the footpath and, after 100 metres, bear right along a gravel track to reach Lodge Farm, another fine old Essex farmhouse (and a Grade II listed building), on the far side of a little green. Keeping on the gravel drive, bear right, passing through the (unmarked) gates of the Copt Hall estate, once the summer residence of the Abbots of Waltham and now partly owned and managed by the Corporation of London.

There are views far over Epping Upland as the drive climbs steadily. When the track winds right towards the farm buildings, keep ahead, across a field corner, to a plank over a ditch about 50 yards from the drive. Cross this and head half-right over a field towards the tiled roof of a white cottage on the far side. This field is usually under crop; it may be easier to skirt around the right edge, passing the farm just away to your right. Once over the stile facing the white cottage just mentioned, turn right for a few metres to the main drive and go left along it as it runs downhill, then on for another 600 yards to a point where it meets a wood on the right. Here you will find a fieldgate (and a footpath sign) beside the trees; pass through this and follow the grassy track that skirts the wood to its upper corner. Here, cross a stile on the left and continue in the same direction, keeping close to the hedge – now on your right – to the top of the field and a ladder stile. Cross this and turn left to follow an enclosed path to another stile and a footbridge over the M25 motorway, which here dives into a tunnel. Cross the footbridge, bear left as indicated by a waymark and follow a short enclosed path to the B1393. Cross this half-left to turn down a gravel track (right) leading towards a cricket pavilion. Follow the track to pass along the front of the pavilion of the Epping Forest Cricket Club. Beyond the practice nets bear left over grass to join a bridleway. Keep ahead along the bridleway as it runs between bushes to meet Theydon Road. Turn left here passing Ivy Chimneys Road, to pass the Forest Gate Inn, a free house with a pleasant beer garden on a green outside.

Continue past the Forest Gate Inn along Bell Common. Ignore footpath signs and keep ahead to the end of where the road is unpaved. At the last house go between white posts and turn right over grass to cross a metalled path and pick up a bridleway heading downhill. Keep ahead along the public footpath as it continues downhill to enter a small wood. Follow the path through the trees as it maintains a fairly straight line south-east to emerge at a road (Western Avenue) in a housing estate. Turn left here. When this joins Centre Drive turn left again and, after 250 yards, turn right opposite No. 77 into an enclosed alleyway, turning left at the end to reach Epping underground station.

Walk 12: End of the Line

Ongar – Greensted-juxta-Ongar – Toot Hill – Coopersale – Epping

---

Much of this walk, following part of the 81-mile Essex Way from Harwich to the capital of Epping Forest, is a mainly flat route in typical Essex countryside starting at Ongar, which until recently was also the end of the Underground's Central line. Little-visited Ongar appeared in the top right-hand corner of the Underground map. On the way to today's end of the line at Epping, the walk passes an ancient log church associated with the Tolpuddle Martyrs and follows a woodland track where deer can often be seen.

Distance: 8.5 or 5 miles.

Map: OS Landranger 167 (Chelmsford) or OS Pathfinder 1121 (Epping and Chipping Ongar).

Terrain: Field paths, bridleways and country roads.

Food & Drink: Clock Tower Café (Tue–Sat 9.30am–2pm) and the Cock (11am–3pm & 5.30–11pm; Sun 12–3pm & 7–10.30pm; M) at Ongar; Green Man (11am–3pm & 6–11pm; Sun 12–3pm & 7pm-10.30pm: M inc. Sunday lunches/G) at Toot Hill; King's Head (12–11pm; Sun 12–10.30pm; M/G) at North Weald Bassett and the Gernon Bushes (11am–11pm; Sun 12–10.30pm; M/G) a quarter of a mile off the route, north end of Coppersale Common. Epping has plenty of pubs and cafés including the Black Lion (11am—1pm; Sun 12–3pm & 7–10.30pm; M/G) and the Forest and Firkin (12am–11pm; Sun 12–10.30pm; M/G) in Epping High Street.

Transport: Central line to Epping (Travelcard Zone 6) then Thamesway bus 200/201 or Townlink 501 (not Sun or Bank Hol) from station to Ongar. (There are at present no rail services from Epping to Ongar.) Return by buses 201 or 501 from North Weald Bassett to Epping. Essex Busline ☎0345 000333.

Start & Finish: Ongar to Epping in Essex. The shorter walk ends at North Weald Bassett.

The bus from Epping passes the former Ongar Underground station (where there is a bus stop) before reaching the shops in the village centre where the walk begins.

ONGAR
The final six miles of the former Central line from Epping to Ongar is single track having been laid in 1865 as part of the Great Eastern Railway which carried milk and produce from the farms to London. The line became part of the Underground network in 1949, although trains continued to be steam-hauled until 1957. The last

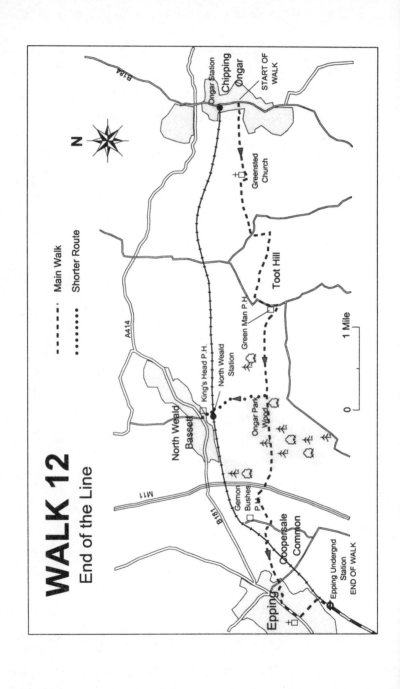

WALK 12
End of the Line

N

Main Walk
Shorter Route

B184

Ongar Station
Chipping
Ongar
START OF
WALK

Greensted
Church

Toot Hill

Green Man P.H.

A414

King's Head P.H.
North Weald
Station

Ongar Park
Wood

North Weald
Bassett

M11

Gernon
Bushes
P.H.

B181

Coopersale
Common

Epping

Epping Undergrnd
Station
END OF WALK

0   1 Mile

Underground train ran on Friday, 30 September 1994, and the line has now been leased to a private railway company.

'Ongar' means 'wooded slope', but the full name is Chipping Ongar, indicating that this was once a market town like Barnet (see page 63). A castle which stood behind the library was built by Richard de Lucy who founded Lesnes Abbey (see page 108). St Martin's Anglican Church is of Norman origin, although much restored in 1884. Oliver Cromwell's niece, Jane Pallavicini, is buried to the right of the altar while to the left there is a tiny hatch through which a hermit could follow services – the cell entrance can be seen outside. In the churchyard to the south is the impressive tomb of Edward Boodle, who gave his name to Boodle's Club in St James's. David Livingstone, depicted in a window in the north side, lived in the room over the archway entrance to the United Reformed Church in the main street. It was from there that he wrote to the London Missionary Society asking if he could go to Africa. One November day Livingstone walked to London and back, leaving at three in the morning and returning after midnight. Jane Taylor, who wrote 'Twinkle, twinkle little star', is buried inside the URC church. The King's Inn with its coach entry dates from the pre-railway era when Ongar was a stop on the coaching route from Aldgate on the edge of the City of London.

Walk down Banson's Lane at the side of the Budworth Hall. At the bottom of the hill is the Cripsey Brook where in summer a kingfisher and dragonflies can often be found. Keep ahead for half a mile along the Longwalk which lost its elms to Dutch elm disease in the 1970s. The way climbs gently to give a distant view (right) of the white Blake Hall mansion, which gave its name to the second station on the Central line.

Beyond a stile, cross the Greensted Hall drive and go through the kissing gate opposite. Keep near the side of the field (right) to go through the gates at the far end. Go forward towards the trees ahead. To the right is a view of Greensted Hall's recently enlarged lake. After passing a (maybe overgrown) pond (left) go through a kissing gate under the trees. Walk ahead up the metalled drive and turn right to find the entrance to Greensted Church.

ST ANDREW'S GREENSTED

The hamlet's full name is Greensted-juxta-Ongar, meaning 'clearing in the forest next to Ongar'. Although recent research has cast doubt on claims that this is a Saxon church, its new Norman dating still makes this the world's oldest log church and the oldest log building in Europe. The chancel arch is Norman and the tower is fourteenth century. The priest's door is Tudor. The tradition that the body of the martyr St Edmund rested here in 1013 while on its way from London to Bury St Edmunds, which had been under threat from the Danes, may refer to an even earlier building. Tolpuddle Martyr James Brine married the daughter of fellow martyr Thomas Stanfield here in 1839 after the pardoned Dorset farmworkers had settled at nearby Greensted Green. The modern wooden font was designed by Sir Hugh Casson. This unique church was depicted on a postage stamp in 1972.

Continue past the churchyard entrance (right) and through Hall Farm. Keep between the farm buildings on a gently descending track. After about 75 yards and just before the bottom of the hill go left over boarding and up steps to enter a field. Keep ahead alongside a hedge and past a huge oak. The path enters a second field and, after a footbridge at the far end, the way is alongside Greensted Wood (right). Beyond barriers there is a road.

Go left for a few yards and then right to follow a path uphill at the side of a wood. Look out for an easily missed stile to the left. Cross this stile and go ahead towards a white building before curving right on a rising path to find a stile under trees. This is the first of a series of stiles. On reaching a crosspath there is a view of Widow's Farm half-right.

Turn right and keep to the right of the pole. Continue ahead past the farm (left) on a high path which occasionally gives views (right) down on to the white houses of Greensted Green where some of the Tolpuddle martyrs settled.

At the end of the long field cross a concealed footbridge and a stile. Continue ahead to another stile and footbridge at a field corner where the way runs inside a fence with a view of Toot Hill ahead. The path briefly crosses a footbridge to run in the field to the right before turning sharp left. Pass the entrance to Weald Lodge to meet a road at a bend. Turn left along the road to pass Weald Farm (left) and walk into Toot Hill passing Mill Lane and a green (right).

TOOT HILL
Toot Hill means 'look-out post'. There is no church so the main building is the Green Man free house noted for its flowers and unusual bar snacks, which include wild rabbit.

Continue past the Green Man, but before the phone box go right over a stile into a field. Bear round to the right and across the centre of the field to the far corner where there is a hidden stile. Follow the path ahead which soon begins to run downhill. On entering another field bear half-left to a narrow gap by a stile. On the far side there is a track. Turn left on this track which runs gently up and down hill between open fields, and then steeply downhill by trees (left). Having climbed up again the track crosses the invisible line of the Roman London–Colchester road to enter Ongar Park Wood ahead.

ONGAR PARK WOOD
Ongar Park Wood dates from at least Saxon times, and after the Norman conquest it was fenced and stocked with deer. There are still occasional sightings of deer, which now roam a wider area.

The Shorter Walk
Those on the shorter walk should turn right at Ongar Park Wood and follow the bridleway just inside the wood. Later, the path is just outside the wood before bearing left along the side of a field. At a gap the way is half-right across the centre of a field with Cold Hall Farm over to the right. Cross a junction of lanes to continue ahead by a hedge field boundary (left). Later, North Weald Station and its signal box can be seen ahead. On reaching the railway line cross the level crossing and follow the path ahead to the station forecourt. Turn right for the main road and go right again to the bus stop outside the King's Head.

NORTH WEALD BASSETT
The manor was held by the Bassett family in the thirteenth century. The village's church is three-quarters of a mile to the north beyond the airfield made famous during

the Battle of Britain when the World War Two pilots rested between sorties at the King's Head near the station. The inn, built in Henry VIII's reign using old ships' timbers, was the home of the village butcher before becoming an alehouse around 1750. In the 1830s it was being called the George IV, but this was changed to the King's Head by 1851. North Weald Station has the only level crossing on the Underground system. The signal box has been restored by the Ongar Railway Preservation Society.

The **main walk** continues ahead on the main track running through Ongar Park Wood. Follow this straight track which crosses over a north–south bridleway and later runs alongside fields to cross the M11 before reaching Gernon Bushes.

GERNON BUSHES
This ancient woodland is managed as a nature reserve by the Essex Wildlife Trust. The pollarded hornbeams long provided fencing and fuel. Just after midnight every 11 November there is a ceremony here involving the cutting of one or two branches to maintain ancient lopping rights. In 1865 and 1866 nearby Epping Forest was saved from mass development by Loughton villagers who stayed up late on 10 November to exercise their lopping rights. Loughton's Lopping Hall was built with lopping rights compensation paid by the Corporation of London, which now owns and safeguards Epping Forest.

Once across the motorway bridge continue ahead for 200 yards to an Essex Way signpost. Turn left on to a boarded path and follow the way through the trees. At a sharp left turn look out for the Essex Way waymark and go ahead up steps and along the side of a playing field. Go through a kissing gate and along a woodland path to reach the road at Coopersale. The model Victorian parish room is immediately to the left, while to the right, at the far end of the village, there are shops and the Gernon Bushes pub.

COOPERSALE
Coopersale House, down the hill to the south, dates from the seventeenth century and succeeds a building occupied since medieval times by the Archer Houblon family. The name 'Archer' was awarded by Henry V in honour of the longbowmen's success at the battle of Agincourt. In the nineteenth century the family was responsible for transforming Coopersale Common from a hamlet into a village by providing a church, St Alban's, opposite Anson's Farm at the top of the hill, and the parish room.

Here at Coopersale, leaving the Essex Way to continue along the road past St Alban's, the walk goes right along the road. But after a few yards turn left down the side of the white house. The enclosed path meets a residential road at a bend. Turn left along Vicarage Road, and at the next corner bear left by The Orchard (2A) to find a footpath beyond barriers. The enclosed way reaches the top of the railway embankment and turns left to provide a panoramic view of London with Canary Wharf and the former NatWest Tower rising above Docklands and the City. Follow the path along the side of the field and go right to cross the Epping–Ongar line.

On the far side keep to the path as it bears round to the left. The landmark here is the hospital's tall chimney. Stay on this path as it passes through a gap and below new buildings (right) to run alongside a sports ground. On reaching the large expanse of grass walk straight ahead towards the red bin by a gap in the hedge. Go down the steps and ahead across the road into Theydon Grove. Once in Theydon Grove take the first turning right by a plane tree on the central island to go downhill, and then the first left to reach a pond. Follow the road round to the right by the pond (right). Ahead is a view of the clock tower of the new civic offices. Cross the road and grass to reach Epping High Street and turn left.

EPPING

Epping means 'forest clearing'. The dominant church dates only from 1889 and was designed by G.F. Bodley, but it is on the site of a Norman chapel served by monks from nearby Waltham Abbey. A window in the north wall shows a monk setting out for Epping. The country town's weekly Monday market started in 1253. Naturalist Henry Doubleday lived on the corner of Buttercross Lane, marked by a blue plaque. Winston Churchill was Member of Parliament for Epping during his wartime premiership.

Walk up the High Street passing the Black Lion (right) and the Forest and Firkin (left) to reach the church. After a few yards turn left into Station Road. The road soon runs downhill. Turn right just before the railway bridge to reach the main entrance to Epping underground station.

Walk 13: Chigwell Circular

Chigwell – Grange Hill

'Chigwell is the greatest place in the world . . . such an out of the way rural place,' wrote Charles Dickens, who featured the village in *Barnaby Rudge*. Today it retains a rural atmosphere but is not so out of the way thanks to the Underground, which makes it just over thirty minutes from the City. This is appropriate, for in Chigwell churchyard there lies the founder of London's public transport. This short walk is across typical Essex countryside from station to station with an optional diversion to a viewpoint offering a reminder of its proximity to the capital.

Distance: 3 miles.

Map: OS Landranger 177 (East London) or OS Pathfinder 1141 (Loughton and Harold Hill).

Terrain: Field paths and rough lane.

Food & Drink: King William IV Harvester (11am–11pm; Sun 12–10.30pm; M/G); King's Head (11.30am–11pm; Sun 12–10.30pm; M/G) at Chigwell. Delicacy café (9am–5pm; Wed–3pm; Sat–6pm) at Grange Hill.

Transport: Central line to Chigwell (Travelcard Zone 5). Return by Central line from Grange Hill (Zone 5).

Start & Finish: Chigwell to Grange Hill in Essex.

Turn right out of Chigwell Station and cross the end of Station Road. The main road runs gently downhill to pass the King William IV (right) and cross Chigwell Brook. The road then climbs out of the valley to pass the Metropolitan Police sports ground (left) and enters Chigwell village. There is a view (left) of Chigwell Hall with its tall chimneys. Pass the Georgian Brook House and Grange Court (right) before reaching the village centre where the King's Head and Chigwell Church face each other.

CHIGWELL
St Mary's, dating from Norman times, has a splendid brass dedicated to Samuel Harsnett, who was vicar here from 1597 to 1605 and inspired Shakespeare, who was writing *King Lear*. In the churchyard is the grave of George Shillibeer, founder of London buses, whose first horse-drawn service ran from Marylebone to the City in 1829. (His grave is on the left of the path running through the churchyard and just beyond the T-junction with the path leading right to Roding Lane.) Also here is John Knight (near end of path opposite west door) of Knight's Castile soap fame. The King's Head is called the Maypole Inn in Dickens's *Barnaby Rudge* where it is

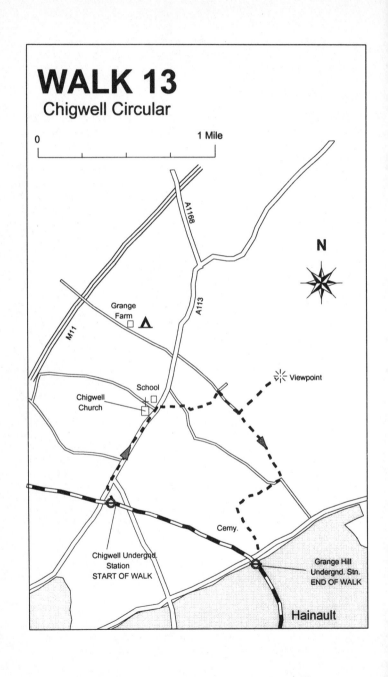

WALK 13
Chigwell Circular

0   1 Mile

A1168

A113

N

Grange Farm

M11

School

Chigwell Church

Viewpoint

Cemy.

Chigwell Undergnd. Station
START OF WALK

Grange Hill Undergnd. Stn.
END OF WALK

Hainault

described as 'an old building with more gable ends than a lazy man would care to count on a sunny day'. Chigwell School was founded in 1629 by Harsnett, who in the same year became Archbishop of York having been Bishop of Norwich. An early pupil was William Penn (see pages 28 and 41), whose family had moved out of London to aid his recovery from smallpox.

Continue past the King's Head (right) and Roding Lane (left) to pass Chigwell School (left). At the zebra crossing bear right up a footpath to reach a stile. Beyond here the path continues ahead in a field. Cross a stile by a gate at a road and go right for a few yards to Lingmere.

Cross the road to a gate. Go ahead for only a few yards before turning right. The path soon runs through trees to enter a field at a corner. Here turn left, with trees at first to the left. Keep forward to go through a gap half-right and enter another field. Bear half-left towards a permissive path post by a pond (left). Follow the curving path past an oak and up to a junction of paths. Turn right to follow the Chigwell County Walk signpost and walk down a track known as Green Lane. At the bottom there is a path signposted Pudding Lane (left).

PUDDING LANE PATH VIEWPOINT

This path runs east to climb to a point 250 feet above sea level which affords a view back to London with the BT Tower and Canary Wharf visible on clear days. To the north can be seen Epping Forest, and just beyond the M11 is the Bank of England printworks where bank notes are produced and old ones destroyed. Follow the wide track, and where it swings into a field go ahead uphill by a hedge (right) as far as a stile.

The walk continues south (past the Pudding Lane turning) down Green Lane, which later narrows. Still keep ahead when the lane opens out again on reaching two cottages. After Hillside (left) the lane bears right to meet Vicarage Lane at a double bend. Go right to follow the pavement, but as soon as there is a pavement on the far side prepare to cross the road with care. Continue ahead past a row of typical weather-boarded Essex houses to the next corner. Go left to pass Puckeridge Cottage (right).

The footpath does a double bend before running ahead by a ditch (left) between fields. To the left is rising ground while to the right there is a view of Chigwell Church with Buckhurst Hill behind. Stay by the field boundary as the path gently descends and follow the path until it turns sharp left to a junction. Here, where there is a glimpse of Chigwell Cemetery (right), go ahead along a path known as Froghall Lane. The straight path leads to a stile at the main road in Grange Hill. Turn right for Grange Hill Station.

GRANGE HILL

The grange and its farm buildings (demolished in the nineteenth century) belonged to Tilty Priory near Great Dunmow in the north of the county. The hill, once part of the Hainault Forest hunting ground, remains only just in Essex, although many of the houses here are in the London borough of Redbridge. The station opened in 1903 as part of the Great Eastern Railway branch line, which became part of the Underground Central line in 1948. In the early steam days a milk train would stop between Grange Hill and Chigwell stations to load fruit and vegetables, grown on the Great Eastern Railway's own farm, destined for Liverpool Street's Great Eastern Hotel.

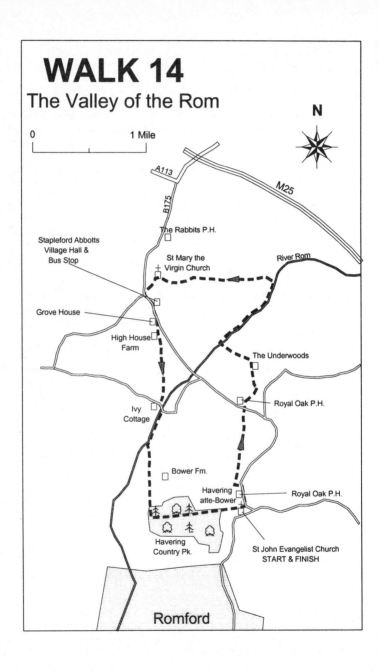

WALK 14
The Valley of the Rom

N

0   1 Mile

A113

M25

B175

The Rabbits P.H.

Stapleford Abbotts
Village Hall &
Bus Stop

St Mary the
Virgin Church

River Rom

Grove House

High House
Farm

The Underwoods

Royal Oak P.H.

Ivy
Cottage

Bower Fm.

Havering
atte-Bower

Royal Oak P.H.

Havering
Country Pk.

St John Evangelist Church
START & FINISH

Romford

Walk 14: The Valley of the Rom

Havering-atte-Bower – St Mary's, Stapleford Abbotts – Havering-atte-Bower

---

This circular walk takes in a pocket of rolling Essex farmland to the north and west of the ancient village of Havering-atte-Bower. In its latter stages the walk descends into the valley of the River Rom before returning to the village by way of a delightful woodland ramble through Havering country park with its plantation of mighty sequoia redwood trees.

Distance: 6 or 3 miles.

Map: OS Landranger 177 (East London area) or OS Pathfinder 1141 (Loughton).

Terrain: Field paths, bridleways and country lanes. Waterproof footwear is recommended as some parts tend to be muddy after rain.

Food & Drink: Royal Oak (Mon–Sat 11.30am–3pm & 5.30–11pm; Sun 12–3pm & 7–10.30pm; M/G) and Teas on the Green (Tue-Sun and bank holiday Mondays 9.30am-5pm; M/G), both Havering-atte-Bower; Royal Oak (Mon–Fri 11am–2.30pm & 6–11pm; Sat 11.30am–3pm & 6–11pm; Sun 12–10.30pm; M/G) and Rabbits (Mon–Fri 12–3pm & 6.30–11pm; Sat 12–11pm; Sun 12–10.30pm; M/G), both Stapleford Abbotts.

Transport: National Railways from Liverpool Street or LT Buses to Romford. Then bus 500 or 502 from outside the train station (Mon–Sat) or from the Market Place (Sun) to Havering-atte-Bower (15 mins). To reach the Market Place (5 min walk) turn left out of the station and keep ahead along the pedestrianised High Street turning right into Market Place. Continue past St Edward's Church on your left to St Edward's Way where, turning left, you will come to bus stop 'H' used by the privatised Sunday service. Current information on bus times is available from Essex Busline ☎ 0345 000333.

Start & Finish: The longer walk starts and ends at the church of St John the Evangelist, Havering-atte-Bower. The shorter walk ends at St Mary's, Stapleford Abbotts, by taking the 500 or 502 bus back to Romford via Havering-atte-Bower.

The bus will drop you at Havering-atte (pronounced 'atty') -Bower's village green (known locally as 'the Green') fronting the Church of St John the Evangelist.

HAVERING-ATTE-BOWER
Havering-atte-Bower is a docile place fanning out around the main street to the north of its village green. The Green, preserved 'for ever and not at any time to be enclosed' by an Act of Parliament of 1811, was originally part of the old royal palace founded here by Edward the Confessor in the eleventh century. Many monarchs visited the

palace, including Henry VIII and Elizabeth I who both used it as a hunting lodge, up to the time of the Civil War, after which it was abandoned and fell into decay. St John's stands on the site of the palace's former chapel of St Mary. A flint-walled Victorian building, it contains a number of interesting memorials as well as a Norman font in Purbeck marble. It's not often open, though, and the best time to gain entry is Sunday morning when there are services. On the Green opposite there's a copy of a seventeenth-century double stocks and whipping post which stood on the same spot and was used to pillory and punish miscreants. The Ducking Pond, where village scolds and witches were once dunked, lies behind the bus stop on the other side of the road. The village school was a charitable institution founded in 1724 by Dame Anne Tipping near the Green, where she gave free tuition to children of the village a century and a half before the Education Act made primary education free and compulsory for everyone. The school, now the Dame Tipping School, later moved to its present site and has expanded since then, but still educates the village's children. The foundation stone from the original building is preserved on the school's exterior.

From the church turn left downhill through the village passing the Royal Oak pub. After 300 yards – and just before the old village school which, with its ancient foundation stones, is worth a look – take a rough tarmac track on the left signed 'Footpath No. 3 Bournbridge'. The track soon bends right and you need to keep ahead following the line of the signed 'Footpath No. 4 Oak Hill Road' which skirts the school's car park and playing field, often being used by Dame Tipping's pupils, and continues along a line of trees to the right. Keep ahead for almost half a mile to a stile. Cross this to pass through a neck of woodland to another stile, beyond which the path becomes enclosed with a paddock to the left. The path then runs along a fence to emerge at the B175 road.

Cross the road to take the path between another Royal Oak pub (which has a beer garden and full-blown seafood restaurant) and a garage, veering right into the pub car park. At the far end of the car park is a well camouflaged signpost marked 'Footpath Nuper's Hatch'. This runs beside garden fences to reach a rough surfaced lane. Turn left here passing first Lyngs Farm, followed by Nuper's Farm, and at the end of the track keep forward through a kissing gate to the left of a house named 'The Underwoods'.

Once through the kissing gate take the path heading left through bushes into a field. Follow a line of trees and stream (left) to a stile. Cross this to enter another field to reach two footbridges over streams. Once across these, turn right to skirt the edge of a field. Now heading roughly north-east with the stream beyond the trees to your right, follow the waymarks keeping ahead across two footbridges over minor streams with the main stream (actually the River Rom) still to your right. At a farm drive turn left and then almost immediately right to cross a gravelled area and renew your direction following the line of trees, still on your right with the stream beyond. Inconsiderate planting by the farmer here often means that in summer you may struggle to keep to the footpath, but Epping Forest Council waymarks will reassure you that you are on the right track. At the end of this field maintain your direction, keeping to the right of a telegraph pole to go through trees to reach a stile with a lane beyond.

Turn left along the unpaved lane to pass farm buildings (right) and, further on, the odd cottage until the end of the lane is reached. Here, proceed forward for a good half a mile over stiles, keeping hedges and fences and the odd tract of woodland to the right. There are fine views over the surrounding countryside of the North Weald beyond the M25 as the path continues west to the church of St Mary, situated to the north of the village of Stapleford Abbotts. Near to the church the hedge turns right, but keep ahead across the field by a path which is usually kept free of crops. Cross a stile on the opposite side into another, smaller, field and follow the grassy path to a metal gate and stile with the church to the right.

ST MARY THE VIRGIN, STAPLEFORD ABBOTTS

A modest Victorian country church minding its own business, St Mary's was visited by eminent architectural historian Nikolaus Pevsner who promptly described it as the 'ugliest church in Essex', a notoriety it has been trying to live down ever since. What apparently provoked the great man's ire was the exterior combination of brick tower and crazy-paved nave. However, those less jaundiced will find within a serene interior with a seventeenth-century pulpit and, in a room off the chancel, a charming miniature fourteenth-century stained-glass window. Depicting Edward the Confessor holding a ring and sceptre, it's apparently a survival from a previous church here on a site which has seen worship since Saxon times. When the church is locked the key is usually available from the former rectory opposite, an elegant Georgian building now known as Old Rectory Farm.

Should you require refreshment at this point, the Rabbits pub lies a quarter of a mile to the north. To reach it take the leafy lane (Church Lane) which runs to the left (or west) of the church and follow it until it joins the B175, where you should turn right. The pub lies a little further along on the right.

Otherwise, to continue the walk retrace your steps for 50 metres from St Mary's Church to a stile. Cross this into a field and turn right to reach a kissing gate. Beyond this follow a farm drive half-left to the B175. Turn left to pass Stapleford Abbotts village hall fronted by a bus stop.

The shorter walk ends here by taking the 500 or 502 bus back to Romford via Havering-atte-Bower.

From the bus stop cross to the opposite side of the road and turn left to head south for about a quarter of a mile. Just beyond the elegant Grove House, with its less compelling ornamental garden pond, go right across a stile to cross a field half-left to a farm track. Keep ahead across the track, passing farm buildings (right), to follow the fence of a horse paddock to the left leading downhill towards the broad valley of the River Rom spread out below. When the track levels, bear right over a ditch and continue in the same direction along the edge of a field to reach, beyond two white metal gates and a stile, a road. Cross the road and turn left taking a signed footpath almost opposite and to the left of Ivy Cottage. This path follows a line of trees with a stream behind (left), for a quarter of a mile, and then crosses a footbridge followed after 50 yards by another. The latter footbridge leads into a field where you should keep ahead along a field path that runs in line with electricity poles. This part of the walk offers a view of the church tower of St John the Evangelist at Havering village on a rise to the left.

Beyond another footbridge the path continues alongside a field fence (left) to a farm track. Keep ahead across the track to follow a bridleway almost opposite which climbs to Havering Country Park. Do not enter by the first entrance, but continue to the second, 50 metres further along, first taking in the fine view over London's East End dominated by the tower of Canary Wharf on the horizon. Turn left here into the country park taking the bridleway into the woods. Twenty yards into the park, where a tree stands in the centre of the bridleway, turn right between posts to another narrower path, and turn left along this.

HAVERING COUNTRY PARK

Roman remains have been found in the park, which later became a deer park attached to the royal palace. In the Victorian era the park was divided between three farms on the estate owned by the McIntosh family, who planted the avenue of Wellingtonia trees, or giant sequoias. Native to the west coast of the United States, the trees were discovered during the California Gold Rush around 1850 and it soon became fashionable for the gentry to plant them on their country estates, chauvinistically renaming them after the Iron Duke who died in 1852. Renowned for their longevity and awesome growing power, the oldest known sequoia is 4,000 years old and the tallest, at Dyerville in California, rises to a mighty 364ft and started life around the time of Christ. Havering's trees, at 140 years old, are comparative striplings, but impressive nonetheless, and this is the second largest plantation of sequoias in the country.

Keep ahead along the path, which can be muddy, as it winds through the dense woodland to reach crosspaths at 'Five Ways'. Keep ahead here along the path (Wellingtonia Avenue) indicated to the village and flanked by imposing sequoias. Beyond two gates you will emerge at the rear of St John's Church. To reach the bus stop keep ahead along the lane to the left of the church which passes in front of the diminutive Teas on the Green tearoom, housed in a line of eighteenth-century timber-framed cottages where, if open, refreshing teas with home-made pastries should be on offer. The stop for buses to Romford faces the village green.

Walk 15: Upminster Fields

Upminster – Great Warley – Cranham – Upminster

'A visit to Great Warley is an experience you will always remember,' claimed John Timpson after featuring its church in his *Country Churches* television series. St Mary the Virgin Church, a memorial to a victim of war, lies just across the London boundary and is the surprise objective on this circular walk from the east end of the District line. This is the countryside of walker and First World War poet Edward Thomas, whose work features dreams of being rich enough to buy Warley's scattered hamlets of Codham, Cockridden and Childerditch. Hamlets do not have pubs, so on this walk walkers may wish to picnic before reaching the Thatched House near the end of the route.

Distance: 8 or 4 miles.

Map: OS Landranger 177 (East London) or OS Pathfinder 1160 (Barking and Romford).

Terrain: Field paths and roads.

Food & Drink: Upminster has several pubs and cafés. The Thatched House (12–11pm; Sun 12–10.30pm; M/G) is at Cranham.

Transport: District line to Upminster (Travelcard Zone 6). Return by Thamesway bus 265 (infrequent; Mon–Fri only) from Great Warley (outside Travelcard zones) to Brentwood National Railways Station. Call Blue Triangle ☎01708 631001 for times.

Start & Finish: Upminster in Essex. The shorter walk ends at Great Warley.

UPMINSTER

Upminster town centre is just south of the station at the crossroads by the church. St Laurence's is mainly mid-Victorian although the typical Essex tower, from where it was possible to observe shipping on the Thames, is partly thirteenth century. The Lady Chapel screen dates from Henry VII's reign and the font was originally in the Abbot's Chapel at Upminster Hall. The east window depicts St Cedd who brought Christianity to Upminster in the seventh century. The white H-shaped house to the west of the church was the Rectory until the new one was built behind in the 1970s – a member of the same family was the incumbent from 1780 until 1970. The windmill at the west end of St Mary's Lane was built in 1804 and worked until 1934.

Turn right out of Upminster Underground station into Station Road. The road becomes Hall Lane as it runs north. Soon there is a view (left) across the Ingrebourne River valley. Immediately beyond the Upminster Golf and Bowling Club entrance (right) go right to reach the Tithe Barn.

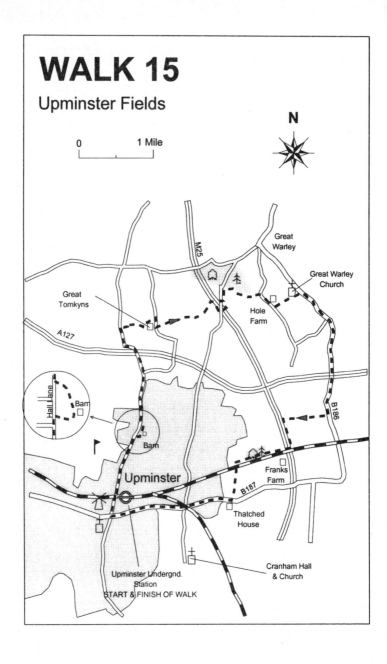

WALK 15

Upminster Fields

N

0   1 Mile

M25

Great
Warley

Great
Tomkyns

Great Warley
Church

A127

Hole
Farm

Hall Lane

Barn

B186

Barn

Upminster

Franks
Farm

B187

Thatched
House

Cranham Hall
& Church

Upminster Undergnd.
Station
START & FINISH OF WALK

UPMINSTER TITHE BARN

The barn was built in the fifteenth century as part of the Upminster Hall estate. The next door Upminster Hall, occupied by the golf club, is mainly Elizabethan. The original house was both a hunting lodge for the abbot of nearby Waltham Abbey as well as a sanatorium for the monks. The chapel survived until 1777.

Continue past the end of the Tithe Barn (right) and ahead through the line of trees on to Upminster Hall Fields. Hall Lane is over to the left. Bear half-left to rejoin the main road at the far corner. Beyond Avon Road (right) there is a grass verge for a short distance before the pavement resumes. Walk past Bird Lane (right) at Pot Kilns.

POT KILNS

The name recalls the brick and tile industry situated here from 1708 to 1930, when clay was dug out on both sides of Bird Lane. A horse-drawn railway ran south from Bird Lane, passing behind Upminster Hall to join the main line at Upminster.

Cross the top of the slip road (right) from the Southend Arterial Road to walk over the bridge spanning the dual carriageway, and follow the grass verge. At another junction go right to find a pavement alongside the continuation of the ancient Hall Lane.

Just before Apple Tree Cottage, a typical Essex-style farmhouse, go right over a stile. Keep ahead and go over a second stile by a gate. Horses, including shires, are often grazed in these fields. At the far end go over another stile on the left. Go down the side of the field for a short distance to go over a stile on the right. Ahead are two oak trees. Keep to the left of these trees to go up a narrow path between blackberry bushes. The long narrow path climbs gently alongside young trees (left) before the way is enclosed by hedges. Go over the stile and alongside the medieval Great Tomkyns (right) to the footbridge to reach Tomkyns Lane. Great Tomkyns is a moated fifteenth-century timber-framed hall house with two-storeyed wings and a seventeenth-century thatched barn. Great Tomkyns Farm is to the left. Turn right, and just before a white fence on the left go left up a narrow path. There is a stile at the top. Keep forward to go over a fence ahead by a bath used as a drinking trough and a gate. Keep by the side of the field as the way rises and falls, with a view (left) down to a pond. The ground rises to a gate at the far end by a wood (left). Go steeply downhill as the path bears round to the right to pass a stile (right).

At the next corner there are two stiles. Take the one ahead to walk uphill with the line of trees (right). There are impressive views to the right across south Essex towards the Thames, where the Dartford Bridge can be seen. At the top of the hill go right to follow the M25 fence downhill to find a stile leading to a metalled bridge. (This links the now bisected Beredens Lane, which once ran from Upminster to Great Warley.)

Once across the motorway go left along a narrow path to reach the lane below a mast. Walk along the lane for a few yards to go right over a stile into a huge field. Turn left to follow the side of the field. At the corner bear round to the right with Coombe Wood. This is also the boundary between Greater London (right) and the county of Essex (left). At the next corner go left downhill with the county boundary. At the bottom of the hill bear round to the right for just a few yards before turning left, with the track alongside a hedge (right). The track meets Hole Farm Lane at a double bend.

HOLE FARM LANE
Once known as Pilgrims' Lane, Hole Farm Lane is part of the medieval pilgrimage route to St Thomas à Becket's shrine at Canterbury. The pilgrims crossed the Thames by ferry at West Thurrock.

Turn right to walk down to Hole Farm, where there are usually plenty of hens and ducks. Walk just past the farmyard to go left along the back of the large barn and past a pond (right). There is a good second view (left) of the timber-framed house. Go ahead over the corner of a field, passing out of London into Essex, to join a metalled road which runs uphill under a power line. At the top there is a glimpse half-left of Great Warley Church across a garden. At the far end go through a gate to meet a road by the Great Warley village sign. Turn left to walk past The Hermitage and reach the church lych gate (left).

GREAT WARLEY CHURCH
At first sight this appears to be a typical Essex church, but inside it is a feast of art nouveau design. St Mary the Virgin Church was built between 1902 and 1904 by a stockbroker as a memorial to his brother who had been killed in the Boer War. The architect was Charles Harrison Townsend, who was also responsible for the Whitechapel Art Gallery and the Horniman Museum. Apart from the pews and choir stalls, the interior is the work of Sir William Reynolds Stephens who used bronze, pewter, silver gilt, black and green marble, enamel and mother-of-pearl for the death and love theme. The golden dove on the spire has the appearance of a parrot. English Heritage is helping to maintain the church, which is open for the 11am Sunday service and every Sunday and bank holiday afternoon. (The main village, known as Warley Street in the early nineteenth century, lies around the green to the north, beyond the church.)

From the church turn right to walk south away from the village. There is a pavement and, just before a road junction, a bus shelter.

The main walk continues across the top of Cotham Hall Lane (right) on to the grass verge and past Bird Lane (left). The start of the pavement is on the London boundary – street signs indicate the change from Great Warley Street in Essex to Warley Street in the London borough of Havering. Continue alongside Warley Rose Garden (right) to pass a school (left). Beyond a group of houses, including a pink cottage (left) and Brick House Hotel (right), the road crosses high above the Southend Arterial Road.

Continue ahead past Church Lane (left) and a Christmas tree plantation (right). After passing Gladstone Cottages (left), and just before the road runs downhill, go over a stile on the right. A signpost points to Moor Lane. Walk ahead across the huge field heading for a point just to the right of the pylon. The path passes the end of a copse known as Hobbs Hole before reaching the M25. Turn left to follow the bank south to the London–Southend railway line. Here, go right under the motorway and ahead along the side of a field by the railway (left). There is a view across the line to the partly fifteenth-century Frank's Farmhouse. At the far end of the field go ahead, following the Upminster

Circular Walk waymark, into Frank's Wood. Walk through the trees, which include coppiced hornbeam, to the far side where the path bears slightly to the right to cross a bridge over a ditch. Keep ahead over the grass of Cranham Playing Field, and head towards the far left-hand corner to find an iron stile leading to the railway. Observe the rule 'Stop, Look and Listen' before crossing the railway line to a second stile. Go forward on a wide boarded path before briefly entering trees and reaching a field. Walk ahead down the side (left) to a stile at the far end leading to a road at Cranham. Opposite is Pike Lane. Go right along St Mary's Lane to pass the Thatched House pub.

THE THATCHED HOUSE

The pub takes its name from an isolated thatched house on the site which farmer James Gates ran as a beerhouse from the late 1860s until his death in 1892. The following year his son sold the house to a brewery. The present tiled building dates from 1910 but still has a homely feel with its inglenook fireplace and logs stacked in the porch. The pub is open all day from noon with food available until at least 9.30pm.

Continue along St Mary's Lane which leads directly to Upminster. On the way it passes under the branch line to Ockenden and Grays. Immediately beyond the bridge there is the lodge (left) at the top of the road to Cranham Hall and All Saints Church.

CRANHAM HALL AND CHURCH

The name 'Cranham' refers to the crane bird, once numerous here. The Georgian house is on the site of the residence of James Oglethorpe, one of the founders in 1729 of the state of Georgia in the US, who is commemorated in All Saints Church, rebuilt in 1873.

Continue ahead to reach the crossroads by Upminster Church. The windmill is ahead on the right. Upminster Underground station is in Station Road to the right.

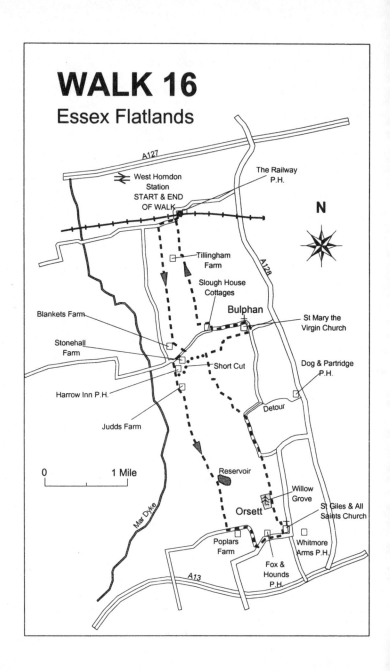

WALK 16

Essex Flatlands

A127

West Horndon
Station
START & END
OF WALK

The Railway
P.H.

N

Tillingham
Farm

A128

Slough House
Cottages

Bulphan

Blankets Farm

St Mary the
Virgin Church

Stonehall
Farm

Short Cut

Dog & Partridge
P.H.

Harrow Inn P.H.

Detour

Judds Farm

0   1 Mile

Reservoir

Willow
Grove

St Giles & All
Saints Church

Mar Dyke

Orsett

Poplars
Farm

Whitmore
Arms P.H.

Fox &
Hounds
P.H.

A13

Walk 16: Essex Flatlands

West Horndon – Orsett – Bulphan – West Horndon

This walk takes in a little-visited tract of countryside secreted away between the conurbations of Upminster and Basildon. A delightful ramble at all times of the year, it's especially so in spring when daffy skylarks career crazily around in the vast Essex skies and hares seem to bolt from underfoot in every field. These flatlands retain a character very similar to the fen country of Norfolk, although the marshes here were only drained in World War Two as part of the agricultural war effort. And if you were thinking that a level landscape is synonymous with monotony, then a walk along these hedgerows bastioned with sturdy oaks and teeming with birdlife interspersed with deep dykes alive in high summer with dragonflies, frogs and waterfowl may well change your mind.

Distance: 10 miles, or 5.5 miles using short-cut.

Map: OS Landranger Sheet 177 (East London) or Pathfinder 1161 (Basildon).

Terrain: Mostly field paths and country roads. Fields very muddy after rain. In summer crops and weeds tend to make some paths difficult. You should also take care using footbridges over dykes as a few are unsteady. No climbs.

Food & Drink: Harrow Inn (Mon–Sat 11am–3pm & 5.30–11pm; Sun 12–10.30pm; M/G), near Stone Hall Farm; Foxhound, (Mon–Fri 11am–3.00pm & 6–11pm; Sat 11am–11pm; Sun 12–4pm & 7–10.30pm; M/G) and Whitmore Arms (Mon–Sat 11am–3pm & 6–11pm; Sun 12–3pm & 7–10.30pm; M/G), both Orsett; Dog and Partridge (Mon–Sat 11am–11pm; Sun 12–10.30pm; M/G), near Ongar Hall Farm; Railway (Mon–Sat 11am–11pm; Sun 12–10.30pm; M/G), West Horndon.

Transport: London Underground (District line) to Upminster, then by train from the same station to West Horndon (one stop) (outside Travelcard zones). To cut out the interminable tube ride from central London it's possible to take the train direct from Fenchurch Street or Barking.

Start & Finish: West Horndon train station.

Arriving at West Horndon train station from London, cross the footbridge over the line to reach and pass through a wicket gate on the opposite platform next to the station sign. Follow the track to the right up to the road where you should turn left downhill. Take care on this road as it is often busy and there are a couple of blind corners. After three hundred yards and just beyond a footpath signed on the right, turn left across fields along another signed footpath. Keep directly ahead across the field – when under crops the way isn't always immediately clear and the farmer tends not to leave a path clear – aiming for a barn close to a power pylon to the right of Tillingham Farm.

Cross the farm road and continue south along the left side of the barn to pick up a hedge on the right. Keep ahead, crossing two fields. In the corner of the second field cross a footbridge over a ditch into a third field with woods to the left and a pond in the centre circled by trees. Cross the field keeping the pond (often dried-up in these times of low rainfall) to your right and then aim for a white marker post and plank bridge on the far side. This stretch tends to be overgrown in summer. Cross the bridge and the field beyond, aiming for another marker post and footbridge. Once across this keep a line to the left of Blankets Farm ahead, picking up the fence of a paddock to the left. This leads to another footbridge over a ditch next to Little Blankets Cottage, whose dogs will probably give you a vociferous welcome.

Go over the footbridge to enter a lane before the cottage gate and turn left for fifty yards to take a signed footpath on the right by the entrance to Drake's Farm. Cross a ditch and head half-left across the field to reach a lattice footbridge over a dyke, and turn right along the road beyond. Pass Stone Hall Farm on the left, and soon turn left to reach the Harrow Inn.

THE HARROW INN

Outside the pub you'll most likely be gruffly greeted by 'Fred', the three-legged labrador, who is a celebrated character in these parts. Fred lost one of his front legs some years ago when, while doing his rounds of nearby fields, he was shot by some unknown hunters who may have mistaken him for a fox. He was callously left for dead and a vet advised having him put down. But Fred proved himself one of life's survivors and went on to make a remarkable recovery. The old pub (run by Alison and Bill Bowerman) is a pleasant oasis in the midst of the surrounding fenland, and besides serving the usual pub grub has an adjoining restaurant with a fixed price Sunday lunch (12–2pm) with vegetarian options.

The Shorter Walk

To take the short-cut, go through a metal gate on the left at the edge of the pub property. Once through the gate head east along the fence around the pub's land to walk along the rear of Stone Hall Farm. A little beyond the farm gate you'll see a marker post and stile ahead, next to a field gate. Cross this and keep ahead with the hedge on your left to cross two more stiles, after the second of which the short-cut rejoins the main walk (see page 102).

The **main walk** continues along the rough, unpaved lane, soon passing Judds Farm on the left. Keep ahead at the end of the track with a ditch and hedge to the left, where there soon appears a public footpath sign marked 'to Orsett'. Keep ahead along the grassy path with the ditch still to the left. At the field corner turn right along the field edge with the hedge and ditch on the left, and follow this for 75 yards to a white marker post, also on the left. Go over the plank footbridge here and then cross the next field aiming roughly half-right to a marker post indicating another footbridge. Cross this and aim for another white marker post and footbridge, again half-right. Then cross a third field keeping roughly straight ahead to another marker post and footbridge. Once over this, keep your line to cross the next larger field which rises and then falls to meet a hedge on the far side. At the hedge turn left (east) along the line of the hedge to reach a low stone bridge. In summer when this field is under crop, the farmer often cuts a path leading directly to the bridge. Cross the bridge and head half-left over the next field in the direction of the hospital, with its tall chimney dominating the horizon.

You will soon spot a white marker post in the far corner of this field and will also be able to make out the low embankment of a reservoir. When you reach the marker post cross the footbridge over a dyke. To the left lies the steep embankment of the reservoir and, if you climb to the top, you should usually spot a variety of waterfowl not accustomed to having their exclusive occupation of this habitat disturbed.

Once across the footbridge, the walk continues south with a hedge and ditch to your left to reach a road junction after half a mile. At the junction turn left towards the house of Poplars Farm, ahead. Passing the house to the right, keep ahead along the road (Fen Lane) as it winds around to meet another road (the B188). Turn left along here and keep ahead to enter the village of Orsett. Just before the church you'll come to the Foxhound pub, with outdoor tables. Beyond the church is the village's other pub, the Whitmore Arms, its name changed from the earlier George to commemorate the last Lord of the Manor here, Sir Francis Whitmore, who died in 1962 aged 90.

ORSETT VILLAGE

A pleasantly rural village whose name may derive from the Saxon 'or' (water) and 'sett' (place), Orsett has a number of ancient dwellings, some dating back to the fourteenth and fifteenth centuries. Over the road from the Whitmore Arms, No. 2 High Road was originally Edward Anson's School founded in 1785 to give 'teaching to six poor boys in Orsett and two each in Hordon on the Hill, Bulphan, Mucking and Chadwell'.

Orsett's main feature is its fine twelfth-century Norman church of St Giles and All Saints with an ancient porch and beautifully preserved south doorway. Inside there's a Saxon stone font and some fine eighteenth-century Italian plasterwork panels depicting the life of Christ. Due to thefts and damage the church is now kept closed. On Sundays (except the first Sunday in the month) it can be viewed for 30 minutes following morning service, which ends just after 12 noon; otherwise you can make an appointment to view by contacting the rector ☎01375 891254, preferably a few days in advance.

From the church take public footpath No. 110, which runs down the west side of the churchyard to become an enclosed path. When you come to a road (Malting Lane) turn left and keep ahead to turn right along a public footpath marked 'to Bulphan', just before Pound Lane and facing Malting Cottage. Beyond the half-timbered Tudor gable of Hall Farm and trees to the left is located the ring-and-bailey earthworks of Bishop Bonner's (a sixteenth-century Bishop of London) Palace, or perhaps hunting lodge, although there's little to see. Keep ahead soon to cross a farm drive to follow a gravel track which skirts the edge of a grove of bat willows.

BAT WILLOWS

Taking its name from the cricket bat, the genus of willow *salix coerulea* (a strain of the white willow) has long been the favoured material for the batsman's friend due to its combination of lightness, toughness, suppleness and resistance to warping. Left to its own devices the bat willow can climb to thirty metres in height, but when grown for making bats it is constantly pruned so that no knots can mar the timber and is felled as soon as the diameter of its trunk reaches 45 centimetres, at about the age of 12. The prized butt length – about 2.5 metres long – is cut off and then cleft by hand into wedge-shaped segments. After seasoning, which ensures even shrinkage, three bat lengths are cut from each segment and are then shaped by hand to make the bat's blade which, when it collides with leather, issues one of the most evocative sounds of the English summer.

Keep ahead, soon joining up with a hedge to the right, to eventually meet a road after half a mile. Walk ahead here following the road (north) for a further half-mile to a sharp right-hand bend.

The walk is now dry from here to West Horndon, but should you require refreshment there's an easy detour to the Dog and Partridge, half a mile east. To get there, swing right with the road, and when it makes a sharp left turn keep ahead along a bridleway (No. 178) to bear right around the ground of Thurrock airfield. Follow a hedge and ditch (right) to reach the pub, sited on the main road (A128). It has a pleasant beer garden with a gaggle of bread-hungry geese.

The walk continues straight on (north) from the bend along a public footpath signed 'Fen Lane'. The path follows a field edge. Where the hedge veers away to the left, walk ahead to pick up another hedge, keeping this to your right. After joining the hedge start to veer gently half-left across the field aiming for a marker post and footbridge about 100 yards to the left of the field's right-hand corner (if the field is under crops the farmer should have cut a path to the marker post). Once across the footbridge aim for another marker post to the left of a line of cypress trees and in front of a barn. Keep ahead along the side of the barn, passing through a narrow gate to proceed across a small field to a stile and footbridge. Once over this, keep roughly ahead across the next field to a stile in the field corner. Beyond this follow a hedge (left) to the left of a long field until you reach a stile, but do *not* cross this.

The short-cut rejoins the main walk here.

Facing the stile turn right (heading east) with the hedge to your left to reach another marker post denoting another stile and footbridge. Cross these and cross the field beyond in a roughly half-left direction. If the field is under crops you will have to negotiate a way round, but you are aiming for the church tower at Bulphan, clearly visible in the distance. As you near the church you will be able to spot a narrow path between a paddock and enclosed grounds on the left. Follow this and it will lead you, beyond a red gate, to the churchyard of St Mary's.

ST MARY THE VIRGIN, BULPHAN

Bulphan's name probably derives from the Anglo-Saxon 'burh fann', meaning a fortified settlement in the marshes, and dates back to early Saxon times. Although the south porch, chancel, nave and belfry are survivals from the original fifteenth-century church of St Mary, it has undergone much restoration since and the present building is largely Victorian – the clock on the tower was added to commemorate Queen Victoria's golden jubilee. Inside the church a fifteenth-century oak altar screen is worth a look. However, it is normally kept locked outside service times, but you could try ringing the rectory (☎01375 891254, in advance if possible).

From the church's lych gate turn left along the road for half a mile, taking care as cars tend to whizz along here. Turn right when you reach China Lane to pass Slough House cottages on the left; the end one has some pargeted decoration with a wheatsheaf on its gable. Keep ahead along an unmetalled track for 20 yards turning left along a public footpath close to a sign marked 'Slough House only'. At the time of writing the sign (PF 142 signed 'to West Horndon') is in a precarious state but the footpath is not difficult to spot.

Cross the field and turn right across a dyke. Where the dyke veers to the right, climb the bank to continue north, following a field hedge on the right. Near the top of this field cross a ditch on the right and turn left, still heading north with the hedge to the left. After half a mile you will arrive at the farm road leading to Tillingham Hall. Turn left here and then almost immediately right just before a telegraph pole (bearing waymarks) to follow a public footpath across a field towards a line of five oak trees.

Keeping ahead along the line of the trees will bring you to a metal stile in a hedgerow to the right of a house and garden. Cross this and the stile beyond to reach the road and West Horndon station, over the bridge to the right. The Railway pub stands in front of the station on Station Road.

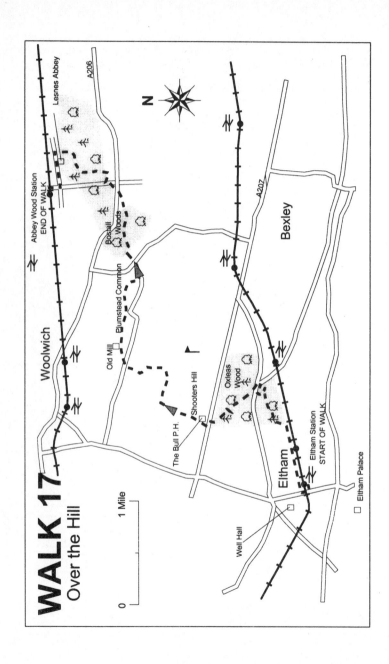

WALK 17
Over the Hill

N

Woolwich

Abbey Wood Station
END OF WALK

Lesnes Abbey

A206

Old Mill

Plumstead Common

Bostall Woods

Shooters Hill

The Bull P.H.

A207

Bexley

Oxleas Wood

Eltham

Eltham Station
START OF WALK

Well Hall

Eltham Palace

0   1 Mile

Walk 17: Over the Hill

Eltham – Shooters Hill – Plumstead – Lesnes Abbey

South-east London's landmark is Shooters Hill, which marks the boundary between London and the Garden of England. This, for centuries the capital's gateway for travellers from abroad, was itself in the country and remnants of the rural past can be found at Eltham, where the walk starts, and over the hill in the former waterside community of Plumstead. The summit of the hill, which conceals a working farm, affords splendid views of the City of London.

Distance: 6.5 or 3.5 miles

Map: OS Landranger 177 (East London) or OS Pathfinder 1176 (Bexley).

Terrain: Woodland paths and roads.

Food & Drink: Tudor Barn (11am–10.30pm; Sun 12–10.30pm; M/G) at Eltham's Well Hall Pleasaunce; Bull (11am–3pm; 5.15–11pm; Sat 11am–3pm & 7–11pm; Sun 12–3pm & 7–10.30pm; M) on Shooters Hill; Old Mill (11am–3pm & 5.30–11pm; Sun 12–3pm & 7–10.30pm; M) on Plumstead Common.

Transport: National Railways from Charing Cross to Eltham (Travelcard Zone 4). Return by LT bus 89 from Shooters Hill (Zone 4) to Blackheath Station; LT Bus 53 from Plumstead Common (Zone 4) to central London or National Railways from Abbey Wood Station (Zone 4) to Charing Cross.

Start & Finish: Eltham in south-east London to Abbey Wood. The shorter walk ends at Plumstead Common.

ELTHAM
A Kentish village into the twentieth century, Eltham has always been known for its palace, described in the fourteenth century as 'a very magnificent palace which the King possessed seven miles from London'. At one time Geoffrey Chaucer supervised improvements. Today's surviving Great Hall was added in 1479. At Eltham Palace Henry V returned after the triumph of Agincourt, Wolsey was made Lord Chancellor by Henry VIII, and Mary's Privy Council met to discuss the defence of Calais. The palace (open Apr–Sep Thu, Fri & Sun, admission £4) was largely destroyed by Oliver Cromwell, who let the hall be used as a barn. The Greyhound in the High Street has a fireplace which may have come from the palace. Thomas Doggett, founder of Doggett's Coat & Badge Race held annually on the Thames, is buried outside the south wall of St John's Church. LCC leader and Cabinet minister Herbert Morrison lived at 55 Archery Road, marked with a blue plaque, from 1929 until his death in 1960.

Turn right out of Eltham Station to walk under the railway bridge to find Well Hall to the left.

WELL HALL PLEASAUNCE

Well Hall, a public garden, was the moated home of Margaret Roper whose father, St Thomas More, was martyred during Henry VIII's reign. The medieval property remained in the family until 1733 when the house was pulled down. In 1899 its eighteenth-century farmhouse replacement (now demolished, leaving the moat) became the home of Edith Nesbit, who wrote *The Railway Children* here, and her husband Hubert Bland, a founder member of the Fabian Society. Visitors included E.M. Forster, Laurence Housman and George Bernard Shaw. H.G. Wells wrote: 'One rushed down from town at the weekend to snatch one's bed before anyone else got it.' In the local paper the couple advertised new-laid eggs on sale at 'Well Hall opposite the Co-operative Stores'. Next to the moat is the Tudor Barn pub which is the remains of Well Hall Farm. Entertainer Bob Hope was born in 1903 at 44 Craigton Road behind the Co-op; the family emigrated to America four years later and the house now has a plaque.

Go right down Dungevan Road, opposite Well Hall. The road rises very gently as it begins to climb Shooters Hill, which can be seen to the left at junctions. Beyond a crossroads, with the noted baker A.J. Ayre on the corner, the road becomes Eltham Park Gardens. After a second crossroads the road bears left to enter Eltham Park North.

Keep forward as the wide path rises giving a view to the left of Crystal Palace mast with central London just hidden behind the hill, but Canary Wharf in view. On the far side of the grass go forward into Shepherdleas Wood. Take the right-hand path which soon joins the Green Chain Walk. Ignore all turnings until coming to a junction with a signpost. Here go left along the path signposted to Oxleas Wood. The path bends round to run near a main road before turning left to the Rochester Way–Welling Way traffic lights. Cross over to go a few yards down Welling Way. Just before the seat on the left go left on a path running into Oxleas Wood. The path is the southern end of Crown Woods Lane and part of the Green Chain.

On reaching a major path junction, where the Green Chain turns right, keep ahead on the metalled path running alongside a wide expanse of grass (left). Beyond a building the path runs just inside the wood before emerging near the top of the hill. Stay on the path to bear round to the left to the viewpoint at the café where there are seats. Here there is a view across Eltham to the North Downs. Walk behind the building to reach a car park and follow the metalled road, still Crown Woods Lane, to a junction with Kenilworth Gardens. Go right to reach the main road on top of Shooters Hill.

SHOOTERS HILL

The name may come from the words 'shaw' and 'tot', meaning 'wood' and 'hill'. The road is the Roman Watling Street and pilgrim road to Canterbury. From here, 432 feet above the Thames, many foreign visitors enjoyed their first view of London. Samuel Pepys mentions seeing a body on a gibbet on the summit in his 1661 diary, and Byron places a hold-up here in *Don Juan*. In *A Tale of Two Cities,* Dickens describes the Dover Mail lumbering up the hill in November 1775 with passengers plodding along in the mud. The mounting stone at the top indicates the original position of the Bull, which was rebuilt a few yards to the west in 1881. The water tower, seen from far away, was built in 1910. A beacon and shutter telegraph preceded the modern radio mast.

The walk continues to the left before going right down Shrewsbury Lane at the side of the Bull. A few yards down Ankerdine Crescent (left) there is a magnificent view of the Thames. Continue ahead along Shrewsbury Lane to pass Occupation Lane (left) which also offers a view. After the fire station (right) and the Roman burial mound by Mayplace Lane (left) the road becomes Plum Lane. Walk on the right-hand side, and soon the pavement leads into the entrance of Shrewsbury Park.

SHREWSBURY PARK

Shrewsbury Park is the former grounds of Shrewsbury House, built for the Earl of Shrewsbury in 1789. Princess Charlotte, the Prince Regent's daughter, spent much of 1799 here. The house was rebuilt in 1923 for community use shortly before the immediate garden became a housing estate.

Follow the metalled path which, on reaching grass (right), joins the Green Chain Walk. Beyond the woodland (left) the path bears left to run downhill by a line of trees (right). At the bottom go over the rough path and ahead on a narrow rough path which stays by a fence to run uphill with occasional views, and then downhill to steps. Go down the steps to Wrekin Road, which soon becomes Upton Road. When level with Olven Road (left) go right down steps into Ennis Road. Turn right to reach a crossroads by the Ship on the edge of Plumstead Common. **To end the walk here** go right for the bus stop.

PLUMSTEAD COMMON

Plumstead comes from the word 'plum', which with other fruit was plentiful here into the nineteenth century. This was a Kentish fishing village and sheep were grazed on the Thames marshes down below to the north of the ancient church dedicated to St Nicholas, patron saint of sailors. The common on the high ground was saved for the public in 1877 by the Metropolitan Board of Works (London County Council forerunner) from being taken over by the Army, who found it a handy exercise ground for Woolwich Barracks. The Old Mill pub opened in 1848 when the attached eighteenth-century windmill ceased producing flour.

Cross the main road (crossing to the right) to pass the Ship (left) and bear right down Old Mill Road opposite Wernbrook Street. The road leads directly across the common to the Old Mill. Go past the pub (left), Plumstead Manor School and the Albert. On reaching Chestnut Rise (left), just before modern Plumstead Parish Church, bear half-right on to a path running across a corner of the common.

Go down the long flight of steps with a pond in the valley below. At the bottom cross the end of a road (left) to take the steps uphill. There are three charming houses to the left. At the top go ahead over two roads to briefly join the main road (right). After a short distance bear left along Bleak Hill Lane. The rough road later bends round to the right. Just before it begins to run downhill to Holly Cottage bear off to the right down steps to rejoin the main road opposite Woolwich Cemetery. Go left past the Alma down to a crossroads. Cross over (crossing to the right) and walk ahead along Waterdale Road to Bostall Woods, purchased in 1892 by the London County Council and described as 'picturesque and charming beyond description'.

Go forward up the steps into Bostall Woods. At the top go right, and after a short distance bear round to the left to follow a path which rises steeply. The Green Chain joins from the left before the path reaches a beechwood at the top. Go forward through the trees using the handy Green Chain waymarks as a guide. The line of the path is soon resumed. Ignore any turnings, and soon the path runs alongside a bowling green (left) and meets a road.

Cross over to bear half-left across the grass heading for the end of the belt of trees. Cross the road and go a few yards further along to find a rough track running into the partly wooded Bostall Heath. Keep forward at a junction by Belvedere Clinic (left, occupying Bostall House) to reach Knee Hill. The Greenwich–Bexley boundary runs down the middle. Go left and then right into Hurst Lane.

Follow the lane until finding a waymarked turning on the left leading into Lesnes Abbey Wood. Ignore all turnings as it runs downhill. The Green Chain turns off to the right by a fenced pond. At the bottom of the hill go right to reach a road. Cross over and take the path ahead, which follows the edge of Lesnes Abbey Wood. Soon there is a hedge to the left. On meeting a junction with the Green Chain, go left through a break in the hedge to see Lesnes Abbey ruins ahead.

LESNES ABBEY

Lesnes Abbey, built with stone brought by ship up the Thames from Normandy, was founded in 1178 by Richard de Lucy, Chief Justiciar of England (see page 81), as an act of penance for the murder of St Thomas à Becket just eight years earlier. The Thames used to flood across the marsh up to the Abbey Road below the bank, and the ten Augustinian monks spent huge amounts of money on the river wall and draining the marshes for pasture. The marsh is now occupied by the tower blocks of Thamesmead. The abbey was closed by Cardinal Wolsey in 1525, ten years ahead of Henry VIII's attack on the monasteries, and some of the buildings were pulled down. The site, overgrown by 1630, was excavated between 1909 and 1913 and 1938 and 1968 and so now the outline of the abbey church and cloister can be seen. Substantial remains include the dormitory stairs and a serving hatch. In spring daffodils, said to have been first planted by the monks, carpet the woods followed by a haze of bluebells shortly afterwards.

Walk through the abbey ruins to the main Abbey Road on the north side. Turn left along the road, and after passing under the flyover go right down Wilton Road to Abbey Wood Station.

Walk 18: The Veil of Heaven

Eynsford – Shoreham – Otford

The 'Veil of Heaven' was painter Samuel Palmer's description in the early nineteenth century of the Darent valley. A more recent resident was historian Arthur Mee, who lived on the hill above Eynsford, claiming the view to be 'a straight mile probably unique on the map of rural England' with 'Roman, Norman, Saxon, Tudor . . . all in a line'. A walk along the Darent (sometimes still called 'Darenth') valley featured more than once in London Transport's *Country Walks* books due to the proximity of Swanley Bus Garage. Again this route follows Mee's line in a valley Palmer would still recognise. Eynsford is pretty enough to have been the subject of a television series called *20 Miles From Piccadilly Circus*. The beautiful Kent village can be reached in just 45 minutes from London's Blackfriars Station.

> *Distance*: 6 or 4 miles.

> *Map*: OS Landranger 177 (East London) and 188 (Maidstone and The Weald of Kent) or OS Pathfinder 1192 (Orpington) and Explorer 147 (Sevenoaks and Westerham).

> *Terrain*: Lanes and field paths.

> *Food & Drink*: Malt Shovel (11am–3.30pm & 7–11pm; Sun 12–4pm & 7–10.30pm; M) at Eynsford; Gatehouse Tearoom (weekends 2–6pm Apr–Sep) at Lullingstone Castle; Lullingstone Park Visitor Centre café (10am–4.45pm; Nov–Feb 11am–3.45pm) at Kingfisher Bridge; King's Arms (11am–3pm; Sat 11am–11pm; Sun 12–10.30pm; M) at Shoreham; Otford Antiques Tearoom (until 5pm; Sun 4pm) and the Bull Inn (11am–11pm; Sun 12–10.30pm; M/G) at Otford.

> *Transport*: National Railways from London Blackfriars to Eynsford (outside Travelcard zones). Return by train from Shoreham or Otford stations to Blackfriars. When buying a day return ticket from London, book to the furthest station on the walk.

> *Start & Finish*: Eynsford to Otford in Kent. The shorter walk ends at Shoreham

Turn left out of Eynsford Station and at the main road go right. Cross over where the pavement ends to continue downhill into the village, passing Willow Cottage (left) just before the Malt Shovel (right). Ahead is the village centre by the church.

EYNSFORD
Eynsford derives from 'Aegan's Ford'. The castle to the north is Norman (ruins open daily, admission free). St Martin's Church, which has a thirteenth-century tower,

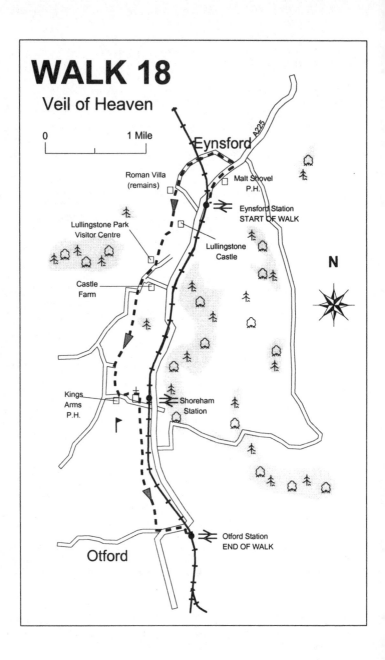

WALK 18

Veil of Heaven

0   1 Mile

Eynsford

A225

Roman Villa
(remains)

Malt Shovel
P.H.

Eynsford Station
START OF WALK

Lullingstone Park
Visitor Centre

Lullingstone
Castle

Castle
Farm

N

Kings
Arms
P.H.

Shoreham
Station

Otford Station
END OF WALK

Otford

retains its Norman influence. The origin of the dispute which led to the martyrdom of St Thomas à Becket in 1170 can be traced back to Eynsford. In 1163 Archbishop Becket excommunicated William d'Eynsford for rejecting the Archbishop's own choice of priest for the village, but William successfully appealed to the king for support. The church stands opposite the ford to create an attractive setting which draws visitors. Children's fishing nets are on sale at the sweet shop. Willow Cottage (opposite the Malt Shovel) was the home of artist Graham Sutherland in the 1930s.

At the church turn left to cross the bridge by the ford. Continue past the Plough to reach Toll Bar Cottage opposite Sparepenny Lane.

TOLL BAR COTTAGE
The cottage was occupied by a toll keeper in the 1850s who probably collected money from travellers using Sparepenny Lane, which must have been cheaper than the main turnpike road on the east side of the Darent. The highland cattle, usually found in the fields beneath the 72-foot-high 1862 railway viaduct behind, belong to the Alexander family who came from Scotland a century ago to the next door eighteenth-century Home Farm farmhouse, bringing their cattle by train.

Continue ahead on a road which is also part of the Darent Valley Way. Where this long-distance path divides, still keep forward on the road, which does not suffer from any through traffic. The road passes under the railway viaduct and rises to give a view over the valley. There is a turning (right) to Eagle Heights Bird of Prey Centre.

EAGLE HEIGHTS BIRD OF PREY CENTRE
The centre has recently opened at Hulberry Farm. The birds include owls, hawks and eagles. Alaska the eagle can often be seen in the sky over the valley. There are flying displays at 12 noon and 3pm. Open Mar–Nov daily 10.30am–5pm; Dec–Feb Sat & Sun 11am–4pm; admission £3.50 (child £2). ☎01322 866466.

At a junction, go forward to pass Lullingstone Roman Villa.

LULLINGSTONE ROMAN VILLA
One of the most exciting archaeological finds of the twentieth century, the villa is in the care of English Heritage. The mosaic floor was discovered in the mid-eighteenth century when a fence was being erected. The clay hill behind the building had slowly slid down to preserve the structure, which was eventually excavated in 1949. The house dates from about AD 80 and during the third century it appears to have been empty for about fifty years. New occupants carried out some restoration and had a mosaic floor laid in the dining-room. Later, but still 200 years before St Augustine's Christian mission to Kent, a room was turned into a chapel for Christian worship. The residence seems to have been abandoned just before AD 420 as the result of a fire. Open daily 10am–6pm (dusk in Oct); Nov–Mar 10am–4pm; closed 24–26 Dec; admission £2.50 ☎01322 863417

Keep ahead past the Roman villa and through the gateway to Lullingstone Castle. The drive passes cottages and stables (right) before reaching the castle gateway (left).

LULLINGSTONE CASTLE

Henry VIII and Catherine of Aragon passed under the Tudor gateway when they came to stay with Sir John Peche, the king's jousting champion and the ancestor of the Hart Dyke family, who live here today. The estate passed to Sir John's nephew Sir Percyval Hart, and in 1738 Anne Hart married Sir Thomas Dyke. Anne's father, who rebuilt the main house, had the stair treads made shallow to assist Queen Anne, who left two chests and a doll here. In 1873 the rules of lawn tennis were devised on the lawn by Sir William Hart Dyke and his friends. St Botolph's, known as the 'Church on the Lawn', is a parish church. The castle and grounds are open Apr–Jun Sun and bank holidays 2–6pm & Jul–Sep weekends 2–6pm; admission £3.75 (OAP £3/child £1.50). ☎ 01322 862114.

Continue past the gateway, and as the road swings left keep ahead to a kissing gate. Follow the path which runs alongside the River Darent. Opposite a footbridge there is a kissing gate (right) leading to Lullingstone Park Visitor Centre (open from at least 11am to 4pm on most days of the year, has a café, toilets, shop and useful information on walking in the area. ☎ 01322 865995). Beyond the visitor centre the path meets a kissing gate by Kingfisher Bridge. Follow the road ahead to pass Castle Farm.

CASTLE FARM

On the site of Shoreham Castle, Castle Farm has grown hops since the seventeenth century. Hop pickers from London used to stay in the sheds by the bridge during the annual picking season. Today's hops are mainly the Fuggles variety, used in the production of lager. Hopbines are sold at the Hop Shop (open Mon–Fri 1-5pm & Sat 10am–5pm), which specialises in dried flowers and grasses.

Continue along the road as it rises to a bend. Here, keep ahead on a path running along the top of a bank above a large hop field (left). At the far end go through a line of trees and down a field to a concrete path. Cross the concrete and bear half-left on a path running across a field which gently rises to the centre. In the far corner go through the gap into the next field and stay by the left boundary. At the next corner go through the kissing gate to follow an enclosed path by the river.

On reaching a lane turn left towards the entrance to a converted mill. At once go right along a short path to cross the river. Turn right on the metalled path to follow the river (right) into Shoreham. Just before reaching the bridge, the now wider path passes the side of Water House (left).

SHOREHAM

Shoreham means 'home in the cleft'. Artist Samuel Palmer came here in 1824 to escape 'that great dust hole' London. After briefly living at Ivy Cottage, he moved into Water House and stayed until 1835. Palmer and his friends roamed the valley footpaths at night, and one of his paintings showing a rabbit on a path is called 'Early Morning'. Another he captioned with the words of Psalm 65: 'The folds shall be full of sheep: the valleys also shall stand so thick with corn, that they shall laugh and sing.' Palmer's Shoreham work was his best, and the best collection of the Shoreham period is at Oxford's Ashmolean Museum where the fragile watercolours are shown in rotation. The ostler's box outside the King's Arms would have been in use during the Palmer years. Cut into the chalk hillside to the west is a great cross remembering the First World War dead.

The King's Arms is over the bridge to the right. The walk continues to the left up the road past Ivy Cottage (left) to the lych gate at Shoreham Church. Walk ahead up the tree-lined brick path to the church porch.

SHOREHAM CHURCH

The church is a Norman building with a 1775 tower. The rood screen is one of Kent's finest. The church's patron is Westminster Abbey, which accounts for the pulpit which once stood in the abbey. Past incumbents include two cardinals. Vincent Perronet, vicar from 1728 to 1785, was a friend of John Wesley who often preached in the churchyard. Perronet's son, Edward, wrote the hymn 'All hail the power of Jesu's name'. A later vicar appears in the Charles Cope painting (at the back of the church) welcoming home his son Verney Cameron, the first man to cross Africa east to west.

Continue past the church (left) to a kissing gate. Turn right to go through a gap by a gate and reach the road opposite the Shoreham Place. Turn left up the road.
To end the shorter walk here continue ahead to Shoreham Station.
The main walk turns right after a short distance (and well before the railway bridge) on to a footpath waymarked Darent Valley Path. Beyond barriers the path runs through trees and soon has a golf course on both sides. Where the fencing briefly disappears, look left for flying golfballs. At a kissing gate go ahead across a cricket field to find the enclosed path continuing south. At a junction with a lane, still keep ahead while the Darent Valley Path turns right towards the river.

Ignore all turnings to reach a stile. The path runs ahead along the side of a field while to the right there is a view down into the valley. Soon the spire of Otford Church can be seen ahead. The path runs down to a wooden stile at a bend on a farm track. Continue ahead on the bridleway, which becomes metalled as it runs directly ahead to meet Otford's main street.

OTFORD

Otford is derived from 'Otta's Ford' where the ancient Pilgrims Way, which runs down the main street, crossed the River Darent. This was an overnight resting place for Archbishops of Canterbury, including Thomas à Becket. The Archbishop's Otford Palace, now much reduced, was rebuilt to rival Cardinal Wolsey's Hampton Court Palace by Archbishop Warham, who crowned Henry VIII. The king stayed here on his way to France for the Field of the Cloth of Gold in 1520, and again when seeking an annulment from Catherine of Aragon. The 1909 church hall (in the High Street) was designed by the vicar's brother, Edwin Lutyens. Opposite is the Bull (named after a papal bull, not the animal) which has panelling and a fireplace said to come from the palace. The pond, once the main water supply, now has carp and is fed by a flow regulated by a flowerpot 400 yards away.

Turn left to pass Otford Antiques Tearoom and the Crown to reach the Willow Dining Room, opposite the village pond. The church and palace are across the junction to the right. Continue ahead past the Woodman to reach Otford Station.

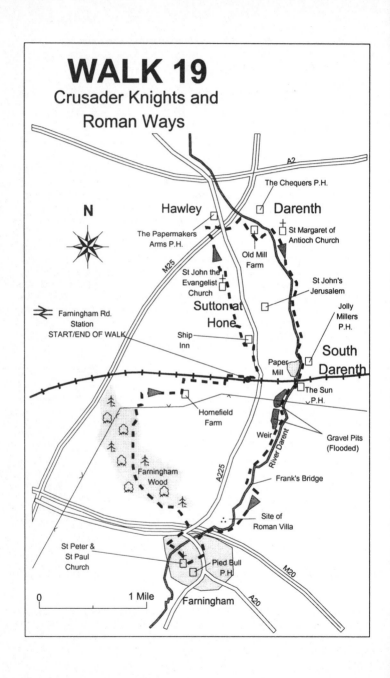

WALK 19
Crusader Knights and
Roman Ways

A2

The Chequers P.H.

N

Hawley

☑ Darenth

The Papermakers
Arms P.H.

✝ St Margaret of
Antioch Church

☐

Old Mill
Farm

M25

St John the
Evangelist
Church

St John's
Jerusalem

Sutton at

☐

Jolly
Millers
P.H.

Hone

Farningham Rd.
Station
START/END OF WALK

Ship
Inn

☐

South

Paper
Mill

Darenth

☐ The Sun
P.H.

Homefield
Farm

☐

Weir

Gravel Pits
(Flooded)

River Darent

Farningham
Wood

Frank's Bridge

Site of
Roman Villa

St Peter &
St Paul
Church

A225

Pied Bull
P.H

M20

0

1 Mile

Farningham

A20

Walk 19: Crusader Knights and Roman Ways

Sutton at Hone – Horton Kirby – Farningham

This is a varied circular walk through the Kent countryside along the lower reaches of the River Darent, where several Roman villas once dotted the riverbanks. Many of the paths you'll be using are the same tracks which once linked these settlements, now mere scatterings of stones beneath the earth awaiting the archaeologist's trowel. The walk also takes in three old churches, includes a chance to spot wildfowl in flooded gravel pits, and passes a charming old farm – a children's delight. An optional detour to St John's Jerusalem, once the headquarters of medieval crusader knights, the delightfully picturesque village of Farningham, and a meander through Farningham Wood are among the walk's other highlights.

> *Distance*: 9 or 4 miles. The shorter walk is effectively the itinerary to the north of the railway line, the longer to the south of it. This arrangement allows the walk to be split into two separate rambles.

> *Map*: OS Landranger 177 (East London area) or OS Pathfinder 1176 (Bexley) and 1192 (Orpington).

> *Terrain*: Mostly low-level walking along riverbanks which, together with the woods on the longer route, tend to be muddy, particularly after rain. One easy climb on the longer route.

> *Food & Drink*: Ship Inn (Mon–Fri 11am–3pm & 5–11pm; Sat 11am–11pm; Sun 12–pm & 7–0.30pm; M/G) and Greyhound (Mon–Fri 11am–3pm & 5–11pm; Sat 11am–11pm; Sun 11am–4pm & 7–10.30pm; M/G) both at Sutton at Hone; Papermakers Arms at Hawley (Mon–Sat 10.30am–11pm; Sun 12–10.30pm; M/G); Hawley Garden Centre coffee shop (Mon–Sat 8am–6pm; Sun 10.30am–4.30pm); Chequers at Darenth (Mon–Sat 11.30am–11pm; Sun 12–10.30pm; M/G); Jolly Miller (Mon–Sat 10am–11pm & Sun 12–10.30pm; M/G) and Sun Inn (Mon–Sat 12–11pm; Sun 12–10.30pm), both at South Darenth; Pied Bull (Mon–Sat 11am–11pm; Sun 12–4pm & 7.30–10.30pm; M/G), Lion (Mon–Sat 11am–11pm; Sun 11am–10.30pm M/G) and Chequers (Mon–Sat 11am–11pm; Sun 11am–10.30pm), all at Farningham.

> *Transport*: Train from Victoria to Farningham Road (outside Travelcard zones).

> *Start & Finish*: Farningham Road train station.

If arriving by rail from London, leave Farningham Road Station by the rear entrance (*don't* cross the footbridge). Go through the gate next to the footbridge steps and follow the tarmac path which crosses a field towards a row of new houses and the Dartmouth Road at the edge of Sutton at Hone village. Turn left and follow the main road into the village until you arrive at the Ship Inn on the left.

The main gate of St John's Jerusalem (see page 118) lies a further quarter of a mile ahead on the right, and you may wish to visit the house and its gardens now rather than make the longer detour later in the walk.

Turn left up Ship Lane immediately before the pub, and then first right along Barfield. Crossing the housing estate, take the second turning on the left (also called Barfield) leading to Barton Road. Turn right here into a cul-de-sac to take a narrow enclosed path to the side of a house in the far left-hand corner beyond a fir tree. Running along the backs of houses with fields to the left, the tower of Sutton at Hone Church appears ahead. A little further along, the path emerges into a field; keep ahead following the track along the edge of a field to where it meets a road before the church. Cross the road and enter the church's peaceful graveyard.

ST JOHN THE EVANGELIST

Set among beech and yew trees, this fourteenth-century church has a high Kentish flint tower and pleasing exterior. However, it has not enjoyed a happy history and a seventeenth-century fire caused serious damage which was compounded by drastic alterations to the body of the church, destroying the original nave, in Victorian times. Only parts of the chancel survive from the earliest period. The church is locked outside service times, although there is not a great deal of interest within.

The route continues through the churchyard passing to the right of the church and down to a kissing gate. Go through this and keep ahead to where the path meets Arnolds Lane. Once in the lane, turn left for 50 yards to an easy-to-miss signed footpath on the right beside a house named 'Thornfield'. This enclosed path, narrow at first, widens beyond a kissing gate when it arrives at a yard with a horse paddock to the left where the local ponies will come to greet you in the hope of a snack.

The path, now metalled, continues to a stile. Cross this, and take the footbridge over the roaring traffic on the M25, towards Hawley. Descend from the bridge on to a fenced path heading north, but turn sharp right at the next crosspath making a dog-leg heading toward the 'London/Dartford' motorway sign. When you emerge at a road (the A225) the walk continues beneath the M25. However, if you're seeking refreshment there's the Papermakers' Arms 50 yards along the road to the left with a pleasant beer garden, alas not quite out of earshot of the M25. Just before the pub the Hawley Garden Centre also has a coffee shop which serves meals and snacks.

Once under the bridge, cross the road and look out for a signed footpath ('to the River Darent') to the right of number 12, the last house in a short terrace. The enclosed footpath finally arrives at a stile. Cross this into a field and bear left towards the motorway embankment, following the line of this to another stile. Cross this stile and turn right along a grassy path running beside the river Darent. Do *not* cross the bridge over the river unless you want to take a short-cut to the Chequers pub. To reach the pub cross the bridge and another beyond and bear right and then half-left across a field to a kissing gate in the field corner. The pub is a little way down Dartmouth Road on the right, and you can pick up the walk by continuing along here to the 'Flagpole' at the end (see below).

If you're not taking this short-cut, follow the grassy path towards the farm buildings ahead. When you reach the picturesque weir at Old Mill Farm with its colony of squawking geese, cross the stile beside it to a footbridge 50 yards ahead. Once across this follow the track along the wall to the lane. To see the farm you will need to turn left, while the walk continues right.

OLD MILL FARM

Owned by genial farmer Jim North, whose family have had the place since 1939, Old Mill Farm is what the countryside used to be like before the age of factory farming and butter mountains. Chickens, geese and guinea fowl scatter noisily in all directions as you enter the unpaved farmyard beside the weir, conjuring up a scene similar to those painted by Constable – even more remarkable when you consider that the madness of the M25 lies fewer than 300 yards from this country idyll. The farm takes its name from an old flour mill that once occupied the site which used a waterwheel to drive its grindstone. The low water levels of recent times would make this impossible today, a result of the water companies carrying out heavy extraction in the area.

Turn right along the farm track after the footbridge, with the wall on your right, to reach a road, where you should bear left. Continue up the road, crossing the river again, where the walk continues beyond the 'Flagpole' on the right. To the left and 200 yards along Darenth Road, if you're seeking refreshment, lies the fifteenth-century Chequers pub with oak beams and beer garden. To visit Darenth Church (see box) proceed uphill for 50 yards beyond the 'Flagpole' – the church is set back from the road on the right.

ST MARGARET OF ANTIOCH, DARENTH

Approached along a path through its graveyard flanked by sturdy horse chestnuts, St Margaret's is one of the oldest churches in the country, and although the first reference to a place of worship here dates from the mid-tenth century, it is likely that a wooden church stood on the site long before this. In the construction of the Saxon building a large number of still visible bricks and tiles were recycled from a Roman villa which lay just to the south of (or behind) the church. The Normans added a chancel (unusually longer than the nave) with an impressive groined ceiling pre-dating the age of vaulting. The church's furniture includes an outstanding twelfth-century Norman font fashioned from stone imported from Caen with fascinating images, including one of St Margaret. Unfortunately, due to theft the church is now kept locked outside service times. Should you want to see inside you could try calling the vicar, the Rev Roger Ford (☎ 01322 227153), from the public phone opposite the church and – if free – he will come and open it.

The walk continues along a footpath behind the 'Flagpole' – often bearing a limp union flag – which slips between a fruit distribution centre and the entrance to a fishing lake. Do *not* go through any gates – the path is a narrow tarmac affair with a line of conifers to the right. The track eventually ascends to some steps leading into a field. Keep ahead along the edge of the field, passing between timber telegraph poles, beyond which the path, often overgrown, leads to a small lake at a clearing. At weekends the tranquillity here may be disturbed by the shrill whinings of model aircraft overhead – enthusiasts use a nearby field for their gatherings.

Follow the track around the lake, actually flooded gravel workings, to another pond signed 'Roman Villa Lake' which correctly indicates that there was once a Roman building here, marked on the OS Landranger map and, given its location by the river, probably a farming villa. It was a significant edifice and its ruins later provided ready-made building material for St John's. The main route continues beyond the lake along the riverbank. However, a detour here would allow a visit to St John's Jerusalem (see box below).

ST JOHN'S JERUSALEM

Beyond a meadow and flanked by a cedar of Lebanon and a magnificent copper beech tree, St John's Jerusalem (chapel and gardens open April–Oct, Wednesday only, 2–6pm, £1) was founded in the late twelfth century by the Knights Hospitallers of the Order of St John of Jerusalem using materials from a Roman villa at Darenth. In the older (or east) part of the present building it's possible to spot fragments of Roman tiles embedded in the walls. The chapel, dating from 1234, is now all that remains of the ancient building founded by these Crusaders, who recuperated here and girded their loins before taking off for the Holy Land and more jousts with the Islamic foe. When the order's lands were confiscated in 1540 by Henry VIII during the dissolution of the monasteries, the Hospitallers decamped to Malta. By the time it was restored as a private house in the seventeenth century much of the earlier building had been cannibalised for building stone. Superstition seems to have saved the chapel then, but not from some later unfortunate Victorian alterations which converted part of it into a billiard room. The house and its wonderful gardens are now in the care of the National Trust.

Detour Route (one-mile round trip): to reach St John's take the path on the right over a footbridge just after the 'Roman Villa Lake' which leads through a small wood to cross a second footbridge followed by a stile. An enclosed path then crosses a field leading to another stile, where you should keep ahead along a pebble track. As you cross a footbridge over a ford St John's is visible behind trees on the left. To gain entry, however, you keep ahead until the track emerges at a kissing gate at the northern end of Sutton at Hone village. Turn left along the main road (A225), passing the Greyhound pub on the right, to the entrance to St John's a further 200 yards along to the left. **If you wish to curtail the walk here** you could continue south through the village to go under the railway bridge, where a right leads to Farningham Road Station.

The main walk continues along the river for a good quarter of a mile before bearing left away from the river to follow a hedge (right) for 50 yards to an enclosed path on the right. Follow the enclosed path to a stile and keep ahead along an unmetalled lane to a white gate and road beyond. Turn right along the road, passing a factory (left). At a bridge over the river keep ahead to reach the centre of South Darenth village. You will soon pass the Jolly Millers pub, with a beer garden on the left and the Horton Kirby paper mill with its foreshortened chimney to the right. Follow the road beneath the impressive railway viaduct to pass the Sun pub on the right.

To end the four-mile walk here cross the bridge over the river and keep ahead at a further junction (across the A225) to arrive at Farningham Road Station.

To continue the walk, also cross the bridge but turn left on the far side to take a path heading south along the riverbank. Keep ahead for half a mile, passing flooded gravel pits on the right where ducks, geese and moorfowl are plentiful. At the half-mile mark you'll pass a disused mill with a weir and bridge over the river. This area is known as Westminster Fields and is the site of another Roman villa.

WESTMINSTER FIELDS ROMAN VILLA AND GRANARY

In 1972, when sewerage work was being carried out in this area, the foundations of a Roman building were discovered which eventually turned out to be a large granary. The path of the sewer was diverted and the site excavated (now backfilled to protect it). A trial trench dug when the sports pavilion nearby was built in the same year revealed a Roman foundation wall, roof tile and mosaic fragments, and this is probably the villa to which the granary belonged, although this will only be conclusively proved when the site is fully excavated. The Darenth valley was popular with Roman farmers perhaps because of its fertility and proximity to the markets of London, about a day's (or night's) wagon ride away. In addition to the other villas mentioned on this walk, Roman villas have also been discovered at Dartford and Eynsford, where Lullingstone Villa is one of the most important in Britain (see p 111). An information board gives details of the excavations and discoveries.

Do not cross the river but keep ahead through the car park of Westminster Fields football pavilion (with public toilets) to a kissing gate in the corner of the field beyond. Here the grassy path leaves the river to cross a field to rejoin it at a clump of trees. Follow the path along this picturesque wooded stretch of riverbank to the brick-built Frank's Bridge. Turn left across the bridge and keep ahead for about 200 yards to reach a metal swing gate on the right beside a cricket pitch. Go through this and follow the enclosed grassy path heading roughly south-west towards the M25 embankment. To the right, beyond trees, lies Frank's Hall, an Elizabethan house which has been renovated as offices. Local residents fought unsuccessfully to keep this path intact when the motorway was built because there is clear evidence of its use by the Romans, probably to reach a Roman villa which stood across the river to the right (see below), as well as settlements at Farningham where more Roman remains have been found.

When you arrive at a kissing gate the path now dog-legs around a paddock and field to follow the riverbank. On the far bank of the river here sat the Roman villa, probably with its own granary and farm. Although investigated, the villa's remains have been reburied to preserve it for posterity. Follow the river bank and pass beneath the motorway to another embankment carrying the A20. Do *not* go under the old bridge but *turn left* just before it along a narrow path which leads to an underpass. Go through the underpass to pass another cricket field (right) and follow an unmade road leading to the High Street of Farningham village. To the left lies the Pied Bull pub, but the walk continues by turning right to pass (left) the church and Manor House and, across the bridge, the Lion Hotel.

FARNINGHAM VILLAGE

Skirted by an uncomfortably close M20 motorway which drones constantly in the background, Farningham has nevertheless managed to retain much of its traditional charm. Mentioned in the Domesday Book, there are quite a few ancient buildings dotted about the village, including the Old Mill on the river. The church of St Peter and St Paul surrounded by yew trees, while founded in the twelfth century, dates mainly from three centuries later. It has a typical Kentish tower (but not the crenellated crown), an octagonal fifteenth-century font and, in the sanctuary, an interesting sculpted Tudor memorial. In the graveyard there's a mausoleum erected by John Nash – designer of Regent's Park and Regent Street in London – for his father, Thomas, who died at Paris in 1778. Slightly further along, the Manor House was once the home of Captain Bligh, captain of the *Bounty* when it was seized by mutineers in 1789; the house is now privately owned and protected by zealous guard dogs, among them a giant St Bernard. The river runs through the heart of the village in front of the Lion Hotel, which has a pleasant terrace. This spot was also where author Charles Dickens spent many an hour with rod and line, fishing for trout.

Keep ahead past the Lion Hotel to the Chequers pub, with a good selection of real ales, at the corner of Dartford Road. Incidentally, this is your last chance for refreshment. Turn right here to reach a roundabout on the A20. Cross this and continue along the Dartford road passing under the M20 motorway. Immediately after the bridge take a tarmac path on the left side of the road, and turn left up a flight of steps to reach the end of a cul-de-sac. Bear left up a short metalled drive to a gate and stile. Cross the stile to gain access to a sloping field and follow the path as it climbs with the hedge to the right to reach Farningham Woods. At the top of the climb do not enter the woods, but bear left along the top edge of the field, taking in a fine view over Farningham and the Darent valley.

When you come to a pair of stiles set in the fence, cross the first stile and take the middle of three possible paths – the one that climbs beyond a gate and a kissing gate. About 20 yards beyond the gate take a left fork and a stepped path to reach a stile. Cross the stile and keep ahead, following the path through the woods and ignoring side paths. At an obvious junction ahead where a path descends to the left, turn right to follow a broad track which soon passes a small clearing on the right and runs near to the edge of a ridge to arrive at some ponds, often dried out in summer, and a gate. Go through the gate and keep forward over a cross track to pass through a second gate opposite. Keep ahead in the same direction for a few hundred metres to the next cross track where you must bear slightly right, then left, to continue in a forward direction to emerge from the woods.

On leaving the woods with a fenced area to your left, turn right along a track which bends to head downhill, passing beneath overhead power lines. At a line of trees, turn right to follow the track as it runs parallel to the power lines, and soon turn left to enter a field. Once in the field turn right, again walking parallel with the power lines to a hedge of alders on the left. Turn left here along the edge of a field, keeping the hedge to your left. At the field corner turn right to follow another track and hedge towards Holmfield Farm, flanked by white sheds, in the distance. When you reach the farm, bear left between the outbuildings to the farm drive. Keep ahead along here, passing a terrace of cottages (left), towards the railway embankment. At the embankment, turn right with the farm drive and keep ahead to a bridge over the railway on the left. Cross this and turn immediately right to follow the edge of a field down to the rear entrance of Farningham Road Station.

Walk 20: Darwin's Retreat

Downe – Cudham – Farnborough

Downe is 12 miles from Charing Cross and the most southerly point in Old Kent to enjoy a London Transport bus service. Horse and bus often meet at the bus stop outside the church in the village where the adjoining fields became the outdoor laboratory for its most famous and controversial resident, Charles Darwin. The shorter walk may be welcome to those who linger longer than intended at Darwin's Down House. Much of this walk is in the Downe parish, although it passes outside briefly to visit hilltop Cudham and ends at the also surprisingly unspoilt Farnborough. The many kissing gates, replacing stiles, have been erected to mark the millennium.

Distance: 5.5 miles or 2 miles

Map: OS Landranger 177 (East London) and 187 (Dorking, Reigate and Crawley) or OS Explorer 147 (Sevenoaks).

Terrain: Field paths and roads, with one very steep climb before the shorter route ends.

Food & Drink: Tea Cosy teashop (12–5pm; Mon closed), George and Dragon (11am–3pm & 5.30–11pm; Sun 12–10.30pm; M) in Downe; Cudham Church (teas 3–5pm on bank holidays and last Sunday in month during BST) and Blacksmiths Arms (11am–2.30pm & 6–11pm; Sun 12–3pm & 7–10.30pm; M) in Cudham; Elsie's Tea Room (8am–5pm, Thu 8am–3pm, Sun closed) and Change of Horses (11am–11pm, Sun 12–10.30pm; M/G) in Farnborough High Street.

Transport: National Railways to Bromley South, then LT bus 146 (not Sun) to Downe (Travelcard Zone 6). Return by LT bus R5 (not Sun) from Cudham (Zone 6) to Orpington Station, or LT bus 358 from Farnborough High Street (Zone 6) to Orpington Station. On Sundays the 320 bus run by LT (hourly from Bromley South) will drop you at Keston Church from where Downe village is a one mile walk along New Hill Road.

Start & Finish: Downe, near Bromley to Farnborough in Kent. The shorter walk ends at Cudham.

DOWNE
The 'e' was added in the mid-nineteenth century to avoid confusion with County Down in Northern Ireland, but Down House, where Charles Darwin lived, retains the old spelling. St Mary's Church, dating from 1291, has two modern windows: the east window depicting the crucifixion by Evie Hone (1950), and one to the right of the main altar celebrating Robin Knox-Johnson's round the world voyage, by Keith Coleborn (1973). Also in the chancel is a plaque to John Lubbock (Lord Avebury), instigator of

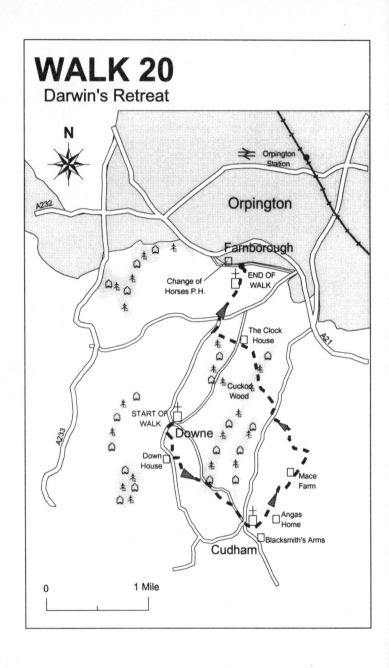

WALK 20
Darwin's Retreat

N

A232

Orpington Station

Orpington

Farnborough

Change of
Horses P.H.

END OF
WALK

The Clock
House

A21

Cuckoo
Wood

START OR
WALK

Downe

Down
House

Mace
Farm

Angas
Home

Blacksmith's Arms

Cudham

0   1 Mile

bank holidays and ant expert, who ceased attending this church when his friend Darwin, who also circumnavigated the globe, was attacked from the pulpit. However, Darwin is now commemorated on the tower by a sundial. The next door Queen's Head sign shows the head of Elizabeth I who was present in the church for a baptism during the second year of her reign.

From the Downe village square walk up Luxted Road. Go left to pass between the entrance to Trowmers and a willow tree. Bear left just before a house to follow a walled path leading to a field. Go ahead down the side of the field and turn right at the corner. After a short distance go left through a gap in the hedge to another field. Over to the left is a farm. Turn right to follow the hedge (right) to a kissing gate deep in the corner. Ahead can be seen the white Down House. Bear slightly left across the field to a stile by the road opposite Down House.

DOWN HOUSE

Down House is a late eighteenth-century farmhouse where naturalist Charles Darwin lived with his large family from 1842 until his death in 1882. He worked on his revolutionary book *The Origin of Species* in the ground-floor study which still has his chair and desk. The publication in 1859 of this convincing challenge to the bible was disturbing to many. Still here are the topical *Punch* cartoons saved by Darwin. It was here that he also explored man's common ancestry with apes for his book *The Descent of Man*. In 1996, the centenary of his widow's death here, the house was placed in the care of English Heritage and the ground floor was restored to how it would have been when Gladstone called in 1876. Upstairs there are extensive displays which include the log of the *Beagle*, on which he spent five years sailing round the world. In the grounds there is the Sandwalk where Darwin walked every morning before eight o'clock. The lawns are one of the best fungi sites in the south-east. Down House is open Wed–Sun 10am–6pm (Oct–Mar 4pm); closed Feb and Christmas period; admission £5, concessions £3.80, child £2.50. Ticket includes audio tour.

Only cross the stile and turn right if visiting Down House. The walk continues past the stile (right) to the end of the field, and then left to follow a fence towards the buildings of Downe Court, occupied by a Venetian glass manufacturer during Elizabeth I's reign.

Go over the stile ahead and forward past the turning (right) to go over the stile on the right. Walk across the grass between the black barn (left) and the line of trees (right) to a second stile. Go ahead past Downe Court Farmhouse and over a concrete road to cross another stile. At once go left. Turn at the field corner, and on reaching a path junction turn left to follow an enclosed path. The fence (left) soon falls away as the path runs gently downhill along the edge of a field to the trees of Hang Grove ahead. Go under a barrier and follow the winding path through the wood. Later the path runs steeply downhill and becomes stepped to reach a road. Turn right for a short distance to pass a white City of London Coal Tax post (see page 141) by a stile at the corner. Cross the stile and look ahead to see the top of Cudham Church's spire. Follow the path which runs downhill cutting the corner of the field. On reaching a stile turn right up the road, which soon rises steeply. Pass a turning (right) to continue up Church Hill to a T-junction at Cudham. There is a bus stop to the left. Go ahead up Church Approach opposite to pass the Oast House and enter Cudham churchyard.

CUDHAM

St Peter and St Paul Church has a Norman nave built by Gilbert de Maninot, William the Conqueror's doctor. The south-east meeting rooms, known as the Warrior's Chapel, is the original Saxon church. St Katherine's Chapel (north side, and now used for overflow seating) was added in the fourteenth century. The spire rests on a Norman tower which, before Cudham was embraced by the London borough of Bromley, was said to have the lightest peal of bells in Kent. The two yews are about as old as the church. The Blacksmiths Arms has a blue plaque recording the birth here in 1867 of music hall comedian Little Tich (Harry Relph), who appeared at the Folies Bergère and influenced Charlie Chaplin. The late nineteenth-century Angas Home, now owned by the health authority, was built as a sailors' convalescent home.

To end the walk here look for the bus stop at the top of the hill. The main walk continues past the church (left) to the large playing field (turn right with the metalled surface only to visit the Blacksmiths Arms, which is on the right just beyond the pavilion). The walk continues to the left to follow the churchyard fence (left) to the corner of the field. Here, go through the kissing gate and cross the Angas Home driveway to find another kissing gate almost opposite.

Bear half-right across a field to a stile. Still continue in the same direction half-right to the side of the field where the path slips into the trees running between oaks and pines (right). The footpath later becomes enclosed and widens before meeting a metalled road at a T-junction. Turn right along the road which bends to pass the white 1910 Mace Farm cottages (left). Here the main metalled way bears left while the walk continues ahead with a concrete surface. This later gives way to a rough surface as the lane runs gently downhill. Ignore a narrow footpath to the right and enter the edge of Foxberry Wood.

At a junction go left on a bridlepath which runs gently uphill to give a brief view across Orpington. Stay on the path as it bends and runs down into a valley and uphill to meet a junction of metalled lanes. Go straight ahead down Snag Lane, passing a house called Southfields (left), to a T-junction by some houses. Turn right to pass a turning (left) and go through a kissing gate on the left to avoid walking on the road. At once turn right to follow the hedge (right). At the far end go through another kissing gate and turn left up a bridleway. After another brief view (right) of London, the path runs between fields and downhill through trees. On entering Cuckoo Wood the path is divided – keep to the left, leaving the right side for horses.

Ignore all turnings as the path runs uphill and briefly into the open. After a short beech avenue go under the barrier and follow the fenced bridlepath across a golf course. The way runs gently downhill to a double bend at the Clock House.

THE CLOCK HOUSE

The Clock House is the former High Elms Farm bought by banker Sir John Lubbock in 1808. The white round building was built about 1850 and contained a wheel which was pulled by a pony to pump water from a deep well to a tank above. The buildings with the clock (facing north) served as stables for High Elms, built nearby in 1882 for

Sir John's son Lord Avebury (see page 121). The mansion was destroyed by fire in 1967 in the period during which his descendant Eric Lubbock (now the 4th Lord Avebury) was the local Orpington MP.

Cross the road to pass the post box (left) and squeeze past the gate to go uphill across another part of the golf course. Later, the path runs through a wood, across a bridlepath and downhill to a road.

Turn right along North End Lane to pass North End Farm. The lane bends to a junction with Shire Lane. Cross over to go through the kissing gate by a farm gate and bear half-right uphill. Go through another kissing gate and keep in the same direction (half-left) to pass the trees (right). On approaching the side of a huge field another path joins from the left. The path bears round to the left to enter Farnborough churchyard. Follow the path through the churchyard (passing Gypsy Lee's grave at the first junction) to the church.

FARNBOROUGH CHURCH

Dedicated to St Giles the Abbot, the church has had its barn-style roof since it was largely rebuilt in 1641 following a storm. The fourteenth-century font survived, and later additions include the tower in 1838. In the chancel (south side) there is a memorial to Thomas Young who translated the hieroglyphics on the Rosetta stone in the British Museum. A window on the north wall shows Reformation martyrs Nicholas Ridley and St John Fisher. On Rush Sunday evening (the nearest to 29 June) rushes and herbs are strewn in the aisle and a preacher is paid 50p to expound on the 'uncertainty of human life'. The origin of the custom was established in Elizabeth I's reign after a drunken man fell into a pond at night and drowned. Gladstone worshipped here when staying with Lord Avebury at High Elms. Buried in the churchyard is Gypsy Lee (Urania Boswell) who lived at nearby Locks Bottom and attracted 15,000 people to her funeral in 1933. The church is open weekdays 2–5pm from Easter to Harvest.

Beyond the church go through the lych gate and along the path to the village.

FARNBOROUGH

Farnborough comes from 'Fearnbiorginga' meaning 'village among the ferns on the hill'. It retains a village feel, although the northern side now merges with Orpington. The junction of Church Street with the High Street was for many years the turning point for London buses, which would be parked next to the George and Dragon coaching inn (now the rebuilt George). The village was on the route to Sevenoaks and Hastings which ran down Church Road to Old Hill at Green Street Green. The Change of Horses stabled the horses, and in the early part of the twentieth century it was the venue for horse auctions when the horses were raced up and down the High Street for the benefit of potential bidders. Elm House, dating from 1819, is the former post office. The annual Farnborough Fair on the first Saturday in September is the successor to the fair held on St Giles Day (1 September) since 1292.

Go ahead to the High Street, where you can catch LT bus 358 to Orpington Station.

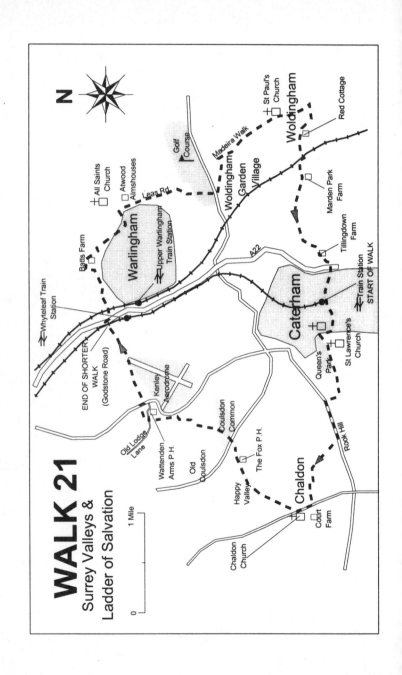

WALK 21

Surrey Valleys & Ladder of Salvation

N

All Saints Church

Atwood Almshouses

Leas Rd

Golf Course

St Paul's Church

Woldingham

Madeira Walk

Woldingham Garden Village

Red Cottage

Whyteleafe Train Station

Batts Farm

Warlingham

Upper Warlingham Train Station

Marden Park Farm

A22

Tillingdown Farm

END OF SHORTER WALK (Godstone Road)

Kenley Aerodrome

Catenham

Train Station START OF WALK

Old Lodge Lane

Coulsdon Common

Queen's Park

St Lawrence's Church

Wattenden Arms P. H.

Old Coulsdon

The Fox P. H.

Rook Hill

Happy Valley

Chaldon

Court Farm

Chaldon Church

1 Mile

0

Walk 21: Surrey Valleys and the Ladder of Salvation

Caterham – Chaldon – Coulsdon Common – Whyteleafe – Warlingham – Caterham

This is a hilly circular walk among the 'pleasant little valleys stored with wild thyme, marjoram, boscage and beeches' described by seventeenth-century diarist John Aubrey. Based on the pleasant country town of Caterham, the full walk is a solid day-long hike, but both this and the shorter version take in the ancient and unusual church of St Peter and St Paul at Chaldon which contains one of the finest medieval wall paintings in Britain.

> *Distance*: 11.5 miles or 5.5 miles. The shorter walk returns to Caterham by bus from Kenley/Whyteleafe on bus 407. Alternatively, London-bound trains stop at Whyteleafe and Upper Warlingham stations nearby.
>
> *Map*: OS Landranger 187 (Dorking, Reigate and Crawley area) or OS Explorer 146 (Dorking).
>
> *Terrain*: Field paths, bridleways and country roads. Three easy climbs and two moderately steep ones.
>
> *Food & Drink*: Fox, Coulsdon Common (Mon–Sat 11am–11pm; Sun 12–10.30pm; M/G); Wattenden Arms, Kenley (M/G; Mon–Sat 11am-11pm; Sun 12–3pm & 7–10.30pm); White Lion (Mon–Sat 11am–1pm; Sun 12–10.30pm; M/G), Old Leather Bottle (Mon–Sat 11am–1pm; Sun 12–10.30pm; M), both Warlingham. Old Surrey Hounds, Caterham (Mon–Sat 11am–11pm; Sun 12–10.30pm; M/G); Wimpy, Caterham (Mon–Sat 10am–10pm; Sun 12–10pm).
>
> *Transport*: National Railways from London Bridge or Victoria to Caterham. The 409 bus runs between West Croydon and Caterham, the 407 between Wallington and Caterham. For the short-cut, trains to London can be taken from Whyteleafe Station (see map) to and London Bridge, or Upper Warlingham Station to Victoria.
>
> *Start & Finish*: Caterham train station.

From the train station turn right to walk up Church Hill. You'll soon pass the East Surrey Museum on the right.

CATERHAM AND THE EAST SURREY MUSEUM
A docile and ancient town dating back to Roman times, it was not until the arrival of the railway in 1856 that Caterham grew to prominence as the home of many city businessmen. The East Surrey Museum (open Wed and Sat 10am–5pm and Sun 2–5pm; admission 30p) has a small collection which documents life and times in east Surrey from prehistory to the present.

At the crown of Church Hill you will pass the Victorian church of St Mary's (right) which was built in 1866 to cater for the burgeoning population of Caterham, now unable to fit into the Norman parish church of St Lawrence (usually open 10am–3pm) opposite, and worth a look if open. Just beyond the two churches and Manor Avenue (the former entrance to the manor house and retaining its stone gateposts) go left at a bus stop to follow an enclosed path into Queen's Park. Bear left where the railings end to follow the metalled path along the backs of houses with a tennis court, bowling greens and sports field to the right. Beyond a small tiled-roof pavilion the path passes through a gap to run parallel to Wood Lane for 75 yards or so, before running downhill to meet Roffes Lane.

Cross Roffes Lane and go ahead up the Heath. After some 250 yards turn right into Chaldon Common Road and continue to a junction with Rook Lane. Turn left along Rook Lane for about 200 yards until the road dips (Rook Hill), and keep alert for a well-camouflaged public footpath on the right beside a street lamp. Pass through a kissing gate on to an enclosed path through woods. After about a third of a mile the path meets a residential road where you should turn left and keep right where the road divides. Just before the road bends go right on to a rough track. After a few yards turn left to follow a footpath signed 'Chaldon Church' which runs down the side of Piles Wood (right). Keep ahead where the trees end to reach Church Lane. Turn right to pass the entrances (left) to Chaldon Church.

CHALDON CHURCH AND THE LADDER OF SALVATION

The charming exterior of the Norman church of Sts Peter and Paul conceals one of the most remarkable wall paintings in the whole country, which is also the oldest known. Founded in 1086 on the site of an earlier Saxon church, a nineteenth-century restoration of the building revealed the wall painting beneath a layer of seventeenth-century whitewash. Dating from the twelfth century and possibly the work of a travelling monk, the 17 x 11ft mural depicts the Ladder of Salvation which souls must climb to reach paradise. The vivid portrayal of demons, the seven deadly sins and miscellaneous sinners being devoured, tortured or boiled in hell's cauldron is contrasted with the entry to paradise where Christ, surrounded by angels, is depicted skewering a prostrate Satan with his cross. A leaflet by Betty Hughes is available in the church and it gives a detailed description of the mural. The church's numerous other features including a rare Cromwellian pulpit, a copy of the twelfth-century church bell – stolen in 1970 and never recovered – and the poignant 1,000-year-old doorstep worn to breaking point by the footsteps of generations of worshippers, are described in a separate leaflet.

The walk continues past the turn-offs to the church where, about 30 yards ahead, you turn right into a field following a footpath signed 'Happy Valley'. This heads half-left across a field. After about quarter of a mile the path passes between two woods to head down to a belt of trees. Walk through the trees to pass a broken wooden stile and follow a hedge (right) to cross Happy Valley, the location of a popular tea garden in Victorian times. Keep ahead, ascending the stepped path opposite. At the top of the climb turn right on to a rough path (signed 'Coulsdon Common') which bears left and becomes metalled. Follow the straight path skirting the common with the hedge to the left and a fitness training circuit to the right. Eventually you will meet a wooden gate. Beyond this you'll enter Fox Lane which soon passes the Fox pub, tucked away behind trees to the right, with a pleasant beer garden.

To continue the walk keep ahead to reach the main road (B2030) at Coulsdon Common. **You have the possibility of curtailing the walk here** by taking the 409 bus back to Caterham heading south, or to West Croydon in the opposite direction. Otherwise, cross over the road to enter the common. Where the metalled path ends, continue ahead on the rough path which bears round to the left through trees. On meeting a road (Stites Hill) go ahead down Rydon's Lane. At the end of Rydon's Lane go over Caterham Drive and up a steep footpath (known as Waterhouse Lane). At the top turn half left up a bank for a short distance before going left at a clear junction along a metalled way.

Soon leave the tarmac by going right past an observatory (left) to a stile. Cross this and keep ahead in the field, but before the far end bear left down to the far corner where another stile leads to a junction of a track and metalled Old Lodge Lane. The Wattenden Arms, with a beer garden, is a short distance to the right. Cross the metalled road to go up steps to Betts Mead. Go right and bear round to the left with the boundary. At the far end turn right to pass some swings and follow a path. Bear left at a fork. The path soon meets houses at Hayes Lane. Go right along the lane and then left by a phone and post box to walk up Golf Road.

At the end of a rough road go through a gateway to enter Kenley Common. Keep ahead on the right-hand footpath, which soon runs past the end of Kenley Aerodrome runway.

KENLEY AERODROME

Kenley aerodrome has a history reaching back into the early days of aviation when the newly established RAF used the field as a base at the end of the First World War. Prime Minister Lloyd George and his officials flew from here to the Paris Peace Conference in 1919 in a converted Handley-Page bomber. Three fighter squadrons were based here in the Second World War and played a vital role in the Battle of Britain. As a consequence it was singled out by the Luftwaffe, and more than a hundred bombs made direct hits on the airfield and hangars causing extensive damage. During the war's latter stages the base was used by a US Air Force squadron (equipped with Spitfires) as well as Free French, Belgian and Canadian air forces. The RAF abandoned the airfield in 1977 and it is now used by a gliding school.

Do *not* bear right beyond the runway but keep forward along public bridleway 36 signed 'Marling's Close' which runs downhill through woods. When the steep path meets a metalled road go ahead across two junctions to reach a footpath over a railway line, which emerges in Godstone Road.

The shorter walk is ended here by taking bus 407 from a stop on the opposite side of the road back to Caterham, or northbound to Croydon. Alternatively, trains to London leave from Whyteleafe station (Charing Cross), reached by turning right for a quarter of a mile along Godstone Road and right at the main junction. To reach Upper Warlingham train station (for Victoria) go left at the main junction up Hillaby Road to find the Station Approach by the bridge.

The walk continues by turning right along Godstone Road and then left to walk up Maple Road. Go under the railway bridge and keep forward to follow the trees on the left. On coming level with the tennis courts (right) turn left into the trees to follow a steep path up the side of the hill. At the top the path runs into the open and across a field to meet a road at a stile. Cross this and go left along the road for a few yards, and then turn right into the entrance of Batts Farm. Keep ahead along the track, and just beyond a terrace of Victorian cottages dated 1897 turn right to walk up the side of these. At a sports field continue in the same direction following a hedge (right) with the rugby pitches to your left. If these are not being used you can head roughly half-left aiming for a telecommunications mast on the field's southern boundary. To the left of the mast, cross a stile into another field and head half-left over the grass to reach another stile in the far corner. Cross this stile and keep ahead over a crosspath to enter an enclosed path to reach the entrance to the Eagle Star sports ground. Keep forward up the short residential road to meet a main road. Turn right to pass the turning (left) to the church, but keep ahead into Warlingham.

WARLINGHAM
A substantial village gathered around its green, there are few things to see, although the thirteenth-century church of All Saints has some interesting features including an ancient font and fifteenth-century wall painting of St Christopher. One of the church's claims to fame is also commemorated in a nineteenth-century stained-glass window portraying Archbishop Cranmer presenting the first English Prayer Book (which he compiled) to King Edward VI in 1549, perpetuating the tradition that Cranmer made the first reading from it here in person, although no proof exists to confirm this. One more certain historical milestone is that All Saints was the first church in Britain to be used for a television broadcast, in September 1950. There are a number of pubs here of which the White Lion dating from the fifteenth century (located on the east side of the green), is the oldest and the most pleasant. If you're thinking of pausing for a drink it's worth noting that this and its neighbour, the Old Leather Bottle, are the last pubs on the walk, which from now on is 'dry' until Caterham (see Woldingham box below).

To continue the walk go past the Old Leather Bottle and the Green (left) to enter Westhall Road (by a garage on the right). Bear left almost immediately into Leas Road. Not far along here on the corner of Chapel Road (left) are the seventeenth-century Atwood Almshouses, founded by local philanthropist Harman Atwood in 1663 and still used for their intended purpose over three centuries after they were built.

Keep ahead along Leas Road, staying alert for speeding traffic, for about half a mile to reach the top of Bug Hill. Leave the road opposite Tydcombe Road by bearing half-left off the road and down a woodland path. Do not turn left before the house but keep ahead at the side of the house (right) to enter a wood, soon emerging on a steep slope overlooking a golf course. This was another popular tea garden in Victorian times until these places went out of fashion, and it was transformed into Halliloo Dairy Farm in 1890. Farmed for five generations by the Fuller family, it fell victim to the European Community's milk quotas and was sold to the golf club in 1994. Bear half-right downhill to cross the golf course. You are aiming for a distant house with two chimneys. Climb over a stile almost facing the house and cross the road (Slines New Road). Do not go up the rough road ahead but turn half-left up the partly metalled drive. Beyond the Coach House (right) the way becomes rougher and steeper to reach High Shaw on the edge of Woldingham Garden Village. Turn left along the road to walk into Woldingham Garden Village.

WOLDINGHAM GARDEN VILLAGE

Woldingham Garden Village started life as a camp to house the Public Schools Battalion of the Middlesex Regiment at the outbreak of war in 1914. Reflecting the rigid class divisions of society at the time, ex-public schoolboys came from all parts of the country to be housed in the camp's timber huts hastily assembled in the autumn of that year. The materials were hauled from the railway station by the Fuller family of Halliloo Farm (mentioned above). Named Dukes Hill Camp, in addition to its use as a training base men from here were also employed to dig trenches at Oxted, just to the south, as part of the outer London defences when enemy invasion was feared. Most of the men trained here soon left for France, and many perished in the carnage of Flanders. Dukes Hill then served as a convalescent camp for the vast numbers of casualties returning from the Somme, Ypres and Passchendaele, and it is reported that on some days the patients were able to hear the roar of the guns from the battlefields of northern France 150 miles away. In 1919 the camp was closed and sold to a developer who converted Dukes Hill into the Garden Village it is today.

At the junction leave Hilltop Walk to go left. When the metalled road later bears right, head for the left-hand side of a garage ahead. Do *not* go left but keep ahead along the side of the garage to follow a narrow hedged path. This crosses another village road to pass a Swiss chalet (left). Later, the path runs between gardens and down steps. To the right there is a parallel bridleway. Keep forward beyond barriers to follow a track known as Madeira Walk with a fine view across the valley to the right. After half a mile the path runs beside a garden and down to join Long Hill. Turn left up the rough lane, which runs gently uphill to St Paul's Church, Woldingham.

WOLDINGHAM

Deriving from the Saxon *Wealda*, Woldingham is mentioned in the Domesday Book. St Paul's Church was built in 1933 to cater for the expanding congregation unable to squeeze into the tiny flint church of St Agatha, half a mile to the south, which although built in the early nineteenth century incorporates elements from a much older thirteenth-century building. There are no public houses in Woldingham. The village did have a pub once, the Hop Pole, but the navvies who came to build the railway in 1881 (including a mile-and-a-half-long tunnel beneath the downs) apparently painted the village red every pay day and the pub was closed down by teetotal landowner William Gilford, who dictated a clause in the deeds of the estate prohibiting 'any public house or building for the sale of alcoholic liquors'. Woldingham has stayed dry ever since.

Continue past St Paul's (left) and, further along, a row of shops to go right, by the green, down Park View Road. Follow the road which, after 250 yards, bears right. A little way beyond here, where the road bears right again, turn left between Hardown House and the Red Cottage (left) to walk down a long stepped path. Cross a stile at the end and continue forward downhill to pass between two trees. Go over a stile and cross Church Road to follow a path (almost opposite) over a railway line. At once turn right with the fenced path, and at the field corner turn left to follow the path towards a stile and Marden Park Farm.

Keep ahead along the line of the path to walk between the farm buildings (indicated by a waymark). Beyond a line of cottages (left) bear right and then left to a gate to follow the farm drive down to a lane. Cross the road and go over a stile between two wooden gates. Climb up the steep enclosed path to walk through a strip of woodland (known as the Bushes) where deer are frequently to be seen, providing they don't catch scent of you first. Go through a gate and keep ahead near a fence (left). Before the end of the field cut the corner to find a stile to the left of a gateway. Keep ahead with the hedge to your left. The way now heads gently downhill with a view of Caterham Church spire on the horizon. You'll soon pass a ruined barn hidden in woods. Climb over a wooden stile to look across a valley to Tillingdown Farm.

Go ahead downhill and climb the farm track on the opposite side to reach Tillingdown Farm. The path runs through the farmyard. Leaving the farmyard by a gateway, turn right at a junction through a (usually open) gate. Go ahead down the lane, but at a gentle double bend, and just before the lane runs parallel to the Caterham bypass (right), go right by a large log in a gap and bear round to the left to find steps. Go down to the dual carriageway.

Cross the road with extreme care and on the far side follow a path into the trees. At a junction go left down a long stepped path into Caterham. Cross a road and go ahead down Timber Hill Road, with grass to the right, to reach the square. On the square there's the Old Surrey Hounds pub, and a Wimpy nearby. Caterham Station lies opposite, in Station Avenue.

Walk 22: Along the Mole

Leatherhead – Norbury Park – West Humble – Box Hill – Mickleham – Leatherhead

---

The climax of this circular walk is Box Hill which has long been a popular place for Londoners to escape to for a day in the country. Red buses used to run to Leatherhead and the Green Line went even nearer. There is still Box Hill's own station at West Humble, handy for the stepping stones over the River Mole. This walk follows the river which rises in Sussex and owes its name to its habit of disappearing underground into the chalk swallow holes here before flowing on to join the Thames at Hampton Court (see Walk 24). Alexander Pope wrote of 'the sullen Mole, that hides his driving flood' and Edmund Spenser suggested that the river was 'like the mousing hole'. Another Londoner who escaped here for a break was poet John Keats, who came in 1817 to avoid noisy children at Hampstead.

Distance: 9 or 4 miles.

Map: OS Landranger 187 (Dorking, Reigate and Crawley) or OS Explorer 146 (Dorking).

Terrain: Parkland footpaths and tracks. One very steep climb.

Food & Drink: Leatherhead has plenty of pubs and cafés. Station Café and the Stepping Stones (11am–11pm; Sun 12–10.30pm; M/G) at West Humble; NT Café (daily all day) on Box Hill summit; Running Horses (11am–3.30pm & 5.30–11pm; Sun 12–10pm; M/G) at Mickleham.

Transport: National Railways from Waterloo to Leatherhead (outside Travelcard zones). Return from Boxhill and Westhumble Station (outside zones) to Waterloo. Surrey Travel Line (for rail and bus information) ☎ 01737 223000.

Start & Finish: Leatherhead. The shorter walk ends at West Humble.

LEATHERHEAD
'Leatherhead' comes from 'Leoda Ride', meaning 'public ford'. The bridge has been here since the thirteenth century, although much of the often repaired structure dates from 1783. The town was not established until the thirteenth century when a weekly market began. The present tower of St Mary and St Nicholas was built about 1480. A tablet on the south wall records a road accident in 1806 involving the Princess of Wales, later Queen Caroline. (The church is open 11am–2pm weekdays.) Buried in the churchyard is Anthony Hope, author of *The Prisoner of Zenda*. Our Lady and St Peter in Garlands Road, noted for its Eric Gill Stations of the Cross, was built in 1923 largely thanks to the generosity of *Picture Post* founder Edward Hulton. The west window featured in the 1992 Christmas stamps. Leatherhead Museum of Local History occupies seventeenth-century Hampton Cottage in Church Street (open

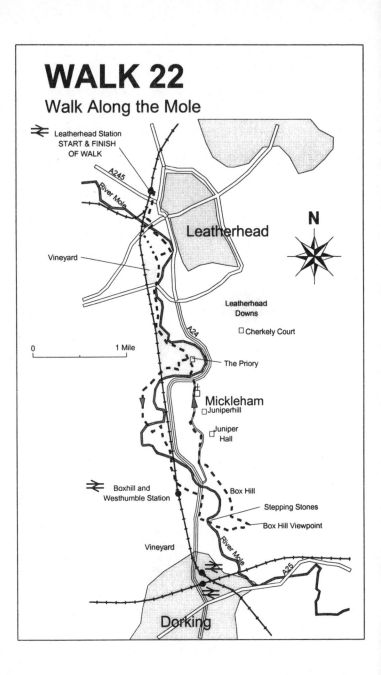

WALK 22

Walk Along the Mole

Leatherhead Station
START & FINISH
OF WALK

A245

River Mole

Leatherhead

Vineyard

N

Leatherhead
Downs

☐ Cherkely Court

A24

0   1 Mile

☐ The Priory

Mickleham
☐ Juniperhill

☐ Juniper
   Hall

Boxhill and
Westhumble Station

Box Hill

Stepping Stones

Box Hill Viewpoint

Vineyard

River Mole

A25

Dorking

Apr–Dec: Thu 1–4pm, Friday 10am–1pm & Sat 10am–4pm; free). The fifteenth-century Running Horse featured in Thomas Skelton's 1517 poem 'The Tunnyng of Elynour Rumming'. The council offices are called Wesley House after John Wesley, who preached his last sermon on the same site one week before his death in 1791. The town is believed to be the model for Highbury in Jane Austen's novel *Emma* – there was a Mr Knightley living here at the time.

Leave Leatherhead station by the 'down' platform and go right to walk down to the bottom of the hill. Cross the road to continue ahead in a park below the embankment (right). At the far end go ahead down Waterway Road to reach the River Mole. From the road bridge there is a view (right) of two railway bridges, the further one carrying the link line to Effingham Junction. The walk continues to the left just before the bridge. Cross the road and go down steps on to the grassy bank. Bear left upstream to find a riverside path leading to the end of the town bridge. The Running Horses is a few yards to the left.

Turn right to cross the bridge and at once go left along a concrete path which leads to a wide grassed area by the river (left). Keep by the water and ignore all turnings. Later, there is a view (right) of Thorncroft Manor, a large white mansion which was rebuilt in 1772 to a design by Sir Robert Taylor and now occupied by civil engineers Brown & Root, although it has been a residence, school and library. Across the water is Thorncroft Island, which includes a bridge with a shell decoration over an inlet. On reaching a road by a bridge (left) go right along the lane to pass the entrance to Thorncroft Manor. Continue past several cottages, but just before reaching Thorncroft Vineyard go left to a kissing gate. At first there is a high wall to the left, while over to the right there is a clear view of the vineyard. Follow the path ahead and, just beyond a pipe crossing the river, go through a kissing gate. A stony path runs ahead to where the path passes under the high Young Street Bridge.

YOUNG STREET BRIDGE

The first was a Bailey bridge built by Royal Canadian Engineers in 1941 to carry tanks which proved too large for Leatherhead's narrow streets. The bridge, named after the commanding officer, was opened by Canadian Prime Minister Mackenzie King. The present one, a few yards south of the original, was declared open in 1978 by the Canadian High Commissioner.

Continue ahead. A kissing gate by a gate leads into a field. Keep forward and the river (left) comes back into view. The way is still ahead with the river over to the left. On the far side the ground rises as the path reaches the field corner. A wide tree-covered track runs downhill to a kissing gate by a gate. Do not stay on the track ahead but bear half-left across the field as the river winds away. At the far corner the river has returned. Here, rejoin the track which is on the right. (There may be a fence to negotiate – look for an orange handle to unhook the wire.)

After a gate, the track joins a metalled estate road (left) before passing Norbury Park Farm and Mickleham Priory. At a junction go right to follow a metalled road uphill. After a second bend there is a wide grass area (right) and a fine view down the valley back to Leatherhead (right). At the junction with the Norbury Park House drive there is a seat.

NORBURY PARK VIEWPOINT

This provides a view north down the valley to Leatherhead where the church tower can be seen rising above the town. Up on the hill to the east Cherkley Court can be seen among the trees. The mansion was home to newspaper proprietor Lord Beaverbrook from 1911 until his death there in 1964. His many visitors included Prime Minister Asquith and opposition leader Bonar Law, who discussed Ireland together, and Churchill, who painted the view from the eleven-bedroom house.

Avoid the turning to Norbury Park House (right) and keep ahead uphill. Just before a barrier turn left down a bridleway. (Ignore an early turning marked 'Druids Grove'.) The way runs downhill through woods including a beech grove. Shortly after a path joins from the left there is a fork. Bear left to a kissing gate at a gateway leading to Swanworth picnic site. Here there is a view across the valley (left) to Juniperhill mansion (see below), and ahead to looming Box Hill. Go ahead through another kissing gate to follow the wide fenced path ahead. After passing Lodge Farm go through a gate on the left. At once turn right down a metalled road to cross the River Mole. Here there is a view back to Norbury Park House (high up on the hill) and home of Leopold Salomons who in 1914 saved Box Hill for public access.

Go ahead on the farm road which turns left to reach Cowslip Farm. At a junction (before passing any buildings) turn right. On reaching Cowslip Cottage (right) keep forward over the grass to go through the kissing gate ahead. Follow the path across the field past an oak tree (right) towards the left-hand side by the railway. Go through the kissing gate and past a left turning under the railway to cross the River Mole on a long footbridge attached to the railway crossing. Continue forward by the embankment, and after the path comes level with the railway line go through a gate and up a short enclosed path leading to the junction of Chapel and Crabtree Lanes in West Humble.

WEST HUMBLE

The archway at Camilla Drive has a plaque recalling Fanny Burney (see page 138) who in 1796 built her cottage 'Camilla' (incorporated into Burney Lodge) here with the proceeds of her novel *Camilla*. St Michael's Chapel is the successor to the ruined twelfth-century chapel (half a mile up on the hill) built for those unable to cross the river to Mickleham Church. Boxhill and Westhumble Station was opened in 1867 and today its booking hall is a cycle emporium, stocked with hire bikes, maps and guides, and a café (open Thu–Mon 9.30am–5.30pm & Wed to 1pm). Cleveland Lodge has been occupied by the Royal School of Church Music since 1996. The Stepping Stones pub stocks Denbies wine produced on the south side of West Humble where England's largest vineyard has the same soil (fertile loam interspersed with flints with an underlay of chalk) as Champagne in France.

To end the walk here look for the station entrance. The main walk turns left over the railway and past the station (right), Cleveland Lodge and the Stepping Stones pub. At the junction with the dual carriageway bear left to go down a slope and through a tunnel under the main road. At the far end go right to follow the road south for 400 yards to a bus stop. Here go left by a National Trust sign to walk down a rough track to the Box Hill Stepping

Stones. Cross the river here, but if the water is running above the stones go right for a short distance to find a footbridge.

BOX HILL STEPPING STONES
Thought to be part of the Winchester–Canterbury Pilgrims Way, the crossing is on the North Downs Way national trail. The present stones were presented to the National Trust in 1946 by Home Secretary Chuter Ede, who lived nearby, and the rebuilt crossing was declared open by Prime Minister Clement Attlee.

Go ahead from the stones. Soon the way, having been joined by the path from the footbridge (left), begins to climb. The main guide is the acorn waymark for walkers on the Pilgrims Way. The rapidly rising path is stepped for much of the way giving views down on to the river and across to the hillside vineyard. Eventually, after passing through yews, the path meets a T-junction. Go right to emerge at the first viewpoint. Continue along the path to reach the main viewpoint.

BOX HILL VIEWPOINT
From here, 563 feet above the River Mole, there is a view over Dorking and further south to Chanctonbury Ring on the South Downs. Planes can be seen taking off from Gatwick. Jane Austen made Box Hill the setting for one of the unsuccessful picnics in *Emma,* and in 1817 John Keats took a moonlit walk here before completing his poem *Endymion* in the Burford Bridge Hotel down below. Box Hill is named after the box trees, although the yew is now prolific. The stone viewpoint, indicating landmarks as far as 25 miles away, is a memorial to Leopold Salomons who purchased the hill for the National Trust. Nearby Swiss Cottage is an early nineteenth-century building where television founder John Logie Baird lived between 1929 and 1932 while carrying out experiments

From the viewpoint platform turn to the right to follow the path uphill towards the NT shop and café, and join the road. Keep forward to go left just before a 'Cyclists Please Dismount' notice at the NT shop approach.

The wide path passes Swiss Cottage (left) before continuing beyond a log. At a junction bear right. Soon there is the simple tombstone of Major Peter Labellière, an eccentric Dorking resident who died in 1800 aged 75 and was buried here upside down at his own request because 'the world is turned topsy-turvy'. Continue ahead with a view, half-left, of Norbury Park House on the hill and west London ahead. On emerging from the trees on to the wide grass sward the view becomes dramatic. Walk ahead downhill, heading for the three trees at the bottom of the hill. There is a glimpse down to the left of a roundabout and the roof of Burford Bridge Hotel. Just beyond the trees at the bottom of the hill there is a clear view to the right of Flint Cottage.

FLINT COTTAGE
Built in the early nineteenth century, Flint Cottage was home to novelist and poet George Meredith from 1867 until his death in 1909. Each morning he walked to the top of Box Hill. His visitors here included authors Robert Louis Stevenson and Henry James. Liberal leader Jeremy Thorpe stayed here as a child during the Second World

War when the house was owned by his great uncle Ralph Wood, a Box Hill Management Committee member. Other visitors at this time included the author and cartoonist Max Beerbohm.

Leave the grass at the T-junction at the bottom of the Zig Zag Road. Go past St Jude's Lodge (right) and up the main Mickleham village street. Walk on the left, and after a short distance go up the steps to a path running at first high above the road. Just past Fredley Manor gateway (left) there is a view across the road to Juniper Hall.

JUNIPER HALL FIELD CENTRE
Most of the building dates from about 1770, although the exterior is nineteenth century. After the French Revolution the house was rented by a group of emigrés including the Count de Narbonne, Talleyrand and Madame de Staël. General D'Arblay, Adjutant General to Lafayette, got to know Fanny Burney (see below) when they tried to teach each other their own languages in the drawing room.

The path rejoins the road opposite Juniperhill mansion.

JUNIPERHILL
Juniperhill mansion was built about 1780 and extended in the following century. It was the last home of Richard Bennett, Prime Minister of Canada from 1930 to 1935, who bought the house from Lord Beaverbrook – both had worked in the same Canadian law practice. On Sunday evenings villagers were invited in to see the latest films sent down by Beaverbrook who lived at nearby Cherkley (see page 136). When Bennett was made a peer in 1941 he took the title Viscount Bennett of Mickleham, Surrey, and of Calgary and Hopewell, Canada. Appropriately, Bennett's butler had been a footman at 10 Downing Street during Asquith's premiership.

Turn left along the road to follow a high wall. The road runs gently downhill to the village centre, where the post office and pub face the church.

MICKLEHAM
Mickleham Church has traces of Saxon work as well as a Norman arch and font. Fanny Burney and General D'Arblay married here on a summer Sunday morning in 1793, and George Meredith married his second wife here in 1864. Lord Bennett, who is buried outside the west door, often read the lesson at services. His arms are next to those of his fellow Canadian Beaverbrook in the Norbury Park pew window (north-east corner) where there is also a tablet to Box Hill donor Leopold Salomons. The post office was established in 1833 and still carries the name of the nineteenth-century postman, Rose. The Running Horses sign shows the 1828 Derby winner which was stabled here and emerged victorious in a re-run after a dead heat. The pub was then on the main London–Dorking road and an hour's ride by horse-drawn coach from the Elephant and Castle.

Continue through the village to meet the dual carriageway. Cross here with great care to enter Norbury Park opposite. The estate path goes over the River Mole and later joins the outward route just before Mickleham Priory. Retrace the way back to Leatherhead. (Remember to bear left at the fork through the gate).

Walk 23: Ancient Woods and Epsom Salts

Ashtead – Ashtead Common – Epsom Common – The Wells – Ashtead

---

This easy walk ambles through what remains of the ancient Ashtead Forest to reach the Wells at Epsom Common, the original source of the famous Epsom salts and in its time a celebrated European spa. In 1995 Ashtead Common was declared a National Nature Reserve in recognition of its status as a unique habitat for a great variety of plants and animals, including roe deer which thrive in the woodland areas dominated by an enormous number of venerable pollarded oaks, themselves a micro-habitat for rare lichens, mosses and insects. With a little forward planning the walk can be extended into the peaceful woods and nature reserve of Prince's Coverts, a Crown Estate property (see box below).

> *Distance*: 4 miles, or longer if visiting Prince's Coverts.
>
> *Map*: OS Landranger 187 (Dorking, Reigate and Crawley) or OS Pathfinder 1190 (Weybridge) and 1206 (Woking).
>
> *Terrain*: Paths and bridleways; tends to be very muddy in certain parts after rain. No climbs.
>
> *Food & Drink*: Woodman (Mon–Sat 12–11pm; Sun 12–10.30pm; M/G), Ashtead; Star (Mon–Sat 11am–3pm & 5–11pm; Sun 12–10.30pm; M/G), near Prince's Coverts.
>
> *Transport*: National Railways from Victoria or Waterloo to Ashtead (outside Travelcard zones). Bus 479 will drop you close to the Woodman, just south of the station.
>
> *Start & Finish*: Ashtead train station.

From Ashtead station use the footbridge to cross the line and leave the station by the narrow enclosed exit at the eastern end of platform one. Woodfield Road bends to the left, but keep more or less ahead following the blue-arrowed bridleway on to Ashtead Common. After 100 yards you will come to a footbridge across the Rye stream. Cross this towards three wide diverging paths. Take the centre path marked by white-tipped posts which takes a north-easterly direction across the common. Keep ahead following the white-tipped posts which, while they lessen the sense of adventure, do mean that it's almost impossible to lose the way.

ASHTEAD COMMON
Ashtead Common has been a woodland resource for at least two thousand years, and evidence has been found for industry and occupation dating back to Roman times. The Romans used the woods as a source of fuel for tile kilns as well as

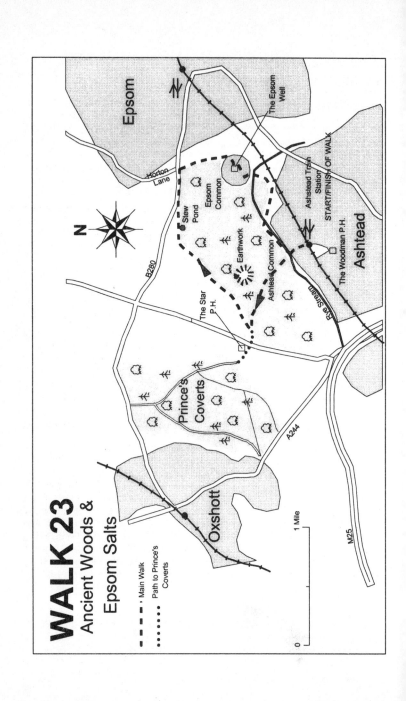

WALK 23
Ancient Woods & Epsom Salts

N

Epsom

Horton Lane

B280

Stew Pond

Epsom Common

Earthwork

The Star P.H.

Prince's Coverts

Oxshott

A244

M25

Ashtead Common

Rye Stream

The Epsom Well

Ashtead Train Station

START/FINISH OF WALK

The Woodman P.H.

Ashtead

- - - Main Walk

· · · · · Path to Prince's Coverts

0   1 Mile

charcoal for hypocausts (underfloor heating from a furnace). In Saxon times the common became the manorial 'waste' on which grazing of deer and cattle was combined with the pollarding of oak trees. Pollarding continued until the arrival of the railway when easily transported cheap coal made it economically unviable. The common still has a thousand pollarded oaks and their great age (many over 400 years old) and gnarled and twisted shapes are a dramatic feature on the landscape. Now under the aegis of the Corporation of London, the common provides a habitat for a wide variety of flora and fauna, the unique nature of which caused it to be designated as a Site of Special Scientific Interest in 1955 and a National Nature Reserve in 1995. An informative leaflet about the common is available from the community woodlands officer on ☎0181 7630464.

After rising gently for almost half a mile, the path levels at an area of 'petrified forest', a part of the common with quite a number of dead or dying trees. Beyond here the path descends down a gully to an exit from the common by a horse paddock with jumping fences. The walk continues between the blue posts to the right, but there is an opportunity for refreshment here by taking the path left to the Kingston Road (A243), where the Star pub lies just to the right. The same path should be taken to visit the Prince's Coverts.

PRINCE'S COVERTS
The Prince's Coverts is an area of picturesque woodland named after Prince Leopold of Belgium who acquired the land in 1821 while resident at nearby Esher after his marriage to the short-lived Princess Charlotte. The area had formerly been known as Stoke Common until it was expropriated as part of the Enclosure movement, and it is now owned and managed for the sustainable production of timber by the Crown Estate. The woods support a rich variety of flora and fauna including wild orchids, 200 different species of fungi and miscellaneous insects, butterflies and birds, as well as roe deer, badgers and foxes. To visit the estate you will need to contact the Crown Estate office at Windsor (☎01753 860222) in advance who (in return for a refundable deposit) will send you a key and an informative leaflet on the coverts which includes a map with a number of suggested trails and details of flora and fauna. While the Crown Estate would prefer keyholders to use the gates to the west and north (Prince's Gate and Highgate Cottages Gate) to gain entry, the gate to the rear of the Star pub, a quarter of a mile up the lane and signposted, may also be opened with the same key.

The walk continues through the blue-tipped posts and skirts the northern edge of the woods for about a mile, passing quite a few of the venerable gnarled and twisted oaks along the way, hangovers from the ancient forest. Keep ahead along this pleasant path following the waymarks for the Chessington Countryside Walk.

COAL TAX POSTS
Along this stretch of the route you will see a number of cast-iron posts painted white and emblazoned with a red cross – the arms of the Corporation of the City of London. Since medieval times the corporation has had the right to levy a tax on any coal being transported across the city boundaries. This duty helped to finance the rebuilding of St Paul's Cathedral and other churches damaged in the Great Fire of London in 1666.

When Parliament passed the London Coal and Wine Continuance Act in 1861, enlarging the metropolitan area where the taxes (now including wine) were payable, these posts were erected to indicate the new boundary.

The path eventually emerges at Stew Pond. Keep ahead with the pond to your right and follow the path as it bends right to climb gently through trees. At a fork after 200 yards take the leftward path towards the B280 road, still following the waymarks for the Chessington Countryside Walk. Do *not* cross the road at the crossing ahead but continue west with the road to your left. Upon reaching a T-junction with a road (Horton Lane, visible left through trees), turn right along a bridleway. After 20 yards the path forks; bear right along a narrower path signed 'summer horse ride'. Ignore any side paths and maintain a roughly southerly direction. The path becomes grassy and passes through a wild stretch of the common. After about a third of a mile bend left with the path to reach the edge of the Wells estate. Cross a gravel path and head half-right to a gate and fingerpost indicating the Epsom Well. Turn right here to enter the Wells housing estate, passing a line of shops to the left. Keep ahead downhill along Spa Drive into a cul-de-sac where, close to a sign for the Wells Centre, you'll find the entrance to Wicker's Way (left), an enclosed path leading to the Epsom Well at the centre of the Wells estate.

THE EPSOM WELL

Standing rather incongruously at the centre of this 1950s housing estate it's hard to believe that this tiny well, recently tarted up with a lantern globe and metal cover, was once one of the most sought after cures in Europe. Discovered by a cowherd in the early seventeenth century, the waters of the Wells soon acquired a reputation for their curative qualities, particularly in the treatment of constipation. Soon crowds were flocking here from all parts of the country and Europe. Samuel Pepys and Daniel Defoe were among the early visitors, and sanitary arrangements seem to have been less than adequate for Pepys described seeing men and women, once they had drunk the waters, seeking privacy in the nearby area and 'turning up their tails'. In the eighteenth century the popularity of Epsom Wells began to decline almost as quickly as it had risen, probably due to the well often drying up because of overuse and the waters becoming putrid. Ironically, in 1951 the well's water was declared polluted and unfit for public consumption, and the industry to which it gave birth died, and Epsom salts no longer come from Epsom.

From the well, descend the steps and turn right to the end of the road, turning left, then immediately right again to the end of Well Way. Turn left here, and take the first right by three trees on a central island to enter a cul-de-sac. At the end of this go through a metal barrier to cross a stream and turn left along a grassy path which bends left beyond a litter bin to head half-right over grass to meet a metalled path signed 'Newton Wood Road'. Bear right along this for 150 yards until you come to a railway pedestrian crossing on the left.

Here, turn right along a bridleway signed 'Rushett Lane' to pass beneath power lines, 200 yards beyond which lies a footbridge over the Rye stream. Cross the bridge and keep ahead on the other bank for a further 100 yards until, where the track swings right, turn left along a path signed 'Ashtead Common'. Flanked by slender Downy oak trees, after a quarter of a mile you'll come to a pair of white marker posts with a gate on the right. Turn left here along a path for 50 yards to make a right by an Ashtead Common noticeboard, passing through a barrier. Follow a track running along the backs of houses beyond a stream to the left, and the wood to the right. After a quarter of a mile, and where the trees end, turn left to find a footbridge over the Rye stream where the walk began. Cross this to return to Ashford train station.

For refreshment, the Woodman pub lies just south of the train station and serves all-day meals as well as tea and coffee. To reach it, cross the station car park to go down steps to a metalled path, heading half-right across a common. Follow this to the pub, about 250 yards from the station.

WALK 24
Hampton Court Deer Parks

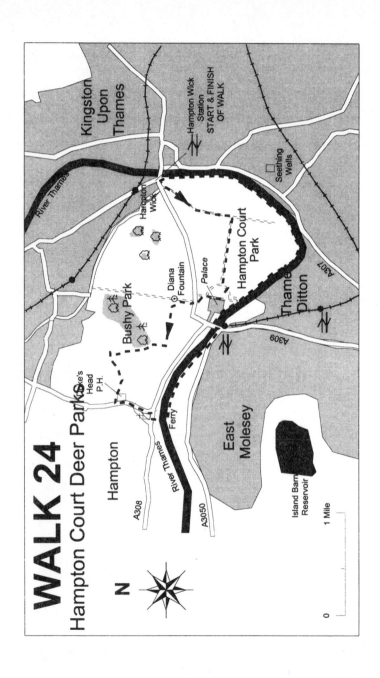

N

0   1 Mile

Kingston Upon Thames

River Thames

Hampton Wick Station
START & FINISH OF WALK

Seething Wells

Hampton Wick

Hampton Court Park

Diana Fountain

Palace

Thames Ditton

A307

A309

Bushy Park

King's Head P.H.

Hampton

A308

River Thames

Ferry

A3050

East Molesey

Island Barn Reservoir

Walk 24: Hampton Court Deer Parks

Hampton Wick – Hampton Court – Hampton – East Molesey – Hampton Court – Hampton Wick

---

Kingston and Hampton Wick were once a day's horse ride from London; now the train ride lasts around thirty minutes. This circular walk takes a route tourists rarely enjoy by approaching Hampton Court Palace from the Long Water where sheep and deer roam. Unless it is a deep midweek winter's day, walkers should be able to cross the Thames at Hampton by boat for the return along the towpath which affords new vistas of Hampton Court and the royal borough of Kingston, where Saxon monarchs were crowned. Although this walk involves rural encounters there are three opportunities for curtailing the walk at good transport links.

Distance: 5.5 or 3.5 miles.

Map: OS Landranger 176 (West London) or OS Pathfinders 1174 (Staines, Heathrow and Richmond) and 1190 (Weybridge, Esher and Hampton Court).

Terrain: Rough and metalled parkland paths and towpath.

Food & Drink: Hampton Wick and Kingston (across the bridge) have several pubs and cafés. There are also plenty of refreshments at Hampton Court Palace; White Hart (11am–3pm & 5.30–11pm; Fri–Sat 11am–11pm; Sun 12–10.30pm; M) in Hampton High Street.

Transport: National Railways to Hampton Wick (Travelcard Zone 6) from Waterloo. Hampton Wick can also be reached by crossing the bridge from Kingston. Return from Hampton Court or Hampton by a choice of buses to Kingston via Hampton Wick. There are railway stations at Hampton Court and Hampton (Zone 6).

Start & Finish: Hampton Wick, at the 'north' end of Kingston Bridge. The shorter walk ends at Hampton Court, Hampton or East Molesey.

HAMPTON WICK
Hampton Wick was for many years a hamlet where the population looked to Kingston for main services. When King Alfred was crowned at Kingston there was a Roman ford linking his kingdom with Mercia on the Hampton bank. A bridge had been erected by at least the twelfth century. Hampton Wick's St John the Baptist Church, only built in the 1820s, is by E. Lapidge who was responsible for Hampton Church (see page 147). Although the Old King's Head is no longer a pub its Henry VII sign survives.

To reach Hampton Court Park from Hampton Wick Station turn left and follow the High Street to the roundabout at Kingston Bridge. Cross the bridge approach to the Old King's Head Studios to find the park gateway on the left.

HAMPTON COURT PARK

Sometimes called Home Park, Hampton Court Park was enclosed by Henry VIII. Charles I rode here in 1647 while a prisoner and slipped out of the gates to make for the south coast. The three-quarter-mile Long Water was dug during the reign of his son Charles II when the avenues of trees were planted. Deer and sheep can still be seen.

Once through the gateway follow the metalled road to the pedestrian gateway by the cattle grid. The park road rises, giving a view of Hampton Wick Pond to the right and a twelve-sided brick ice house to the left. Keep right where the road divides before the first view of Hampton Court Palace. At the second fork bear left. After half a mile the road runs between the Long Water overflow (left) and the end of the Long Water. Turn right here up the bank to follow the side of the Long Water (right) with the palace ahead at the far end. On reaching the end bear left with a fence to a large gateway. Go through one of the two side gates to cross the canal bridge. Walk straight ahead through the formal garden to the palace.

HAMPTON COURT PALACE

A Knights Hospitallers house, the palace was rebuilt by Cardinal Wolsey to be his own residence. As he began to lose royal favour Wolsey presented this new palace to Henry VIII who brought five of his six wives here. He is said to have been playing tennis here when he received confirmation of Anne Boleyn's execution at the Tower of London. His daughter Elizabeth I enjoyed gardening here, where she often celebrated Christmas. The vine, the world's oldest and largest with roots watered by the Thames, was planted in 1765 for George III under whom Hampton Court ceased to be a royal residence. (Grapes are sold in the shop at the garden entrance in late August and early September.) William IV began the first guided tours for visitors and Queen Victoria opened the main rooms for free public viewing a year after her accession. Now the palace is open daily but, no longer a royal residence, it is in the hands of the Historic Royal Palaces Agency which operates a hefty admission charge; £9.25, children £6.10.

On reaching a palace entrance turn right along the Broad Walk with the palace to the left. After passing the royal tennis court (left) go left through a small gateway and at once bear half-right to walk through a garden (known as the Wilderness) to pass the maze and reach the Lion Gate by the King's Arms.
To end the walk here look for bus stops.
To continue the main walk cross the road on the crossing (right) opposite the Liongate Hotel to enter Bushey Park.

BUSHEY PARK

Bushey Park is a 1,000-acre deer park enclosed by Henry VIII. Today there are about 200 fallow and 125 red deer. (The young found in the bracken in the summer months should never be touched, as this will lead to the mothers abandoning them.) The stags enjoy the conkers in September before the October rutting season. The north–south Chestnut Avenue was planted for William III to be a grand approach to Hampton Court Palace. The Diana fountain, carved by Fanelli for Charles I, was placed on the avenue as part of Christopher Wren's plan for a Versailles-style garden.

The pedestrian entrance is on the left of the gateway. Walk ahead, keeping near the road, to reach the huge water area surrounding the Diana fountain. Here leave the traffic by turning left on a little-used side road. Keep on this straight park road running west down a young avenue. On reaching a T-junction, go right. The metalled path runs alongside a garden to cross the Longford River, which was dug for Charles I in 1639 to bring water from the River Colne at nearby Longford to feed the Bushey Park ponds. Here the river runs through the Waterhouse Woodland Gardens created in the 1940s. Continue ahead, ignoring two paths bearing off to the right. The way becomes rough as it runs ahead across open ground. Where the way divides keep forward past a line of trees (left). At a junction the path meets Cobbler's Walk at a point where it begins to run east as a rough path.

Turn left along the metalled path to a gateway where Cobbler's Walk, named after the cobbler who saved the right of way in 1754, becomes Duke's Head Passage. Go through the wooden gate, and after a short distance there is the Longford River (right). The path crosses the river at a bend and later reaches a gate next to the Duke's Head. Turn left past the pub, and where the road divides keep to the left fork to pass the White Hart.

To end the walk here look for the bus stops.

The main walk continues past the White Hart. Here cross the road to walk past Penn's Place (right) to enter the churchyard and follow the path round to the south side of the church, where there is a view of the river.

HAMPTON
There has been a riverside church here since at least 1342, although the present St Mary's building by E. Lapidge (see page 147) only dates from 1831. When the church is locked the interior may be seen through St Luke's Chapel, which is entered by way of the west door. The glass doors, adorned with an Eric Fraser depiction of the Annunciation, are a memorial to the *Radio Times* artist who lived at Penn's Place until his death in 1983. The house has a stained-glass window by Fraser showing Edward VI and his nurse Sibell Penn, who lived on the site. Riverside Garrick's Temple (downstream) was built in 1755 for actor Richard Garrick who lived in the house behind. Artist John Zoffany (see page 152) visited in 1762 to paint Garrick and his wife at the Temple dedicated to Shakespeare. The Bull, rebuilt in the last century, has been next to the church since at least Henry VIII's reign.

Walk down the steps to the high pavement and turn right to the Bull. Cross the road to the boatyard and take the ferry to Hurst Park on the far side. The Hampton ferry has run since at least 1519, and now operates weekdays 7.30am to 6pm and weekends 11am to 6pm. (During winter weekdays the service may be restricted to early morning and 4 to 6pm. If the ferry is not operating, walkers should return to the road to go right downstream past the church to Hampton Court Green and right to Hampton Court Bridge. Hurst Park, on the south bank, was a racecourse until 1960.

Once on the Surrey bank, turn left downstream with the river to left. Here, the towpath is also the Thames Path. There is a fine view of Hampton Church and, just beyond Garrick Ait, there is a view of Garrick's Temple on the Hampton Bank. The towpath surface is rough until reaching the entrance to the cricket ground (right). Soon after there is a view between Tagg's and Ash Islands of a Swiss cottage.

TAGG'S ISLAND

Once Walnut Tree Island, Tagg's Island is named after Royal Waterman Tom Tagg who ran a boatyard and hotel there in the nineteenth century. Later, Fred Karno covered the island with his leisure complex. The Swiss cottage on the far bank was brought from Switzerland in 1899.

Continue along the now metalled towpath to reach the weir and Molesey Lock. The path continues ahead below the road before joining the pavement by a bus stop at East Molesey.

EAST MOLESEY

East Molesey takes its name from the River Mole (see Walk 22) which joins the Thames just downstream of the station. Bridge Street indicates the line of the old main road before Hampton Court Bridge was realigned. The first bridge was built in 1753 and pedestrians paid a halfpenny (double on Sundays) to cross. The charge stayed until 1876, and the tollhouse can be seen as part of the Mitre Hotel opposite. The present Hampton Court Bridge opened in 1933. The railway station is now called Hampton Court.

To end the walk here you turn right at the bridge to Hampton Court Station.

The main walk continues across Hampton Court Bridge to reach the Mitre Hotel. Use the crossing ahead before going right downstream on to the wide towpath alongside Hampton Court Palace (left). Soon, the River Mole can be seen entering the Thames while the towpath affords a superb view of Hampton Court Palace's recently restored Privy Garden. Before the Thames turns north, the path runs between Thames Ditton Island and, on the towpath side, the Pavilion.

THAMES DITTON ISLAND AND THE PAVILION

The island is now covered by 48 timber houses and bungalows which hide the village on the far bank with its thirteenth-century church and a riverside inn dating from the same period. By the towpath there is the Pavilion, designed by Wren and built in 1700 for William III to entertain in; it later became the home of Queen Victoria's father.

After passing Seething Wells, a suburb of Surbiton on the far bank, the path reaches Raven's Ait.

RAVEN'S AIT

Raven's Ait, an island watersport centre, was an osier ground in the nineteenth century where reeds were grown for making baskets. The name derivation is uncertain, but Seething Wells on the far bank recalls the therapeutic springs there. Hart's Ferry operates downstream of the island on Sundays.

On the far bank there is the Italianate tower of St Raphael's on the outskirts of Kingston.

KINGSTON-UPON-THAMES

Turk's boatyard is on the edge of the town where Royal Waterman Mike Turk's ancestor maintained a salmon weir for Henry VIII. The River Hogsmill, which rises near Epsom, flows into the Thames just upstream of the Bishop-out-of-Residence pub, which is on the site of a house used in the fourteenth century by Bishop William of Wykeham when travelling between Winchester and Southwark. Behind is the tower of Kingston Church which overlooks the square where a market operates under a Charles I charter which allows no other within a seven-mile radius.

From the Coach House there is a metalled road known as Barge Walk which eventually runs up to the roundabout on the north end of Kingston Bridge. Either cross the bridge to enter Kingston or go along Hampton's High Street to Hampton Wick Station.

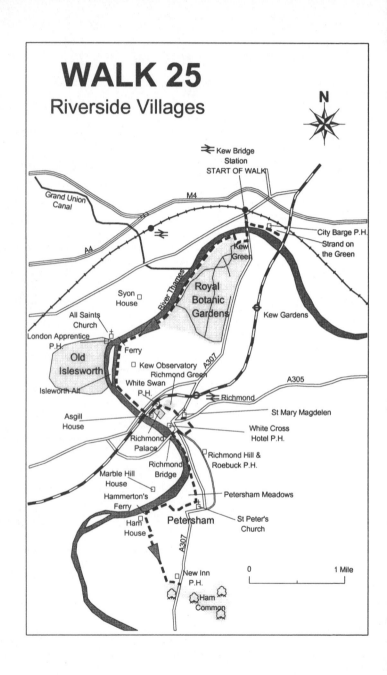

WALK 25
Riverside Villages

N

Kew Bridge
Station
START OF WALK

Grand Union
Canal

M4

City Barge P.H.

A4

Strand on
the Green

Kew
Green

Syon
House

Royal
Botanic
Gardens

River Thames

Kew Gardens

All Saints
Church

London Apprentice
P.H.

Old
Islesworth

Ferry

Kew Observatory

Richmond Green

A307

A305

White Swan
P.H.

Richmond

Isleworth Ait

St Mary Magdelen

Asgill
House

White Cross
Hotel P.H.

Richmond
Palace

Richmond Hill &
Roebuck P.H.

Marble Hill
House

Richmond
Bridge

Hammerton's
Ferry

Petersham Meadows

Ham
House

Petersham

St Peter's
Church

A307

New Inn
P.H.

0   1 Mile

Ham
Common

Walk 25: Riverside Villages

Kew Bridge – Strand on the Green – Kew – Richmond – Petersham

---

Not quite qualifying as a country walk, although in parts it has a decidedly country feel, this ramble along the Thames is included for the sheer variety of scenery and sights en route, not to say the changing scene along the river itself. Among possible visits are the Kew Botanic Gardens and, near the end of the walk, two fine seventeenth- and eighteenth-century mansions. This is a good walk for short winter days or when the weather is uncertain.

Distance: 6.5 miles, or 4 miles if concluded at Richmond (tube, buses and trains).

Map: OS Landranger 176 (West London area) or OS Pathfinder 1174 (Staines).

Terrain: Riverside paths, some metalled others not. Some mud after rain, no climbs.

Food & Drink: City Barge (Mon–Sat 11.30am–11pm; Sun 12–10.30pm; M/G) and other pubs at Strand on the Green; London Apprentice (Mon–Sat 11am–1pm; Sun 12–10.30pm; M/G), Isleworth; White Swan (Mon–Fri 11am–3pm & 5.30–11pm; Sun 12–10.30pm; M/G), Angel and Crown (Mon–Sat 11am–11pm; Sun 12–10.30pm; M/G), Café Mozart (daily 9am–7pm), White Cross Hotel (Mon–Sat 11am–11pm; Sun 12–10.30pm; M/G), Roebuck (Mon-Sat 11am–11pm; Sun 12–10.30pm; M), all Richmond; Coach House Café (March–Oct daily 10am-6pm), Marble Hill House; Orangery cafeteria (April–Oct Sat–Wed 1–5pm), Ham House; New Inn (Mon-Sat 11am–11pm; Sun 12–10.30pm; M/G), Ham Common.

Transport: National Railways from Waterloo to Kew Bridge Station. Kew Gardens train station and underground are also possible, but you will need to walk half a mile north along Kew Gardens Road and Kew Bridge Road to reach the start of the walk. The 237 and 267 buses pass Kew Bridge Station.

Start & Finish: Kew Bridge Station (Zone 3) to Richmond (on the shorter walk) or Ham Common (both Zone 4).

From Kew Bridge Station turn right outside the exit and cross the traffic island towards the east side of Kew Bridge. Do not cross the bridge but bear left into Strand on the Green, passing a small terrace of shops (left). Keep ahead to follow the road as it bends left along the riverbank for about 200 yards until you meet a sign indicating Strand on the Green, fronting the river.

STRAND ON THE GREEN
Strand on the Green, originally a cluster of eighteenth-century fishermen's cottages, is one of this stretch of the riverside's most picturesque but little-known corners. Proceeding downstream or east along the terrace of dinky, bijou residences fronting the river, Zoffany House at No. 65 takes its name from the Swiss painter Johan or, as

he became, John Zoffany, a celebrated artist who lived here from 1780 until his death in 1810. The disciples in his 'Last Supper', now hanging in St Paul's upstream in Brentford, are portrayals of the local fishermen who lived here. Poet Dylan Thomas was another sometime resident at Ship House Cottage (No. 56), and writer Nancy Mitford once lived at Rose Cottage (actually at No. 84 Thames Road alongside the Café Rouge restaurant). Further along again, the City Barge pub dates from 1484 and takes its name from the Lord Mayor of London's barge which used to be laid up here. Long familiar with the dangers of surging tides, it has an impressive steel door to prevent the bar from being flooded. Quite a few of the dwellings here have taken similar precautions, including a curious half-door at No. 49 through which the inhabitants must scramble to gain entry. The Bull's Head, just to the east of the railway bridge, is another ancient hostelry where Oliver Cromwell once took refuge to avoid arrest by the forces of the king. He gave his pursuers the slip by escaping along a tunnel to the island opposite, now called Oliver's Eyot (island) and home to colonies of herons and cormorants.

Retrace your steps to Kew Bridge and climb the stairs to the bridge to cross the river. Cross over the road at the zebra crossing on the south bank and continue ahead past the former King's Arms (currently a pizza restaurant) and the Rose and Crown pub to walk along the north side of Kew Green.

KEW GREEN

The Church of St Anne was built in 1714 and enlarged by George III who in 1805 added the 'Royal Gallery'. The portico, designed by Wyatville, was added in 1836. In the graveyard can be seen the tombs of Thomas Gainsborough, the eighteenth-century painter, beneath the fourth window from the west end on the south side, as well as that of John Zoffany (see above), between the eastern end of the church and the road. During the reign of George III many of the imposing Georgian houses surrounding the green were built to house members of the court. On the north side of the green – used as a cricket pitch in summer – is Kew Herbarium, a collection of seven million dried plants and specimens from all over the world, alas open to specialists only.

Keep ahead along the top of the green to reach the main entrance to the Royal Botanic Gardens (see box). No longer costing a derisory single penny (the price of entry from the 1930s until the early 1980s), if you intend to visit the Gardens you can rejoin the walk by using the exit at the Brentford Ferry Gate. If you are not visiting the gardens, take a right along Ferry Lane, signed 'Brentford Ferry Gate', and at the end join the river towpath turning left to head upstream.

ROYAL BOTANIC GARDENS

The Royal Botanic Gardens (open daily from 9.30am, closing times vary according to season; adults £4.50, £3.00 concessions, £2.50 children) is a great open-air entertainment where exotic trees, plants and flowers from all parts of the world are displayed in a marvellous setting. The gardens were started by Prince Frederick Louis, but it was his spouse Augusta who, after Frederick's death, started a nine-acre botanical garden in 1759. This was considerably enlarged during the reign of her son George III, and again after 1841 when it was acquired by the state. Following further expansion during the reign of Queen Victoria, by 1904 the whole 300 acres of the present gardens had become established as an institution of scientific research, as well as a centre of education and relaxation. Architect Decimus Burton designed the main gates, the Palm House and the Temperate House. A leaflet describing the gardens is included in the admission price.

Continue along the towpath for about half a mile, passing the Brentford Ferry Gate where visitors to the Botanic Gardens can rejoin the walk. To the right across the river is the entry to the Brentford arm of the Grand Union Canal (see p 54) opened in 1794, which once carried a multitude of goods brought up river from London's docks to Birmingham. A further half a mile brings you to a fine view of the colonnaded east front of Syon House beyond a meadow on the opposite bank.

SYON HOUSE

Topped by the flamboyant lion whose outstretched tail is silhouetted against the sky, Syon House was founded in the fifteenth century for the Bridgettine monastic community sponsored by Henry V. It is named after the holy hill of Zion on which the city of Jerusalem stands. After the dissolution of the monasteries the building was seized by Henry VIII, and Catherine Howard, Henry's fifth wife, was imprisoned here before her execution. After Henry's death in 1547 his body rested at the house where it was mauled by dogs – perhaps a revenge inspired by simmering local resentment at the monastery's earlier desecration. In the same year the house was acquired by the Duke of Somerset, the real power behind the throne during the minority of Edward VI. When accused of treason by John Dudley, the duke was executed and Dudley was presented with the house and the title of Earl of Northumberland to go with it. The earldom was upgraded to a dukedom in 1750, and the first duke employed Robert Adam to renovate and decorate the house, and Capability Brown to landscape the gardens. In the nineteenth century the Tudor brick frontage was encased in Bath stone and the enormous lion, which once fronted the family's Northumberland House in the Strand, set in its present position. The house, with its richly furnished interior and gardens, is open to the public in summer.

The path now becomes attractively wooded, and roughly half a mile beyond Syon House there is a glimpse, through the trees to the left and beyond an obelisk, of Kew Observatory, built by Chambers in 1768 for George III to observe Venus. The stone obelisks mark the south and magnetic south points used when time was measured here. Soon, the Syon Pavilion appears on the opposite bank.

SYON PAVILION

A Georgian construction built in 1803 over a Tudor boat house, Syon Pavilion was a gift from the 2nd Duke of Northumberland to his wife, who used it to hold tea parties in one of its three rooms before taking a river trip. The house's eight-oared barge was also moored here and was used throughout the nineteenth century to ferry the members of the family along the river to their house in the Strand. Now a private dwelling, the balustrade on the roof was added in 1961.

Just beyond the pavilion and also on the far bank is Old Isleworth and the London Apprentice pub. In summer at weekends and bank holidays a ferry

(May–Sept, 50p each way) allows a visit to Isleworth. Ring the bell provided beside the bench if the ferryman is on the far shore.

ISLEWORTH

There may have been an ancient pre-Christian chapel on the site of the church of All Saints, whose elegant pinnacled tower rises above Old Isleworth across the river. However, the tower is all that remains today of the fifteenth-century church destroyed by arson in 1943. The new building now attached was designed by Michael Blee and opened in 1969. A large sundial on the wall replaces an earlier one which used to show the time not only here but also in Jamaica, Jerusalem and Moscow. The bodies of many of the 1665 plague victims were brought by barge from the city and buried in the churchyard. There's an underground passage running from the church to the nearby London Apprentice pub, which takes its name from the apprentices of the London livery companies who used to row up here on their annual leave day. In the Eights Room on the pub's first floor there's a fine Italian plasterwork ceiling dating from 1600. Other visitors who came here included Henry VIII, Elizabeth I and Charles I and erstwhile distinguished artistic residents number Hogarth, Turner and Van Gogh.

Continue along the west bank passing the island of Isleworth Ait, now a nature reserve, to reach Richmond Lock, an impressive chunk of late nineteenth-century Victorian engineering in its livery of cream and jade paintwork with a footbridge and sluices to control the water level. Then, go under Twickenham Bridge. Beyond the railway bridge, and to the left, lies Asgill House.

ASGILL HOUSE

Asgill House, which Sir Nikolaus Pevsner describes as 'a Palladian villa of great charm', was designed by Sir Robert Taylor and completed around 1760 for Sir Charles Asgill, Lord Mayor of London. One of the last of its type to be built overlooking the Thames, the house was given the distinction of being painted by Turner.

Turn left up Old Palace Lane, passing on the left the attractive eighteenth-century White Swan pub which was constructed, incidentally, with stone taken from the ruins of Richmond Palace. Just beyond the pub go right into the chestnut-shaded Old Palace Yard.

RICHMOND PALACE

Richmond Palace was rebuilt by Henry VII, who changed the name of the village from Sceon to Richmond, after his earldom derived from Richmond, Yorkshire. In 1541 Henry VIII granted the palace to his divorced wife, Anne of Cleves, and in 1603 his daughter, Elizabeth I, died here. It was from a window above the entrance that a ring was dropped, to signal the Stuart succession, to a horseman who sped north to James VI of Scotland. During the reign of Elizabeth, Shakespeare staged performances of his plays here. The Roundheads ransacked and dismantled much of the place after the execution of Charles I in 1649, and it is hard to believe today that the palace once covered ten acres. The buildings that remain were reconstructed from the ruins.

Go through the historic gateway (bearing Henry VII's coat of arms) to reach the elegantly spacious Richmond Green, once the scene of Tudor jousting and where George III was partial to watching cricket. On summer weekends spectators still lounge on the grass to watch matches between local teams. Turn right and take the footpath across the green just before Maids of Honour Row, built in the early eighteenth century by George II for the ladies-in-waiting of the then Princess of Wales. Crossing the green you're aiming for the centre of the terrace on the west side, not the corner. This will bring you to Brewers Lane, a narrow alleyway lined with shops. At the end of this cross George Street and go left for a few yards to walk up Church Court (by Tesco). Passing the Angel and Crown pub, the Café Mozart and Houben's, a rather good second-hand bookshop, ahead is the Church of St Mary Magdalen. Keep ahead past the church to Paradise Road.

ST MARY MAGDALEN

The flint and stone tower is partly fifteenth century, but most of what remains visible today is the result of a substantial eighteenth-century restoration, with further alterations in the early years of this century. The late sixteenth-century Cotton brass on the north wall is the earliest memorial; Robert Cotton was an Officer of the Wardrobe to Mary I and Elizabeth I. Edmund Kean, the celebrated early nineteenth-century tragic actor who collapsed and died on stage at Covent Garden in 1833 while playing Othello, was buried here when Westminster Abbey refused to take the body because of his final alcoholic years. A slate slab in the north-west corner indicates the vault containing his remains.

To end the four-mile walk turn left along here to take the second left (Eton Street) downhill. Bear half-right at the bottom to cross the road into a small alley known locally as 'The Passage', and at the end turn right along The Quadrant. From the bus stop on the opposite side of the road bus 65 will return you to Kew and Kew Bridge. Otherwise keep ahead for 200 yards to the combined rail and underground stations (right) for the tube, North London line and trains to Waterloo.

To continue the main walk cross Paradise Road and go left. Just beyond Eton Street (left) is Hogarth House.

HOGARTH HOUSE

Built in 1820 as Lord Suffield's country residence, Hogarth House is noted today as the former home of Leonard and Virginia Woolf. In 1917 they founded the Hogarth Press on the kitchen table, a period during which Virginia had taken up printing as a form of therapy after a nervous breakdown.

Backtracking slightly to before the junction and beyond a metal barrier, walk south up the unsigned Vineyard Passage beside the modern Vestry House. Deriving its name from a period in the seventeenth century when this spot was famous for its vines, the alleyway is now flanked by a burial ground. On reaching the street named The Vineyard, turn right and follow it as it bends around to the left. Ahead, on the right, lie Bishop Duppa's Almshouses.

BISHOP DUPPA'S ALMSHOUSES

Bishop Duppa, chaplain to Charles I, retired to Richmond after the king's execution. The almshouses were built on the hill in 1681 as a thanks-offering for the bishop's safety during Cromwell's regime. The entrance is part of the original building.

Keep ahead, passing on the right a charming Georgian house beyond a gate which was once the residence of Bernardo O'Higgins, early nineteenth-century South American revolutionary and liberator of Chile. After the nineteenth-century Church of St Elizabeth of Portugal with its neo-baroque tower, you emerge on Richmond Hill.

RICHMOND HILL

Long a fashionable address, the eighteenth-century Irish dramatist Sheridan lived at Downe House (No. 116) with a commanding outlook, George IV spent part of his honeymoon at No. 3 The Terrace (at the viewpoint), and the eighteenth-century painter Sir Joshua Reynolds lived and died at Wick House, next door. The view from the top of the hill attracted many artists, including Turner. It can be enjoyed over a pint by turning left when you emerge on the hill to reach the Roebuck pub, whose customers are allowed to take their glasses over the road to The Terrace to admire the Thames valley panorama.

Turn right downhill, taking in an evocative neon-lit Odeon cinema (right) built in 1930, only three years after the first talking picture was shown in New York. Turn left into Bridge Street, opposite.

RICHMOND BRIDGE

The oldest Thames bridge in London, the five-arched Richmond Bridge was completed in 1777 replacing the horse ferry – note the milestone-obelisk at the end nearest the town. Tolls were levied until the last shareholder died in 1859: 'Pedestrians half-penny, one penny if accompanied by a wheelbarrow; one-horse vehicle 8 pence but one shilling on Sundays. A drove of calves, hogs, sheep or lambs 6 pence a score.' The bridge was widened in 1937. Turner painted the bridge from the far bank. To the north side of Richmond Bridge the atmospheric White Cross Hotel provides an opportunity for a break for refreshment. It's reached by taking the steps descending to the right side of the bridge and following the waterfront for 100 yards.

The walk continues down the steps on the left side of the bridge to turn left and upstream. Just beyond the Three Pigeons restaurant (recently fire damaged), the path becomes separated from the river by a lawn. On meeting a crosspath go ahead through a turnstile and follow the metalled path across Petersham Meadows. On the far side the way becomes enclosed between hedgerows. On meeting a lane at a bend the walk continues to the right, but go ahead to visit Petersham Church.

PETERSHAM

Although mentioned in the Domesday Book, the village is mainly seventeenth and eighteenth century. The charming St Peter's Church contains elements, including parts of the chancel, from its original thirteenth-century predecessor, but what you see today is mostly the result of a Georgian rebuild. A delightful interior (open for visits Sun only 3–5pm) has curious box pews and galleries as well as an entertaining triple-tiered Jacobean monument to lawyer George Cole, portrayed recumbently lording it over his wife and child below. George Vancouver, who discovered Vancouver Island while sailing with Captain James Cook, lived in Petersham and is buried by the churchyard's south wall.

Turn right before the church to follow the wide lane which becomes narrow and enclosed beyond plant nurseries (left). It soon crosses River Lane to lead on to a cross track. Go half-right to follow another rather leafier enclosed path with a wire fence to the left enclosing a sports field. Ignore a stile on the left and cross a footbridge to join the river towpath. To the right there's a fine view of Richmond Hill with the Star and Garter disabled seamen's home, built in 1924, on its crest. Across the river there is a glimpse of Marble Hill House.

About 150 yards along the towpath a signed path on the left leads to Ham House. Almost opposite is the Hammerton ferry landing (ferry daily all year 10am–6pm or dusk, 40p each way) should you wish to visit Marble Hill House. If there's no sign of the boat call, 'ferry' to the Hammerton barge moored on the far bank, and the boatman will come and get you.

MARBLE HILL HOUSE

Designed in the Palladian style by Robert Morris, Marble Hill House (open daily, April–Sept 10am–6pm; Oct–Mar Wed–Sun only 10–4pm; adults £2.50, children £1.30, concessions £1.90, English Heritage members free) was built in the 1720s for Henrietta Howard, the mistress of George II. Poet Alexander Pope was a frequent visitor here and had a hand in laying out the house's fine gardens, now disappeared. The white and gold Great Room was modelled on Inigo Jones's single Cube Room at Wilton House in Wiltshire. Unlike nearby Ham House (see below), nothing remains of the house's original furnishings and it is presently decorated with period paintings and furniture from elsewhere.

To reach Marble Hill House from the ferry landing on the west bank, turn left along the metalled path and just beyond where it bends to the right, go through a gate (right) into Marble Hill Park. Turn left along a path and then right to pass the Coach House Café, followed by the fascinating ice-house (right), the eighteenth century's version of a refrigerator, followed by the entrance to Marble Hill House.

The walk continues by the path on the left to Ham House. Go through trees and across a green to reach the entrance.

HAM HOUSE

Described by the eighteenth-century diarist John Evelyn as only 'inferior to few of the best Villas in Italy . . . and furnished like a great Prince's', Ham House (April–Oct Sat–Wed 1–5pm; free access to gardens daily; £4.50 adults, £2.50 children, £12 family ticket) was built in 1610 as a modest manor house and in 1672 passed into the hands of Elizabeth Dysart, a countess in her own right. A high society doyenne, together with her husband the Duke of Lauderdale (a member of Charles II's cabal cabinet), she radically extended and embellished the house, decorating the interior in a flamboyant baroque style and adding many fine paintings and tapestries. Today the house and its interior furnishings are much as the countess left them, and the seventeenth-century formal gardens, laid out on a Union Jack ground plan, have been restored to their former elegance. The house is now a National Trust property. The house's Orangery cafeteria lies close to the mansion's own ice-house, and has a pleasant garden terrace.

The walk continues along the left (or east) side of Ham House outside the grounds. This path and bridleway eventually arrive at a crosspath. Go right here to head half-left over grass towards trees. Beyond the trees, and opposite an enclosed path with signs prohibiting horseriding and cycling, swing left to go south between trees along another path with railings behind the trees to your right. Cross a road to keep the same direction along another footpath and bridleway to reach Ham Common and its pond surrounded by elegant houses and attractive cottages.

On reaching the common, turn left to follow the road which soon bends right to a junction with Upper Ham Road (A307). Turn left again to find a small wooden bus shelter and bus stop. Bus 65 from here goes to Richmond Station and Kew Bridge. Just beyond the bus stop lies the New Inn, with outdoor tables, if you're looking for refreshment.

Walk 26: Along the Thames

Staines – Penton Hook Nature Reserve – Laleham – Chertsey

This is a short Thameside walk between two former country towns now enveloped within the Greater London area. Along the way Penton Hook Island's nature reserve, an opportunity to see some interesting birdlife, and the ancient village of Laleham make rewarding diversions.

Distance: 4.5 or 2 miles.

Map: OS Landranger 176 (West London) or Explorer 160 (Windsor).

Terrain: Easy riverbank walking which can be muddy in parts after rain and on Penton Hook Island.

Food & Drink: Angel, 24 High Street (Mon—at 7.30am–11pm; Sun 12–3pm & 7–10.30pm; M/G), and the Packhorse, Thames Street (Mon–Sat 11am–11pm; Sun 12–3pm & 7–10.30pm; M/G), both Staines and both offering tea and coffee; Three Horseshoes, Laleham (Mon–Sat 11am–11pm; Sun 12–10.30pm; M/G);. Boat House, Chertsey Bridge (daily 11.30am–10.30pm; M/G), serving tea and coffee; Crown Hotel, Chertsey (Mon–Sat 11am–11pm; Sun 12–10.30pm; M), tea and coffee served.

Transport: National Railways from Waterloo to Staines, or buses.

Start & Finish: Debenhams department store, High Street, Staines, to Chertsey train station. The shorter walk terminates at Laleham from where the 218 bus goes back to Staines.

Arriving by rail from London, to reach the start point cross the footbridge to the right and follow a tree-lined lane signed to the Arts Centre and bus station. Follow the lane to the end, about 200 yards, then take a left under a bridge into a car park. Once under the bridge turn right to cross the car park keeping a ramp used by vehicles entering the multi-storey car park to your left. The rear of a Marks and Spencer store appears over the road to the left. Follow a path out of the car park to a junction. Cross the traffic island to turn left into the High Street to reach Debenhams. Over the road from Debenhams the Angel Inn is one of Staines' oldest hostelries, dating back to the twelfth century as a tavern before its later conversion to a coaching inn.

Turn left down Thames Street at the side of the Debenhams store. Just beyond the Thames Lodge Hotel and Pack Horse pub (right), with a pleasant riverside terrace, go under a railway bridge to find the Thames and the riverside path. Keep ahead downstream and after a short distance there is the late nineteenth-century Church of St Peter's, Laleham on the left. The far bank is in Surrey. After three-quarters of a mile the river bends eastwards, and a further half a mile beyond you reach Penton Hook lock and island nature reserve.

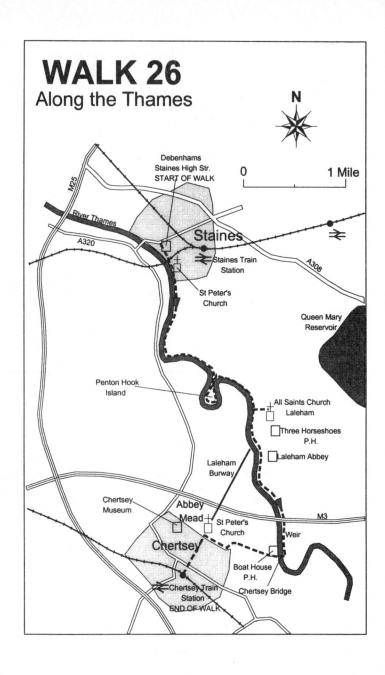

WALK 26
Along the Thames

N

0   1 Mile

Debenhams
Staines High Str.
START OF WALK

M25

River Thames

A320

Staines

Staines Train
Station

A308

St Peter's
Church

Queen Mary
Reservoir

Penton Hook
Island

All Saints Church
Laleham

Three Horseshoes
P.H.

Laleham Abbey

Laleham
Burway

Chertsey
Museum

Abbey
Mead

St Peter's
Church

M3

Chertsey

Weir

Boat House
P.H.

Chertsey Bridge

Chertsey Train
Station
END OF WALK

PENTON HOOK ISLAND

This tight loop in the Thames is perhaps the most impressive meander on the river's length. The densely wooded island, now a nature reserve administered by the Environment Agency, is reached by crossing the weirs behind the lock. Among birds to be seen here are five species of warbler, numerous thrushes and finches as well as kingfishers, herons, woodpeckers and great crested grebes. One curiously common bird in these parts is the ring-necked parakeet, a former cage bird introduced from India which has multiplied and thrived in the wild. Butterflies and plants such as sedge and purple loosestrife are also to be seen in season. A map board at the entry to the island illustrates its paths as well as the location of a new wetland habitat constructed by the Agency to encourage a wider variety of amphibian and birdlife.

Continue along the riverside path beyond the lock for half a mile, passing the Thames Water intake. Where the road leaves the water keep ahead along the riverbank (signed 'Public Footpath Laleham ¼ mile'). To visit Laleham go left ahead down Blacksmith's Lane or Vicarage Lane. Just along from the parish church in Laleham is the Three Horseshoes pub, which serves food and has a pleasant beer garden and conservatory.

LALEHAM

Laleham's name means 'branch and river bend', and the village is mentioned in the Domesday Book of 1086. Laleham House, to the south of the village and now converted into luxury flats, was once the seat of the Lucan family. The Church of All Saints dates back to the twelfth century with sundry later additions, and has a number of Lucan connections. If you obtain the key (see below) the simple interior supported by stout clunch (a form of chalkstone) pillars holds, in its north-east corner, the Lucan chapel. A descriptive leaflet on the church is available. In the graveyard outside, the Lucan family tomb lies at the church's eastern end between flanking yew trees, and a stone marks the grave of the third earl who ordered the disastrous charge of the Light Brigade into the valley of death at Balaclava in 1854, when only 200 out of 700 men survived. Whether or not the seventh earl – who disappeared in 1974 after the murder in suspicious circumstances of the family nanny – ends up alongside his ancestors remains an open question. Incidentally, he and his successors are still patrons of the living here, but in the awkward circumstances surrounding his disappearance the Archbishop of Canterbury has appointed the last two vicars. Another grave of note is that of Matthew Arnold (close to the porch on the south side), the Victorian poet and author of *The Scholar Gypsy*, among many other works. The gravestone inscription, however, seems to throw more glory on his father, the famous headmaster of Rugby School. When the church is closed the key is available from the vicarage in the Broadway to the rear of the church and just beyond the Turk's Head pub on the same side.

Return to the riverside path and keep ahead, following the riverbank. The ferry that has crossed the Thames here since the sixteenth century closed down in the 1980s after 400 years of operation, which is a pity as it allowed you to enter Chertsey along the Burway. Continue ahead with the park and campsite on your left to eventually pass under the M3, followed by a weir and lock. Now you are in sight of Chertsey Bridge, an elegant seven-arched eighteenth-century construction somewhat tarnished by the clashing copper-topped lamps added to celebrate its bicentenary in 1985. Cross the bridge – passing the Boat House pub and restaurant with riverside terrace – and keep ahead along Bridge Road into the centre of Chertsey to reach the Crown Hotel, another opportunity for refreshment, and St Peter's Church.

CHERTSEY

Chertsey is a once small country town now caught up in the enveloping sprawl of London's suburbia. A Benedictine abbey was built here in AD 666 and in the ninth century the Danes murdered the abbot and 90 monks as well as destroying most of the buildings. The abbey was rebuilt and became famous for its encaustic (burnt-in colour) tiles which can be seen in St Peter's Church, the Chertsey Museum (see below) and the V & A. The abbey was demolished after its dissolution by Henry VIII and the stone used to improve Hampton Court. Although St Peter's Church on Windsor Street dates from the fourteenth century, it was substantially rebuilt in a jarring Gothic during the nineteenth – save for the fourteenth-century tower and chancel – when the nave was replaced and the floor raised. The memorial chapel to the right of the chancel has a few of the encaustic tiles mentioned above. The abbey's bells are also ancient. One, dating from the fourteenth century and transferred to the church from the abbey after the dissolution, is used to ring the curfew (at 8pm) from Michaelmas in September to Lady Day at the end of March. The Chertsey Museum (Tue–Fri 12.30–4.30pm, Sat 11am–4pm, admission free) lies further along the main street at Cedar House, 33 Windsor Street. A small but interesting collection comprises archaeological finds from the surrounding area as well as medieval tiles, a display of costumes and accessories and an oral history library on tape.

To reach the train station, turn down Guildford Street (opposite the eastern end of St Peter's Church) and keep ahead across three junctions to the station on the right.

Travelling in London

The Underground
The London Underground (the Tube) serves all parts of central London and runs for 20 hours every day. Every line has its own name and colour so it's easy to find your way around the system. The Tube is divided into six fare zones. Zone 1 covers central London. You can buy your ticket from the ticket office or ticket machines at any Underground station. Make sure you have the correct ticket to your destination, including all the zones you will pass through, before you begin your journey, or you will be liable to a £10 Penalty Fare. Many stations have automatic ticket gates. If the value of travel on your ticket is used up at the end of your journey the gate will open for you but the machine will keep your ticket. Please try to avoid the busiest times. These are between 0800–0930 and 1700–1830 Mondays to Fridays.

Buses
With 17,000 bus stops all over London you are never more than a few minutes walk from a bus route. There are two types of bus stop:
Compulsory: Buses will always stop unless they are full (except for Night Buses which treat all bus stops as request stops).
Request: To stop a bus you must put out your hand in time for the driver to stop safely. A bus might not stop if it is already full. When you want to get off a bus at a request stop ring the bell once in good time to let the driver know. Most buses are red but some are painted in other colours.

London's bus network is divided into four fare zones. Please ensure you have the correct ticket for your journey, or you will be liable to a £5 Penalty Fare. Pay the driver or conductor or show your Travelcard or Bus Pass.

Fares and Tickets
Travelcards give the freedom to make unlimited journeys on the buses, Underground, Docklands Light Railway and most National Railways services in the London zonal area. There are several types of Travelcard.

One Day Travelcard
Valid after 0930 Mondays to Fridays, any time weekends and public holidays. Not valid on Airbus, Night Buses and other special services like tourist buses. You can buy One Day Travelcards up to seven days in advance.

Weekend Travel
Save 25 per cent on the price of two One Day Travelcards. Valid for both Saturday and Sunday, or for any two consecutive days during public holidays. Available in the same zonal combinations as One Day Travelcard. Not valid on Airbus, Night Buses and other special bus services.

Family Travelcard
Available for up to two adults travelling with between one and four children.

Each member of the group receives a ticket, with adults paying 20 per cent less than the normal Travelcard price; children's tickets cost 60p. Members of the party do not need to be related, but must travel together at all times. Not valid on Airbus, Night Buses and other special bus services.

Weekly Travelcard

Use any time, day or night for seven consecutive days. Not valid on Airbus and other special services. You also need a Photocard – see Photocard section.

You can buy Travelcards at Underground stations, London Transport Information Centres, National Railways stations in the London area, and at selected newsagents.

LT Cards

LT Cards give you the freedom of the Underground (except north of Queen's Park on the Bakerloo line), Docklands Light Railway, and all daytime bus routes in the London area displaying the London Transport Bus Service sign. LT Cards are valid all day, and have no time restrictions. Not valid on Airbus, Night Buses and other special services.

Carnet

A book of ten single tickets available from Underground stations and valid for travel on the Underground in Zone 1 only. Adults save £2 over the cost of buying single tickets. Tickets can only be used once but can be used by anybody in your party. Each ticket must be validated before use, by passing it through the ticket gate or validator at the start of each journey.

Children

Up to two accompanied children under age d five can travel free on buses, and all children under five travel free on the Underground. There are reduced rates for five-to-15-year-olds, see Photocard section.

Photocards

Adults and children need a Photocard to buy a weekly or longer period Travelcard or Bus Pass. 14- and 15-year-olds need a Photocard to obtain any child rate ticket Photocards are free. Just take a passport size photograph (and proof of age for 14- or 15-year-olds) to any Travel Information Centre, Underground station or selected newsagent. The 16-17 Photocard entitles the holder to a discount of 30 per cent when buying a ticket from the 16-17 range.

For full details of all London Transport tickets, including the range of bus passes available, pick up a copy of the *Fares and Tickets* leaflet from any Travel Information Centre, Underground station or selected newsagent.

London Travel Information Centres

Call in for travel advice, free maps, leaflets and timetables giving full information about London Transport services. You can buy Travelcards or Bus Passes or book sightseeing tours and attractions. Travel Centres sell guidebooks and souvenirs too.

All Travel Centres are open between 0900 and 1700. Some offices open earlier and close later.

Travel Information Centres are located at: Euston and Victoria* rail stations; King's Cross, Liverpool Street, Oxford Circus, Piccadilly Circus, St James's Park and Heathrow 1, 2, 3 Underground stations; in the passenger arrival halls of Terminals 1, 2 and 4** at Heathrow Airport and at Hammersmith and West Croydon bus stations.

*Closes 1900 Daily **Closes 1500 Daily.

For 24-hour advice on planning your route in London and for fares and timetable information call London Travel Information 0171 222 1234 (personal 24-hour service) or 0171 222 1200 (recorded information).

(Photocopies of the advertisement below are acceptable)

MORE WALKS IN THE LONDON AREA

Many local authorities and other organisations in and around London produce their own walks and guidebooks, most of them free. Listed below are the addresses of some of these.

Bexley London Borough Planning Department, Wyncham House, 207 Longlands Rd, Sidcup, Kent DA15 7JH (0181 303 7777 ext. 4788 fax 308 4912). Produces a number of leaflets detailing walks in the Bexley area and provides information on the Green Chain - a network of footpaths linking woodlands and commons spread across four boroughs in south-east London.

British Waterways Customer Services, Willow Grange, Church Road, Watford WD1 3QA (09123 226422 fax 201400). Information on the Grand Union Canal and walking along its whole length.

Downlands Countryside Management Project, Highway House, 21 Chessington Road, West Ewell, Epsom, Surrey KT17 1TT (0181 541 7282 fax 541 7206). Leaflets describing walks in north Surrey including the Mole valley and North Downs.

Epping Forest Country Care, Epping Forest District Council, Civic Offices, High Street, Epping (01992 788203 fax 650036). Produces a pack of ten walks in the Epping Forest area for a small charge.

Havering Countryside Service, Mercury House, Mercury Gardens, Romford, Essex (01708 772582 fax 772696). Walks in the Romford and Upminster areas.

London Borough of Barnet Leisure Services, 1 Friern Barnet Lane, London N11 3DL (0181 359 3052 fax 359 3011). Produces a range of walks pamphlets for the Barnet area including one covering Section 16 of the Loop (London Outer Orbital Path).

The London Walking Forum (0171 213 9714; fax 248 2583). A partnership of local authorities, government agencies and voluntary organisations, whose aim is to promote a network of green walking routes within and around Greater London. The Forum awards the London Walk kite mark to waymarked walks which meet minimum standards and also coordinates the 24 section 150 mile London Loop and its guide leaflets.

Merton Council, Civic Centre, London Rd, Morden, Surrey (0181 543 2222 fax 545 3237). Series of free pamphlets detailing walks in the Mitcham and Merton areas.

The Ranger Service, Epsom & Ewell Borough Council, Town Hall, The Parade, Epsom, Surrey KT18 5BY (01372 741191). Walks around Epsom.

Royal Borough of Kingston, Dept. of Environmental Services, Guildhall, Kingston upon Thames KT1 1EU (0181 547 5500 fax 547 5521). Has information on walks in the Kingston area including the Hogsmill River walk.

Thames Valley Groundwork Trust, Colne Valley Park Centre, Court Drive, Denham, Uxbridge, Middlesex UB9 5PG (01895 832662 fax 833552). Produces pack of eight walks around the Colne Valley for a small charge.